The Blessed

sharon mcmahon moffitt

The Blessed

a sinner reflects on living the christian life

GRAND RAPIDS, MICHIGAN 49530 USA

We want to hear from you. Please send your comments about this book to us in care of the address below. Thank you.

ZONDERVAN™

The Blessed
Copyright © 2002 by Sharon D. Moffitt

Requests for information should be addressed to:
Zondervan, *Grand Rapids, Michigan 49530*

Library of Congress Cataloging-in-Publication Data

Moffitt, Sharon McMahon, 1947-
    The blessed : a sinner reflects on living the Christian life /
    Sharon McMahon Moffitt.
            p. cm.
    Includes bibliographical references.
    ISBN 0-310-24638-5
    1. Christian life — Meditations.   I. Title.
BV4501.3.M64 2002
248.4 — dc21

2002008300

All Scripture quotations, unless otherwise indicated, are taken from the *Holy Bible: New International Version*®. NIV®. Copyright © 1973, 1978, 1984 by International Bible Society. Used by permission of Zondervan. All rights reserved.

Scripture quotations marked MESSAGE are taken from THE MESSAGE. Copyright © by Eugene H. Peterson 1993, 1994, 1995. Used by permission of NavPress Publishing Group.

Scripture quotations marked NKJV are taken from the *New King James Version*. Copyright © 1979, 1980, 1982 by Thomas Nelson, Inc. Used by permission. All rights reserved.

Interior design by Todd Sprague

Printed in the United States of America

02 03 04 05 06 07 08 /❖ DC/ 10 9 8 7 6 5 4 3 2 1

For Don
Tell the truth and stand back

Timshel

Transl. "thou mayest" in East of Eden
by John Steinbeck

Cities in the wilderness,
Merton called them the *glittering*
towns that spring up overnight
in the desert . . . the brilliant and sordid
smiles of the devil
upon the face of the wilderness . . .

The wilderness
God created, the nothingness
into which he cast his children
there to wander, to meet him and be alone
with him. At one
with him. Atonement.

The wilderness in which he is fully
aware the devil lies
in wait for us, smiling with promises
he cannot keep, lying
in wait for our ignorant arrival.

There to wander forty years in despair,
with nothing save this: the will to choose
with whom you will yoke your hopeless self
for Life. *This then is our desert: to live*
facing despair, but not to consent.

Timshel.

Sharon McMahon Moffitt

Contents

Blessedness

It is a spring day in South Puget Sound, a Sunday, and there are whispers of good things on the way after a long winter. We survive the lightless days up here between fall and spring—soggy earth and leaves turned dangerous on the patio in their slimy decomposition—by treating this time as a season of advent. We wait. We dry our shoes on the hearth and wring ourselves out over and over again, because we know something better is coming. We know we will get up one morning to find tulip trees heavy with the juicy heft of magnolia blossoms, mothers ready to give birth. And from the kitchen window, we will look out one morning to see the forsythia on fire in the corner of the garden and daffodils popping up out of the compost heap like dandelions. We will kneel before clumps of trillium, western wake-robins who return each year during Holy Week to unfurl their triune petals, first white, later tinged with blood. Things that can't be paid to grow anywhere else thrive here, thanks to the rains, and as winter huffs out its final breaths, I watch for a perennial bluebell that thrusts herself up through a crack in the cement at the bottom of my back stairs every year, reminding me, as I rush out to engage in the business of life, to stop, repent of my winter whining, and give thanks.

On this particular spring day, my heart is a burgeoning magnolia blossom, full and rich and ready to break open. I am sitting in my usual place in church next to my sons, Patrick and Michael, and my husband, Don. But today is not an ordinary Sunday. This morning our beloved Mona kneels before the baptismal font on the chancel in front of us. Her name is Monicah, actually, and she is Patrick's girlfriend, though today she becomes more than that. Today, she becomes our sister in Christ.

I am never unaffected by Mona's beauty. She is an absolute original in both appearance and spirit. A cataract of copper hair falls in wiry ringlets to her waist. Her skin is the color of cream, her eyes, dollops of rich chocolate. She is the embodiment of femininity, though there is nothing froufrou about Mona. She possesses at once the strength and vigilance of one who has seen and heard too much too soon, and the meekness of one who has lost all of the encumbrances of naivete. When she laughs, it sounds as if the laughter comes from her toes, and when she cries, it's as if something inside her has come undone. Though life has brutally thrust her into dark, scary places, and she knows the pain of despair, she keeps looking for, and finding, beauty to sustain her, carry her farther along. This morning as she kneels before the baptismal font, I want to stop time and bid a painter to come and capture this vision on canvas. Remembering it now, I am filled with joy—a clear, high note of bliss cradled in the bosom of a deeper chord of low, fine music.

My first encounter with Mona was, in truth, a non-encounter, but I recognized it as a moment I should store in a safe place.

Something in me knew I would take it out later and hold it up to the light, as I am doing this morning. Patrick was fourteen years old at the time, and we were new to the Northwest, transplants from the arid glory of the Colorado prairie to this mysterious, moist, emerald landscape. The move may have been hardest on Pat, occurring as it did smack in the middle of middle school, when one's social survival from one day to the next is dubious at best and life depends on your getting through the day without embarrassing yourself to death. He was handling it with grace. I was proud of him. In truth, he was faring better than I.

He came in from school one day to tell me he'd been smitten from across the orchestra pit by "the most beautiful girl" he had ever seen. An aspiring cellist. I was charmed but not keenly interested. He'd demonstrated a lively appreciation for God's handiwork in the creation of the female of the species for a long time. Whenever he spoke of pretty girls, he was partial to superlatives—it's a family curse—and though I noted the remark, I thought nothing more of it until, weeks later, while we were driving through a neighboring community, he exploded with energy. "Mom, Mom ..." he stuttered, "there she is! The girl I told you about." He pointed to a nearby corner, but alas, Mona had disappeared around it. I would have to wait to see this vision of loveliness, who, as it turned out, already had a steady boyfriend and so was unavailable anyway. I attempted to pick up the thread of conversation that had been underway before the Mona sighting when I realized Patrick had all but vanished. "Pat?" I jostled him. "Anybody there?" Shaking himself loose, he turned with glassy eyes. "Sorry," he said with a sigh. "I just lost all the feeling in my legs."

It took them three more years to break down all the adolescent barriers that seemed determined to keep them apart, things like acute shyness, zits, insecurities, bad timing, bad hair. Finally, early in Pat's senior year, we looked up into the nosebleed section of the bleachers at a football game one cold October night and spotted them straddling the bench seat, facing each other, unaware of the score—or the game, for that matter—or the presence of hundreds of strangers; they appeared to be mesmerized by the commingling of their breath in the night air. I nudged Don in the ribs and pointed. It was obvious love was afoot.

Odd as it sounds, their union immediately received an unusual amount of attention from friends and neighbors. It seemed significant to others, who observed their courtship with keen interest. It certainly wasn't because theirs was a remarkably fluid and harmonious affair; it wasn't. It gave the pleasure not so much of a gently ambling stream but of a tumultuous, vibrant Rocky Mountain river running clear and cold and galumphing headlong over boulders to make its way home. Everything about their courtship, good and bad, was punctuated by passion. It just seemed like they were supposed to be together, so much so that when, during college, they decided nothing was working right and went their separate ways, everyone I told looked absolutely crestfallen, as if they'd learned of yet another divorce in the community. But I've gotten ahead of myself.

In the weeks following the football game, Patrick brought Mona home often. I don't remember not loving Mona, so I'm tempted to say I loved her instantly. It feels as though I did. We learned that she had spent part of the previous summer in an ashram in upstate New York, so we wondered how she and Pat would hammer out their religious differences if they continued to see each other. Meanwhile, I made vegetarian versions of whatever we were eating and prayed a lot. I was surprised when she came to me one day and asked if I'd be interested in teaching a Bible study for her and some friends who wanted the scoop on Jesus. I liked the idea, though I was a bit apprehensive at the notion of being their guide. I take James' admonition regarding teachers very seriously and certainly did not want to misinform or mislead these young women in matters of life and death. Reluctantly, I said yes, praying that God would cover my ineptitude with grace.

After many months of study, discussion, and prayer, sometime during the Lenten season Mona decided to sign on with Jesus. I am trying here to avoid all the salvation cliches: "she was saved," "she welcomed Jesus into her heart," and "she became a Christian." The mere hearing of these bits of canned Christianity chafes me even today. I think it's baggage lugged along on my personal journey out of childhood, forever strapped to memories of women like an old Sunday school teacher who accidentally dropped her mask of hypocrisy in my presence one day to reveal a hateful, arrogant bigot lurking under her very white skin. This woman loved to go on about people getting saved and giving their lives to Jesus, apparently unaware of how much damage she did by living a life that lacked spiritual integrity, and doing it right in front of the children. She'd have done less damage if she'd run around stark naked screaming obscenities.

In any event, Mona had given Jesus the high sign, and today she is making a public profession of her newfound faith. As we sit here, I catch myself smiling at the memory of an ex-nun friend telling us of the bizarre moment in the convent when she sat down to have her hair shorn, and the old nun making ready to do the deed asked her if she was ready to "go all the way with Jesus."

Mona's inner child is never far beneath the surface. As she stands on the chancel this morning, she is at once a stunningly beautiful woman and an achingly vulnerable child. Baptisms always make me cry, and I warned my husband and sons that I might embarrass them today and that they'd better not give me any grief about it. Memories, vivid and alive, leap into my mind. Mona sitting cross-legged on our living room sofa with the Bible open in her lap, her head tilted as she framed yet another probing question about Jesus; Mona, firmly grasping the hands of her friends as we prayed each week, friends two of whom stand beside her on the chancel today to publicly profess their faith. I remember Mona's dark eyes, sassy and irreverent, as she cracked a joke about my becoming a circuit preacher and driving from college town to college town with a blinking neon sign on the roof of my car: "Jesus is coming and boy is he ticked!" And I remember those same dark eyes wet with tears and bright with anticipation as we approached the communion table the night she chose to publicly profess her faith.

I am breaking up inside; my resolve to be stoic is an iceberg about to calve in the heat of a blazing August sun. I want everyone present to know what I know about the journey that brought this intelligent, vibrant young woman to this place. I want everyone to know this is not a girl who makes promises lightly, nor glibly says things she doesn't mean. I wait with bated breath to hear what she will say when asked to share a word about her feelings on this occasion. I should have known there would be nothing saccharin or sentimental in her remarks. I should have known she would avoid the cliche and go straight for the poetry. I should have been prepared, but, and I love God for this, I could not have guessed what she would say.

"I feel," she says with a clear voice and humble confidence, "as if every cell in my body is about to be changed."

———

I do not consider myself a theologian, unless you take the word by its roots—one who studies the things of God. Perhaps it would be more apt to call me a theophile, but I don't think that's actually a word. I have spent a fair number of hours in my Bible. In fact, during the crisis that brought me to my knees and, subsequently, back to God, at the urging of my big sister, Linda, I virtually crawled into the Psalms like a feverish child crawls under a favorite quilt, and did little but feed on God's Word until I felt strong enough to emerge and step into the world again. My first desert experience, I guess. I've read an ample number of books and poems *about* God, and I love to converse with anyone who shares my endless curiosity about him and longs to have a real relationship with him, a relationship that is at once earthy and divine, which is to say, of course, a relationship with Jesus.

It surprises many of my peers to learn that many high school and college people are seeking God these days, and I don't mean a treacle god, smooth and easily digested, a god who generously doles out mercy but has no interest in justice—in other words a god rewritten to suit one's personal theology, what Frederica Mathewes-Green called her Frankenstein God. The young people of whom I speak seem weary of a diet of sweets that satisfies temporarily but leaves them craving something savory, something with a distinct taste and texture, something they can chew and swallow, digest into their bodies, absorb. They are looking for energy and life. I know all this because small bands of these people, beginning with Mona and her friends, have sojourned through my living room over the past several years in their search for such a god. Every year, when students ask me if I plan to continue holding the Bible study, I say yes, despite lingering doubts about my competence. I say yes because I think I should, and I expect God to use what happens in my living room for good.

The result has been a continuous flow of vibrant, youthful energy moving through our home as students have met to talk and read and pray, to gather grain and make bread; to find validation for something within that they really already know, or at least suspect—that the road to happiness as dictated by our culture is the wrong road. Something in us knows that our hunger for happiness will not be satisfied by sex, money, power, and prestige and that the bumper sticker theology which proclaims "He who dies with the most toys wins" really is just a joke after all. What if, we ponder, there is something more important than money and prestige? What if relinquishment and surrender ultimately provide more happiness than power and acquisition? There is something in Mother Teresa's craggy countenance we crave for ourselves despite the buckets of hard-earned cash we dole out to buy products that promise us a face like Madonna, and I don't mean Jesus' mother. We struggle between what we think we need—approval and acceptance from peers, and truckloads of stuff—and what we know in our hearts we need—God. I have a close friend, a good Christian woman, who knows full well that the ethos of her workplace is contrary to everything she believes about life and God, and yet a part of her longs for the approval of her colleagues there. Such is our nature. We never quite overcome our longing to gain entrance into the popular crowd.

These Bible students seem to be motivated by a nagging possibility that there is a different way to live. Their energy infuses my environment with light. It informs my personal spiritual quest, humbles me thoroughly and continually, and gives me hope for the world. Being in relationship with them has brought healing as we mutually agree to risk and be vulnerable, to confess our sins and share every manner of trial and jubilation life serves up. With so many other demands on our time, it has not always been easy to keep the fire going, but we've managed, I suppose because we know it's good for us, and good for the Body.

At that first gathering, we decided to read the gospel of Matthew (I can't remember why) and quickly found ourselves immersed in a deep discussion of the Beatitudes, found in the fifth chapter—Jesus' opening remarks in what we know as the Sermon on the Mount. The word *beatitude* is derived from the Latin *beatus,* which means "bliss," more frequently translated "happiness," though it is, I think, less than precise to use these words synonymously. *Bliss* has such limited usage in contemporary life that it's practically meaningless except as a synonym for personal happiness. "Follow your bliss." I understand that this phrase originated with Joseph Campbell, though it, like so many things, has been thoroughly reduced by ad-men into just one more call to self-gratification. More bumper sticker theology. In Scripture, though, it suggests something divine, beatific, something that transcends the mundane notion of happiness. Something more like joy, perhaps.

I'm not wild about translating *blessed* as "happy" either, though some prominent Christian scholars seem okay with it. My uneasiness with this translation was heightened when I perused William Barclay's commentary on Matthew's gospel, in which he explains that the Greek word for blessed, *makarios,* describes a godlike joy, something out of this world. It relates directly to the Isle of Cyprus, which "was so lovely, so rich and so fertile an island that a man would never need to go beyond its coastline to find the perfectly happy life."[1] He goes on to point out that the English word *happy* derives from the root *hap,* which means "chance." Blessedness, because it comes from God, is a constant, a sure thing, whereas happiness is subject to the whims of fortune. I don't like happy as a synonym for blessed because I'm concerned it will reflect the contemporary connotation of the word, the driving force behind our culture's idolatry of anything that makes us feel good, from first-class coffee to casual sex. It's an unsavory extension of the values that defined the zeitgeist of the '70s—"If it feels good, do it"—and frankly, I bear a measure of personal shame for my part in the mess we left for our children to clean up in our posthippie, self-indulgent haste to exit that hedonistic era and lunge headlong into the self-promoting moral anarchy that permeates our thinking and defines many of our choices today.

This maniacal striving for happiness seems to me a shallow, temporary, corporeal sort of thing derived largely from gluttonous appetites which must be satisfied instantly and results in embarrassingly conspicuous consumption as opposed to something of God, something simple, intransigent, and eternal, a kind of spiritual sans souci, a life free of unnecessary encumbrances, a life of, well, bliss that might be ours if we choose to make it so. Life in a blissful kingdom sounds like a fairy tale, of course, fantastic and unattainable, unless you're Donald Trump or Mickey Mouse or, better, willing to entertain the possibility that a kingdom is something within, as opposed to something out there, waiting to be procured. Or maybe, given God's artistry, it's both. A careful reading of this sermon suggests, though, that Jesus was not so much placing the emphasis on the reward we would someday receive if we behave ourselves now—namely heaven—

so much as he was describing what we might experience here, today, if we choose to live life his way. It would seem that bliss is not so much a place, then, except in Carefree, Arizona, where I'm told it's a street name, as it is a state of mind and heart and soul, a condition of blessedness.

Spelunking for a deeper understanding of the word *bliss* resulted in my sense that at its root it's about largesse and suggests fullness and satisfaction, maybe a bit like the satisfaction an infant feels having been nursed and burped, ready to settle in for a peaceful little postprandial nap. It further suggests a sort of completion and integration, wholeness. Blessed are you. Filled. Satisfied. Whole. And free from worry. At rest *and* unaffected by the judgment of the people around you regarding the way you choose to live. It's been my experience that the real challenge of living in Christ is in doing so in a world that thinks you've lost your mind, a world that hears the word *Christian* and recoils at the caricature of a smarmy televangelist bilking widows out of their Social Security checks. I hate that. Frequently, after identifying myself as a Christian, I want to snag the person I'm talking to by the collar and quickly explain all that I am *not* before he beats a hasty retreat, presuming I am no doubt eager to return to work on my "I Hate Homosexuals" home page while I pitch aluminum cans into the nearest landfill. No one likes to be on the receiving end of prejudice, not even Christians.

I remember one young woman, as we opened our pages to the Beatitudes and read through this litany of blessedness the first time, looking up from her Bible and saying simply, "Ouch!" People usually react to this passage in much the same way they react to the Ten Commandments before they realize they are, in fact, a love letter from a father to his children detailing what is good for us and warning us of things that will cause us pain. Most of us, after reading the Beatitudes carefully, decide that surely we are not to take them literally, because if we are, we might as well fold up our tents and go home.

I suppose this is as good a place as any to point out that Dallas Willard, author of *The Divine Conspiracy,* insists that people have misunderstood the Beatitudes—what have become for many "nothing less than pretty poison"—for centuries. Given the context in which this sermon was delivered, he writes that the Beatitudes are merely a rhetorical method of proclaiming to the masses the quintessence of the gospel—God's love is available to all comers, including the poor and the needy, the crippled, the blind, and the disenfranchised.[2] I absolutely and humbly defer to Willard as a superior teacher and scholar and couldn't agree more that this is the salient feature of this passage. Jesus was throwing the doors to the kingdom wide open. I just don't think that's all there is to say on the subject. I'm a poet and a creative-writing teacher. One of the things I point out to my students is the economy of poetry: good poets derive as much from a line as they possibly can. Great poems are richly textured and usually layered with meaning. A poem is also slightly altered each time a new reader explores it, because each reader brings something unique to bear on the experience. Certainly the Bible—the Living Word—qualifies as great literature. What Dallas Willard says about the Beatitudes is true, and I believe that beneath that truth there lies something more.

And it's this. In one very important sense, Christ, our divine role model, actually lived the Beatitudes. Born fully human in the humblest of circumstances, he lived a simple and virtually impoverished life. We know he was an obedient child who appeared to honor only his Father in heaven above his earthly parents. Like all good Jewish boys, he was steeped in Scripture. As a young man, he appeared to have no interest in acquiring either wealth or prestige. He was a loyal friend who wept openly when he learned of Lazarus' death. Fully God, Jesus was pure of heart, of course, and could not bear cruelty, injustice, or hypocrisy, and yet the mercy he showed to others has never been equaled. He was the ultimate peacemaker in that the very purpose for his presence on the planet was to reconcile God and man, and his reward for doing so was to die a shameful death at our hands.

I think believers are called to assume, or at least to seek, the posture of the Beatitudes as we come before God. But it's not about "salvation-by-attitude," as Willard calls it. The Beatitudes describe the blossoming character of one who has given himself or herself over to God. They invite us to purge ourselves of all the stuff that fills us up, to become empty jars, vessels God will happily fill with his very self if we'll let him. But to do so will mean upending ourselves and pouring out the booze and drugs and sex and bungee jumping and any of the various and sundry highs, including respectable things like work and church service, that so engage us we haven't room for anything else.

Debates on this subject are not new. They are rooted in an eternal struggle aptly illustrated by the conflict between Augustine and Pelagius in the fifth century. Though my understanding of the ways in which these theologians differed may be somewhat less than scholarly and suffer a bit from oversimplification, the gist of the conflict is something like this: Augustine, a man of lusty appetites, insisted that man's propensity to sin and generally make a mess of things is innate and cannot be modified by anything less than grace and redemption, while Pelagius believed that a loving

God would never give us more to do than we are capable of, so we must have it in us to live up to his commandments. In the world of orthodox Christianity, Augustine's wisdom prevailed, for without divine aid, God's laws are certainly beyond the grasp of the human hand, and even more important, there looms this question: What need have we of the cross if we have it in us to obey God's laws on our own?

Pelagius, eventually declared a heretic, found a wide hearing among humanists, who extended his arguments to say that we are all basically good, though capable of evil, and what we need to do is listen to the Obi-Wan Kenobi in us as opposed to the Darth Vader, and we should make it through life relatively unscathed. Americans tend to believe our lives are our own business, that we are captains of our fates and should take Frank Sinatra's advice to do it our way, without regrets. For most, God has pretty much disappeared from the discussion altogether. We can do anything we set our minds to, or better yet, we can do *everything,* as some people had us believing—like the woman in the old TV ad who brandished her frying pan like a six-shooter while she lustily bumped and ground her way through a jingle in which she proclaimed that she could not only bring home the bacon but fry it up in a pan, feed it to her family, make love to her man, and then get up the next day and do it all over again! Every time I saw that ad, I wanted to quietly retire to the bathroom and slit my wrists.

To presume that with enough effort we can muster up the goodness to live as the Beatitudes suggest is certainly beyond my feeble imagination. And believe me, I tried it, like Sisyphus trying to get that cursed rock to the top of the hill in Hades, only to have it roll down right on top of me. Repeatedly. I'm a slow learner. And because it seems too big a challenge for just about anybody short of Superman, many readers simply choose to skip stones across troublesome little rivulets of Scripture like the Beatitudes, preferring something a tad more manageable. It reminds me of King Jehoakim, who, as he listened to the prophecies of Jeremiah read to him from a scroll, sliced away all the things he didn't like with his penknife and tossed them onto the fire until, alas, the entire thing was aflame. But anyone engaged in a thoroughgoing study of Scripture will find they have to skip a lot of stones across a lot of rivers if that's going to be their approach to the Bible. Jesus' teachings, time and time again, rob us of comfort and agitate us with outlandish imperatives: turn the other cheek, give the guy who's suing you your coat *and* your cloak, make amends with people who have hurt you, turn your back on your mother and father, and—my personal favorite—*don't worry!* Surely Jesus did not mean for us to take this stuff literally, any more than he means we shouldn't lust after our neighbor's spouse or covet his stuff. It's un-American.

Maybe our problem grasping all this lies in our belief that blessing should, by definition, feel good. We grow up hearing our mothers admonish us to count our blessings, meaning we should keep a running tally of all the good things we've been given and forget about the bad things, despite the fact that some of the most profound blessings come out of pain and struggle. I'm thinking of the story of Jacob recorded in the thirty-second chapter of Genesis. Knowing he was in line to receive a blessing, Jacob wrestled with a mysterious man all night long, so determined was he to receive his blessing.

It's important to note here that the confrontation seems to have its origin in Jacob's character rather than God's. Some of us just don't have the good sense to simply accept gifts that are there for the taking. I guess we feel as though a struggle will somehow make us more worthy. Who knows why we do the things we do? But God, ever patient with even his high-maintenance children, agreed to participate in the dance until morning, when he gave Jacob the blessing he was after. But not before giving him a painful tap on the hip, along with a new name. Herein, I believe, lies the essence of true blessing. It comes as part of transformation, specifically our willingness to be changed by God. Jacob was commanded to say his given name, which meant "deceiver," before he would be christened with his new name, Israel, which some scholars translate "Prince with God." Others say "strive with God." Apparently the literal translation of Israel as used here is "God prevails." What matters is this: Jacob was transformed by this blessing, changed from a man known as a deceiver to a man who walked with God. And it's very important to note that when he walked away from this engagement, he walked with a limp. Jacob's utterance was nothing less than a confession of the sin that defined his life before he gave it to God. And his blessing was the beginning of sanctification. When Jesus spoke of the blessed life, he was not speaking of mere obedience any more than he was talking about a life of ease. He was talking about a life that has gone under the knife. A life blessed by God, then, appears to be something far beyond what we might consider "the good life."

I had a Baptist Sunday school teacher in maybe the sixth grade who pulled a long face when I asked her to explain what it meant in the Bible to work out our salvation. "If," I queried, "a person 'gets saved,' then once you're saved, what's left to work out?" I don't remember her answer, only that she looked at me with that look teachers reserve especially for incorrigible middle-school kids who ask annoying questions. This one was etched on my heart for a long time until, in an epiphanous moment, it dawned on me that the root of the word *salvation* is the same as the root of the word *salve,* and I remembered an old-timey hymn I had always found curiously comforting about a balm in Gilead. "Salvation is not just about being rescued," I exclaimed, "it's about healing!" It's for people who are sick and broken and wounded— and have a loving father, Abba, who longs to heal and comfort them. It goes beyond the rescue into the rehabilitation. God doesn't just scoop you out of the floodwaters and sit you on a rock and abandon you there to start reading your Bible, stop sinning, straighten up, and fly right. The day you say yes to God, the day you turn and reach out for him, is the first day of a healing process that will take time, as all healing does. And as all healing does, it may hurt sometimes.

This is not a trek for spiritual lightweights. In his introductory remarks to the writings of Blaise Pascal, Os Guinness writes, "A sickness of our age is that we have fit bodies, but flaccid minds and vacant souls."[3] Everywhere I go, I see people jogging, riding bikes, kayaking to work, and rappeling off man-made rocks for recreation. Would that we were all as concerned about our spiritual fitness as we are about our bodies. Because, ironically, though we are promised rest in Christ, it is clear we are called to be participants in our life with him. In fact, the first thing that happens when we come to the place of deciding to live differently is a physical turning, a choice to step into a dance that will change us forever. *Repentance.*

What better place than on the mount to initiate a dialogue with young men and women who claim they long to walk the high moral ground in a culture that expects them to get the best grades, do the most community service, participate in the greatest number of extracurricular activities, make it into the best colleges, and pull down a six-figure salary before turning thirty? Year after year, I escort my young friends to sit at the feet of Jesus and hear this unsettling, countercultural description of God's kingdom, and it is to this place that I return in these pages to share what we have gleaned over time. They've been brave souls, these kids, many of whom are now out there living as adults in the world, working, getting married, and having children, remembering, perhaps, the challenges that were placed before them by Christ—to live in the world but be not of it. And to be blessed.

Blessed but not shielded from the insults of a world that thinks we're terminally old-fashioned and have essentially lost our minds. Jesus clearly meant for us to work out our salvation *in* the world, despite a persistent longing to cut ourselves out of the herd and wait for the Second Coming. It's tempting, and actually easy enough to do, to bug out, find an enclave of like-minded people who believe exactly what you believe and live exactly as you live and embrace rigid rules of accountability so that no one strays far from the party line. What could possibly be wrong with building a safe haven, growing organic vegetables, and sharing chores? People make this choice all the time. Flower children, white supremacist groups, people who flee the world to live in ashrams and other sundry communal habitats such as Waco and Jonestown and even, dare I say it, some pretty regular churches around town. The problem with all these communal situations is that they tend to lend themselves to a nasty sort of spiritual and psychological inbreeding, and the sordid result is usually a deformity of self-righteousness, a carbuncle, inflamed and oozing hatred. I'm not sure what the psychological explanation for this is, but I know what the scriptural one is. We are broken people who, left to our devices, gravitate toward sin like flies to honey, as well as to piles of other pungent things. Given a cesspool in which to live, we will take root and grow. Jesus never meant for us to go into hiding, and believe me, more than once I've let him know in no uncertain terms how I feel about this, when the world is simply too much for me. When my inner world is simply too much for me and I'm looking for a way out.

But no matter where I look in Scripture for permission to isolate myself, I cannot find it. Instead I find things that strike again that chord of knowing—that to subject oneself to healing will mean a measure of suffering. I stumble upon riches such as the prayer in the seventeenth chapter of John that Jesus prayed on behalf of his beloved disciples and, by extension, each of us—not that we would be taken out of the world but that we would be protected from the Evil One as we carry out the work of God *in* the world, and would be sanctified, made holy, in the process. The high moral ground, I've come to believe, is a place of sacrifice and submission—outdated words in the lexicon of our time. We are called to live in the world and make disciples *as* we are being healed (not after we get it all right, I hasten to add). In the act of repentance, we give ourselves over to be made new in Christ's image. This is the promise we are left with as Jesus leaves us in the hands of the Holy Spirit, the one who he promised would come alongside us and see us to the end of the age.

We're promised a divine helper, one who will sustain us in the same sort of tension that existed between Augustine and Pelagius, a tension that tugs at us from one side, insisting that we must somehow show God we are worthy of salvation and be perfect at the same time that it tugs at the helpless child inside each of us, who knows we can do nothing outside of accepting grace. We live in the tension that directs us to love others as we love ourselves and simultaneously dictates the death of self so that

Christ might live in us. The Christian life is not for those who cannot abide paradox.

Indeed, it is mystery itself that sustains many of us in what Sören Kierkegaard calls our "restless faith," perhaps because it portends a God whose goodness we are permitted to witness, as Moses did from the cleft of a rock, but whose being is too grand, too glorious to be seen with the naked eye, and too large to be contained within the confines of our wee little biodegradable skulls. As I flip through the archives of images stored in my mind of the faces of godly men and women who have gone before me, it is clear they were people who embraced the marvelous mystery of the faith, people who found their peace in the largesse of God, as suggested in these lines from a poem by Scott Cairns.

> The comfort lies in fingering the incoherent for the true.
> The comfort lies in suspecting more than the evidence allows.
> My only rule: If I understand something, it's no mystery.[4]

They were able to embrace the mystery of God despite living in a culture that sometimes seems to put all its hopes in science and technology, in knowledge it can fully grasp and contain. They understood that embracing mystery isn't about mere acceptance of that which we don't know, about grudgingly accepting what appears to be missing and cryptic, but instead is about recognizing what is present—a very real God who is unknowable at the same time he is all that we know for sure.

When You're Little in Your Own Eyes
Brokenness

It's 1985 and I am meandering along Lido Beach near Sarasota, Florida. Air travel once again has wreaked havoc with my reality, catapulting my family and me from the cold, arid climes of the Colorado prairie to this pristine beach on the Gulf of Mexico. Meandering is not something I do a lot of back home these days, where I take care of two active sons in the prime of childhood. Most of my life is spent either in the car or cracking the whip over the kids as they sit at the piano. I hope they will thank me later, or at least not hate music altogether. But this week we've been invited to forget school, forget the piano. We're in Florida to play while my husband attends a medical conference, and we may as well have been shipped to another planet for the difference between this place and home.

The sky is blue, but not the thin cerulean of a Colorado sky. Emerald undertones deepen it, pull it toward the earth. The air at night is warm and redolent of things heavy with wetness, blossoms as full and round as their names: magnolia, bougainvillea. There is so much to learn. Years of an untraveled life once led me to presume that all oceanic bodies are the same, but I am discovering otherwise. This lush expanse of roiling sea, for instance, is warm, and as colorful and alluring as a parrot, quite unlike the forbidding gunmetal gray of the North Sea off the coast of Whitley Bay in England, where we spent a summer many years ago. And nothing like the bathwater waves that lap up on the shore of the eastern seaboard off Hilton Head Island, where I once stood, with childlike glee, watching a pair of dolphins slip-slide past me one morning. These gulf waters are not like the thundering surf at Cape Cod—cattle stampeding the shore—and they bear little resemblance to the frigid expanse of the Pacific off the eroding coast of Washington state, where we will eventually live. What all these bodies of water do have in common is their power and vastness, and the way each causes me to experience my smallness, my frailty.

I am essentially alone, the kids yards away engaged in a giggly game of tag with the suds of breaking waves. I stand and look hard across the big water, try to imagine life being played out on the far side of the gulf on another beach, equally foreign and unfamiliar to these prairie-white feet, feet that just days before padded unprotected across the frozen tundra of my front yard to snag an errant football that had been lying in the bushes since Super Bowl Sunday. It was as if a web of frost had been woven underneath the brown grass there, causing the turf to crackle as I gingerly made my way across it. The sound of winter in Middle America. It's difficult to believe that winter continues there while I stand here, toes sunk in warm, white sand. White. Until I came here, I presumed all sand was gray and cold, stones ground fine by perpetual wave action and the battering of time. These white sands are, according to hotel literature, broken shells—beaten to imperfection, I philosophically conclude, by green rhythms and the moonwashings of ten thousand years. I can't quite believe the array of shells that lie before me, and the people combing the beach for them intrigue me.

I conclude that the collectors look like experts, though I muse I haven't a clue what a shell expert should look like. Whoever they are, they mean business and seem to know exactly what they're looking for as they stoop to scour one patch of beach after another, hurling their discards over brown shoulders, gingerly placing the keepers into trugs and baskets. I wonder if they are local artisans who make trinkets to sell in one of the myriad gift shops nearby. Some, perhaps, are tourists, but their deep tans suggest this is home to them, and their approach to this task suggests more of harvest than treasure hunt. I trail one of them for a time and stoop to collect the shells she leaves behind.

Savoring the luxury of time and a moment of solitude, I grow contemplative as I scrutinize these broken shells, and I am struck not so much by their flaws as by their loveliness. Though the unbroken ones are beautiful, unquestionably exquisite symbols of survival, the broken ones, the ones with holes in their thin walls, reveal delicate spirals and hidden treasures that would be indiscernible had their outer shells remained intact. I am drawn into their tiny interiors and dumbstruck by the delicacy with which each has been designed.

Perhaps it is because I feel the tectonic plates of my marriage shifting and know a breaking is about to occur that I am drawn to these shattered specimens. I find myself thinking about the walls I have so carefully constructed to conceal the flaws of my life. Intuitively, I know they are about to be tested and found unworthy, about to have holes punched in them by the truth. The enormous effort Don and I have put into presenting a picture-perfect family is about to be rendered a colossal waste of time and energy. On some visceral level, my body knows what I have refused to acknowledge, that the flawless exterior of our lives is about to be pounded by the surf and we will be laid waste, broken shells for every passerby to see, for treasure hunters in search of perfection to reject. I can sense that the chronic tension and conflict is about to come to something, moving us toward a moment when we will have to face the consequences of choices we made in our youth, and we won't be able to keep things neatly packed away any longer. Perhaps what I know is that all my quiet, unspoken fears are about to be validated. We're no different than anyone else. All my efforts to avoid the pain of being fully human have been vanity. It's as if my solar plexis is emitting faint signals, a sort of Morse code from central operations saying that the jig is just about up and the two of us are going to wake up one morning to find that we've been slammed onto the shore in a heap. My fighting spirit ebbs like the tide.

Perhaps it is the weight of this burgeoning awareness, rooted in truth, that leads me, amid these profound suspirations, to find a sand speck of hope in the loveliness of broken shells. All I know is that I feel a kinship with these rejects scattered at my feet, and I begin to make a small collection of my own. Soon there is a rhythm to my gathering which serves to empty my tired mind and relieve me of all thought. I walk, stoop, scoop, and hold my treasured specimens up to the light. Suddenly, a line from one of the psalms lights like a feather on my sunburned shoulder: "The Lord draws near to the crushed in spirit."[1]

> *Blessed are the poor in spirit,*
> *for theirs is the kingdom of heaven.*

For a person whose temperament tends toward melancholy, Jesus' opening declaration should provide a ray of hope. And in fact, when all is said and done, it does. The trouble is this first beatitude appears to be so counter to the American way of thinking that finding anything good in it requires time and reflection. Americans are known for their strong spirit, their spunk, their bold, minuteman defiance of the odds. And we don't have much patience for people who are down and can't seem to get up. By and large in this culture, anyone ailing with the dis-ease of despair can count on getting everything from a gentle scolding to a boatload of free advice—a plethora of aphorisms reminding her to look on the bright side. Friends tend to rush us to treat symptoms before we've given much thought to causes. Sadly, the most outspoken of all of the folks handing out free advice is liable to be a Christian. I remember finding it ironic when my friend, who had lost her son in an automobile accident, told me that she asked her husband to spirit her out of the church one Sunday morning because she had begun to lose her composure. Because her son had been dead two years, she thought people would think she was wallowing in her grief. I had two thoughts in quick succession. The first was a question, really. If you can't cry in church, where *can* you cry? The second was this: Christian friends *do* send out lots of messages suggesting that a person must not be a very *good* Christian if she can't "let go and let God" and do it pretty darn fast.

To exacerbate the problem, one of the nastiest aspects of melancholy is guilt, which acts as food for the monster that's bringing you down in the first place. Depression, clinical or otherwise, makes the people around you uncomfortable; they want you to cheer up. They *need* you to cheer up. I've even heard cheerfulness cited as one of the fruits of the Spirit, though I can't find it as such in my Bible. Joy is one of the fruits, of course, and just as folks translate *blessed* to mean "happy" in contemporary, self-indulgent terms, they likewise translate *joy* to mean "good cheer," which is to reduce it to something much smaller than what it really is.

Like it or not, while Eeyore makes for a charming cartoon character, he does, after all, get left off the party list. I have always been ashamed of my tendency to drift into eddies of melancholy, and more than once I've been accused of wallowing in it, looking for trouble where there is none, making mountains out of molehills.

It reminds me of the time I decided to try Weight Watchers several years ago. I should have known not to go. I'd been before and decided it wasn't for me, but my friend, along with thousands of people over the last few decades, had achieved such good results using the plan that I thought maybe I'd changed and it could work for me too.

After parking the car at the local recreation center, I sat behind the wheel for a while, working up the courage to join the stream of women going into the meeting hall. I hoped I wouldn't see anyone I knew, and marveled at the way some of the women seemed to be using this as an occasion to socialize with friends. I hung my head in legitimate shame when I realized that my snobbery was fully operative. I thought I was too good for this, and that's the awful truth. I swallowed my pride and went in. The presenter for the day didn't help matters. She was so unbearably cheerful and perky I found myself looking for signs of an incision at the base of her neck, proof she'd been spirited off to the men's club like a Stepford wife and turned into June Cleaver. (Did anyone *ever* run the vacuum cleaner in high heels and pearls? Did the makers of that show have any idea what they were doing to future generations of women when they directed Barbara Billingsley to serve Wally and the Beave their afterschool milk in stemware?) You think I've digressed, but no, these are the thoughts that were running through my mind as I squirmed in my seat and looked for the nearest exit sign. But I was trapped.

Before I knew it, I was standing in line to weigh in. One by one, women stepped onto the scale and blushed to hear the numbers that confirmed what they already knew—they were still fat, though some were gleeful to learn they'd shed a pound or a part of a pound. Working the program. Tears of shame pushed their way into my eyes but were suddenly transformed into tears of anger (a survival tactic that has worked well for me over time) as I watched the woman in front of me step onto the scale and heard the weigh-in official say, "Uh oh, missy. You've been a bad girl this week, haven't you?"

Had I heard her right? Missy? Bad girl?

"No," I wanted to say as the fantasy me grabbed the woman by her frilly lapels and pushed her up against the wall. "*You're* the bad girl—for treating this woman as if she were a naughty child that you caught stealing from the cookie jar. For humiliating her in front of her friends. For being shanghaied into this whole stupid conspiracy that convinces women that nothing they do, absolutely *nothing,* matters if they are overweight. Never mind that they are doctors, lawyers, world leaders; they must still wear a scarlet letter, a giant red *F,* if, heaven forbid, they're *fat.* Hester Prynne's sin of adultery no longer warrants such treatment; it's okay to sleep around as long as you're not fat!" Of course, I didn't say any of these things, and thank goodness I didn't push anyone anywhere. Except for myself, whom I pushed out of line and propelled out the back door to stumble through the parking lot and climb into the safety of my car, where I threw a temper tantrum.

I would have a similar experience after an Overeaters Anonymous meeting, as I continued to search for help with this nuisance of a body which was really starting to get on my nerves. Again, overcome by shame, I left the meeting in tears, though this time I wasn't angry. This time I was just landing with a thud at the bottom of the pit. I don't know what I'd expected that morning. I guess I'd thought I'd get lots of love and sympathy and a few helpful tips on weight control, though it's hard to believe I could have been so naive. I sure wasn't prepared to hear that I might be addicted to eating, that perhaps I found my comfort and protection in food. Nor was I prepared to hear that my "issues" were all entwined with my husband's and that perhaps the two of us needed help. It appeared that the jig was closer and closer to being up.

Shortly after leaving Colorado and moving to Washington, events finally forced us to square off with the foreboding I'd felt on Lido Beach. We sought counseling. It had always been easy for me to rail at Don about what ailed him. His failings were patently obvious to me, and at last, I thought, he was prepared to own them. And he did. With unflinching courage, he stepped into the light, and I thought our troubles would soon be behind us. I'd never even heard the word *codependent,* and I certainly wasn't prepared to hear that I was as big a part of our problems as my husband. Hadn't I always been the one to hold our emotional lives together, the one with all the insight, all the answers? Things were not going according to my plan.

Sitting there in that OA meeting, when they talked about taking the first step—admitting you're powerless over food and your life has become unmanageable—I was not ready to hear it. To admit I was powerless over food would mean I had to admit I was powerless, period, and I'd spent a lot of time in the laboratory powering *up* the self I'd considered battle-ready, a woman who could survive in a world that often unrolled in tragic ways. I was a self-made bride of Frankenstein—not the prettiest girl in town, but steely, if necessary, and tough.

I'd learned how to be tough from my mom. In fact, all my role models were people who were tough, folks you couldn't keep down. Indeed, the picture of a person poor in any way—body or spirit—does not jibe with what I was taught, and it doesn't jibe with the American way. It bears no resemblance at all, for instance, to the characters created by turn-of-the-twentieth-century author Horatio Alger, whose all-American protagonists inspired our predecessors to grab life and go for the gusto. These fictionally empowered boys could do anything they set their minds to, including pull themselves up by their own bootstraps, an image which confounded me so much as a child that when my mother alluded to it, her point was almost entirely lost on me as I tried to imagine someone fallen down, struggling to right himself by tugging at his boots. Her point was that such people didn't need anyone's help to get by. They were anything but lacking in spirit, seemingly the very antithesis of the people to whom Jesus promised the keys to the kingdom.

Such stories gave shape and substance to the values sculpted and bequeathed to us by our grandmas and granddads—good, decent folks raised by immigrants who came to America from every corner of the planet and landed on these shores penniless, their only resources being their imaginations and the grit of their spirits.

My grandma and granddad had to move their family into a tent during the Great Depression after Granddad lost his store, and when they finally did move into a more substantial dwelling, it was a one-room apartment over a tavern. My uncle Bud told me it was his job to escort his little brothers to the toilet downstairs by maneuvering them through the drunks in the bar. Life was anything but easy for these people, and it's hard to imagine the double-barreled misery of the children of slaves who, though finally unchained, found themselves both penniless and despised. That anyone survived sometimes seems miraculous. And yet they did, and they survived because they were strong. For them, "Get tough or die" was more than a bumper sticker; it was code, and it left little room for the puny in spirit.

My mother certainly came from this stock, and it saw her through many trials and an immense tragedy. I was a mere toddler when my father committed suicide in 1949, leaving Mom, at age thirty-three, to raise six children with only a diploma from Scottsbluff High School to her name. Somewhere she gathered the strength to face all the small-town gossip and shame, punctuated by the pastor's public lament over the fiery destiny of my father's soul. Somehow, she herded her forlorn and fatherless little tribe into the future. I didn't fully appreciate what she had accomplished until, during my husband's residency, I grudgingly accepted the bulk of parental responsibility for a brief time for just two children and thought I was going to die.

Mother would explain to us later that though she managed, she did succumb to a period of numbness, a "year on ice," she called it, following my father's death. The first time I encountered Elizabeth Barrett Browning's poem about grief, I thought of my mom:

> . . . like a monumental statue set
> In everlasting watch and moveless woe
> Till itself crumble to the dust beneath.
> Touch it; the marble eyelids are not wet.
> If it could weep, it could arise and go.[2]

For Mom to crumble would have meant the disintegration of our family, and though I was too little to register the particulars of her counsel, I understood that the fibers woven into the fabric of our family were toughness, pride, loyalty, and love. The wit and grit of our Irish ancestors would enable us to survive this crisis, and there was little time to ponder anything *but* survival. When floodwaters are swirling around your ankles, there's hardly time to contemplate your navel. You grab whatever debris is floating by and ride it to dry land, and to heck with feeling sorry for yourself. We couldn't afford it, and there would be time enough later for us, each in our own way, to experience the pain of this tragedy that in many ways defined our lives. In the hour of our plight, no one was going to see us cry. Nothing in my mother's upbringing allowed for unchecked grief, viewed for the most part as self-pity. Attentive to the laws of nature, in which the lame and disabled get eaten for lunch, getting fit and staying strong seemed the wise thing to do. It would be years before I would come to understand that tears of weakness are the stuff from which real strength is made. But though I wish Mom had known it was okay to cry, I'm grateful to her for teaching me what she knew about survival. I can't really imagine her facing this awful tragedy any other way. *Because* of Mom's spirit, we survived.

The whole thing is very confusing, and it's made even more confusing when you consider that in Luke's account of this sermon, the blessing was given to the poor—period! In other words, we are supposed to be not only poor in spirit but poor in pocketbook as well. "Blessed are you who are poor. . . . But woe to you who are rich."[3] Talk about un-American. Where in the world do Horatio Alger's boys fit into God's plan, anyway? To suggest that we should be anything less than well fed and content seems patently unpatriotic. The story of Jesus' encounter with the rich young ruler poses serious problems for those Americans hoping to reconcile their acquisitive lives with God's Word.

But reconcile it we must, if we are going to be Christians of integrity. The connection between physical poverty and spiritual poverty is really pretty obvious when you think about it. Money and power give the illusion of independence and indestructibility. When we're sitting on top of the world, it's hard to accept that we're no different than the homeless woman digging through the Dempsey dumpster looking for empty cans, or the schizophrenic muttering paranoia as he lumbers down the street. Hard to believe that our money can't somehow help us buy our way out of anything, even death. Hard to believe that the playing field will be leveled at the morgue and that when all is said and done, the Donald Trumps of the world will lie side by side with the rescue mission bums on those cold slabs.

It turns out the word Jesus uses here does, in fact, suggest abject poverty. According to Barclay's commentary on Matthew, the word describes "the man who, because he has no earthly resources whatever, puts his whole trust in God."[4] Were we to take this literally, we would have to conclude that hundreds of thousands of believers, people who live comfortable, some even opulent, lives are unworthy of God's blessing, that only the Mother Teresas of the world or monks who have taken oaths of poverty are candidates for the kingdom. And maybe I'm tinkering with the truth when I say this, just covering my own middle-class behind, but I don't think that's the case. I sure hope not. What I do think, though, is that the rich and the comfortable usually have a harder time humbling themselves before God than the poor and destitute.

I am reminded of a conversation I had several years ago with a friend who has since passed away. Her name was Phyllis Lee, a beautiful African-American woman with whom I taught school. She told me about an acquaintance, also black, who absolutely recoiled at the image of slaves portrayed in most movies. Men, women, and children working in the cotton fields to the rhythm and sway of spirituals, those bluesy laments that enabled them to keep a steady pace at their labors as well as claim some measure of hope in what must have seemed an utterly hopeless situation. It irked this modern young black woman to imagine her ancestors oppressed by white Christians who had robbed them of their homes, families, and cultural identity and replaced them with a story about some long-ago, far-away white guy named Jesus, who loved them and would redeem their savage souls one day, welcoming them into some sort of unfettered celestial paradise as long as they were good little slaves now and did what they were told. I understood her reaction. Who among us does not experience a surge of pride when the beleaguered cinematic hero finally stands up in the face of sure death to declare his freedom, refusing to be shamed one more time? We identify with this hero; this is the guy we want to be in the face of oppression, not some shuffling, cowering old uncle whose spirit and back are broken, who hobbles off each night to his slave quarters murmuring mantras about a someday savior, who, I hasten to add, could have kicked the stuffing out of the Sanhedrin and knocked off Pilate all at the same time if he'd wanted to. I certainly wanted him to. I still want him to.

But pondering all this today, I wish I could ask those slaves, long dead and gone, what they found so comforting in the figure of Jesus. What about him gave them hope? Something in their circumstances gave them the ability to see what others could not see. And what Jesus is talking about here, I think, is the clarity of vision afforded by poverty. Poverty suggests an empty vault, and for many of us, until our vaults are empty, we think we have no need. And what the melancholy among us sometimes know, though may not be able to articulate, is that coming to the end of our resources may be our only hope for coming to the beginning of something more substantial than self. "I cry out to the LORD with my voice; with my voice to the LORD I make my supplication. I pour out my complaint before Him; I declare before Him my trouble."[5]

Our problem with this, as with much of Scripture, arises from the way we apply contemporary meaning to the language of the Bible. We read "poor in spirit" and immediately take it to mean "loser." We assume that *weakness* and *humility* are synonyms. I'm thinking that what makes this all seem so impossible boils down to our misunderstanding of the word *spirit*. When we hear it, understandably we think of vigor and strength. When our spirits are high, we're strong and capable; when they are low, we're weak and ineffectual. To be high-spirited, then, is a good thing, a virtue, something highly sought after. It suggests energy and zest for life.

To be spiritual is also a good thing. In fact, spirituality is enjoying something of a comeback in America these days (though religion is still highly suspect). Just look at Richard Gere. When he was named sexiest man alive by *People* magazine a few years ago, much was made of the fact that he is supposedly deeply spiritual. Spiritual *and* sexy? Be still my heart!

Actually, the word *spirit,* as it appears in Scripture, means "wind" or "breath." In 2 Samuel, the word used is *ruach,* a word that does indeed suggest strength and power. In Romans, Paul uses the word *pneuma* to describe that part of a person that is able to respond to God. What's central to both is that each has, as its source, God. So maybe what Jesus wanted folks to ponder was where their power comes from. And maybe there's a big difference between a vigorous, hearty spirit and an egocentric, haughty one. Hubris.

Americans tend to shun anything that asks us to submit or to subject ourselves to anyone, including monarchs. For us, to submit *is* to shuffle, and to be silent is to consent. But Jesus didn't shuffle or cower. When the occasion called for it, however, he did submit, and he consented—to do his Father's will rather than look out for his own well being. And there, as Hamlet would say, there's the rub. Many of us, tutored by parents and grandparents who limped through the depression, believe we must vigilantly look out for ourselves, because no one else is going to. Though we may like the idea of God and Jesus and all that they stand for, to actually throw our lot in with them, to trust them down here in the midden of our daily lives, to actually obey them, seems patently unwise and downright foolish. In *Amazing Grace,* Kathleen Norris traces the etymology of the word *believe* to discover that in its original Greek form it means, simply, "to give one's heart to."[6] Believing that Jesus existed, even accepting his divinity, is not the same as giving our hearts to him, a gesture very few of us are willing to make. We may long to heed Paul's admonition to the Corinthians that "the foolishness of God is wiser than man's wisdom, and the weakness of God is stronger than man's strength."[7] We may want to embrace the poetic paradox that tells us we are strong when we are weak, that we will live if we permit ourselves to die, but most of us think, realistically, that we dare not appear defenseless in this dangerous, wicked world. We dare not identify too literally with Christ.

It doesn't help that liars and false prophets throughout history have shamelessly misrepresented Christ. This bogus representation of Jesus is a grievous thing that can only be explained, I think, by the presence of God's enemy among us, known as everything from the Prince of Darkness to Satan. Jesus referred to him as the Evil One. Pretty much everyone has an opinion about evil, and though we don't all come down in exactly the same place about how it is manifested in the world, pretty much everyone who accepts its existence agrees that deceit is the devil's calling card; lies are his lifeblood. And he will stop at nothing to pervert the truth. We are all aware of the egregious manipulation of Scripture that has resulted in perverse practices such as slavery and the Holocaust. We are haunted by the very idea that someone could torture and kill in Jesus' name. But Satan set the precedent in the desert for the abuse of power and the manipulation of Scripture, and he delights in anything that suggests the world has gone berserk with hatred. God hasn't been behind any of these horrible events, past or present. Murder and mayhem are Satan's poison, and the only antidote, in my experience, is Jesus Christ. Only by spending time in humble quietude with him, only by leaving our prayer closets and living obediently and trusting his promises about how the story turns out, can we hope to keep evil at bay.

And while no compassionate person wishes adversity on any living creature, and we can't pretend to understand why God permits suffering, it's clear that people who have been driven to their knees by one hammer or another are in a better position to recognize the compassionate Shepherd for who he is than those who have lived lives of relative ease and have the illusion that they are somehow responsible for their good fortune. It's tempting sometimes to think that death-row inmates and other down-and-outers, or miserable souls caught in the throes of grief, "get religion" as a way of rationalizing their circumstances and easing their pain, easy to think of religion as the opiate of the oppressed. But I think it far more likely that the story of Jesus' suffering at the hands of oppressors, as well as his extension of mercy to the thief on the cross, resonates so deeply within the emotionally and spiritually bankrupt—people who have lost all hope and have no reason to believe that anything will ever change, people drained of all human resources, unencumbered and undistracted, people who appear to have had the stuffing kicked right out of them—that they are suddenly able to see Jesus for the real savior that he is and claim, through him, the kingdom of heaven. When suddenly we are robbed of everything and the foundation beneath our feet is crumbling, we know where to go.

Perhaps Christians need to spend more time with believers who have seen the underbelly of life. I once heard someone suggest that the ambience in our local churches should feel a lot more like that of the corner bar and a lot less like a museum of saints. I presume he was thinking of the welcoming and earthy atmosphere of the local tavern as opposed to the sometimes snobbish and crystalline atmosphere that seems to permeate our vestibules and narthexes. It concerns me that those of us who work with the youth in our Christian community fall into a trap of trying to cultivate young believers who resemble hothouse flowers we can proudly wear on our lapels like prom corsages. I fear that we perpetrate, without meaning to, a kind of spiritual perfectionism among our youth that leads them to try to balance themselves atop precarious pedestals, a fall from which could be deadly. I am not suggesting some sort of moral dumbing down in our church programs, just that we get off our pharisaic high horses and get down in the dirt with real people as Jesus did. It grieves me when I hear people say they don't feel like they should go to church because they are so screwed up or their lives are such a mess, or they don't have a decent outfit to wear, or they don't want the people sitting next to them to smell the smoke on their clothes. These are the Mary Magdalenes and well-women of our time! When you sit next to me, you are sitting next to a woman who smelled like stale smoke for over twenty-five years and didn't turn her heart toward God until all other options were shot.

I'm not suggesting we dim the lights, serve beer, and light the smoking lamp at church, though some folks seem to think we are dangerously close to the edge of this envelope when we permit amplified musical instruments in the sanctuary—and, heaven help us, trap sets! What I am suggesting, I guess, is that whatever your view on contemporary Christian music—and I'm sure you have one—it is high time we all pause, take a deep cleansing breath, and look to Jesus to see how we're supposed to conduct ourselves, whether we're at church or in line at the grocery store.

Sometimes getting outside the church building helps. Not long after I went to that OA meeting, I read about a group called

Adult Children of Alcoholics that was meeting in a church basement near our home. Maybe there, I thought, I could get some answers. It was pretty hard to sit through that first meeting, pretty hard to tolerate the diverse depictions of these folks' higher powers, everything from nurse logs in the Olympic rain forest to New Age nabobs. I swore I heard rumblings from the graves of my dead Sunday school teachers. Somehow I managed to sit still, and I'm glad I did. What I came away with was my first glimpse of the beauty of a broken spirit. Bereft, these people formed a community with others like themselves who had discovered that their cisterns were empty. Suddenly the connection between the first of the Twelve Steps and the first beatitude was obvious. "We admitted we were powerless . . ." "Blessed are the poor in spirit . . ."

In *Addiction and Grace,* Gerald May suggests that people are easily addicted to anything that will make them feel satisfied, if only temporarily, and warns that even serving God can interfere with the greater aim of knowing him. It's hard to believe God would have us repent of service to the church, unless one rethinks what is really involved in repentance. I noted an interesting connection between the words *repent* and *comfort* recently in the *Spirit Filled Life Bible.* In Psalm 23, the word *comfort* is *nacham,* which in its original use suggested a deep sigh such as that associated with repentance. Scott Cairns, in a poem that appeared in issue 31 of *Image: A Journal of the Arts and Religion,* explores the Greek word for repentance, *metanoia,* and poses the interesting notion that perhaps repentance is not so much a turning *away* from sin as a turning *toward* God. All this mysteriously dovetailed for me the other night as I pondered what seemed to me to be a revolutionary idea. What would happen if we simply turned away from all the things we have and all the things we do and all the things that eat up our time and energy, allowed everything to fall away so that we might turn ourselves fully and completely to God? If, one by one, we let it all go, from our preoccupation with our sexual orientation to our social causes to our addictions? What would happen if we actually chose to find our comfort in the Lord?

As I'm writing this, I'm thinking a lot of readers are going to get a little squeamish about emulating recovering alcoholics in their quest for holiness. I don't think we're very honest about our attitude toward alcoholics, really. We want to believe all the stuff we hear about how alcoholism is a disease and it's not the addict's fault any more than it's a diabetic's fault that he has diabetes, but deep down, I think we still see alcoholism as a condition of moral inefficacy. Some part of us believes that the alcoholic isn't so much sick as he is weak. Once again we get entangled in a semantic gill net, confusing weakness with humility. But I think what we really disdain about these people is their admitted dependence, on each other and on God. Most folks in recovery attend a meeting weekly, some daily. They need it; they need each other. Americans aren't keen on that much dependence. On the Fourth of July, we fill the night sky with fireworks to declare our *in*dependence. It's the hallmark of our American culture.

Assuming, though, that we are able to get in touch with our broken, sinful selves, most of us are likely to quickly permit the epiphany to fade like a photograph left in sunlight, so we can reclaim life on our own terms. There are just some sins we're so attached to, so downright fond of, that relinquishing them is too painful to bear. Especially anger and bitterness. For some reason, we especially like to hang on to those. The big one, of course, is pride.

I've been rereading the story of Saul in 1 Samuel this week, in which a pattern of human behavior is clearly evident. It seems the Israelites were not satisfied with God as their sole sovereign. Like middle schoolers clamoring for brand-name shoes, they wanted a king like all the other kids had, so God revised his plan and gave them what they wanted. He gave them Saul for a king (though he warned them there *would* be trouble in the end), and then he poured out every manner of blessing on Saul and his charges. Pretty soon, the once-humble king began to get puffed up about his power. He started to believe his own press and second-guess the directives of God. So hungry was he for the plaudits of the world, he forgot the creator from whom all good things had come. Eventually, he would allow fretful, wicked spirits to have their way with him. Incredulous when things began to fall apart, he was thrown into despair. At the climax of his reign, when he had ignored God one too many times, he gushed forth in his own defense but was silenced by the prophet Samuel, who reminded him, "When you were little in your own eyes, were you not the head of the tribes of Israel? And did not the LORD anoint you king over Israel?"[8]

We're all like Saul. When we get full of ourselves, all grown up and self-assured, we think we know better than God what to do; when our consolation abides in the praise of men rather than in the approval of God, we give ourselves over to fretful spirits and forget the very God who has been so gracious and generous to us and who so much wants to be in relationship with us. Blaise Pascal, reflecting on human nature, observed that "our desire for the esteem of those around us is such that pride will dominate us even in the midst of all our miseries and errors. We would even die gladly, provided people talked about it."[9]

Samuel's confrontation of Saul foreshadows Jesus' admonition that unless we come to God as children who, though sometimes obstinate and stubborn, generally recognize their need for help, we are bound to miss the kingdom being offered to us. This is particularly significant if what I remember hearing from the pulpit of a Methodist church many years ago is true—that a more faithful translation of the word for kingdom is king*ship,* suggesting not so much a place as a posture of dependence, a submission to an authority higher than our own.

Paradox abounds. On the one hand, we are expected to be strong enough to pick up a cross and follow Jesus, while on the other, we are told to be as little children. The truth lies in the tension between these two. Even a very small child can manage to pick up a heavy object, assuming she is not too proud to ask her father (or mother) for help. When Saul was childlike, he understood he needed the Lord. When he became egocentric and proud, he fell.

In Luke's account of Jesus' sermon, Jesus says, "Woe to you who are rich, for you have received your consolation."[10] To be consoled is to be comforted, and comfortable! In fact, the NIV translation of this verse reads, "Woe to you who are rich, for you have already received your comfort." Remember those quiz shows of the '50s? There was always the grand-prize winner, but there were never any losers because everyone went home with at least a consolation prize. I believe what Jesus is warning us about here is the danger of thinking we're big winners when, in fact, we're settling for the consolation prize. When Jesus warns those who are rich in spirit, he is addressing those of us who like to think of ourselves as self-made men and women who take our comfort in the trappings of the world: waterfront homes, luxurious automobiles (and unlimited oil supplies), the best foods and wines, custom-designed wardrobes, Oscars on the mantel, gobs of money in the bank, gorgeous kids in the best schools, and every other little thing that reveals what we really value. The danger here is not in folks being happy but in what we deem happiness, and in presuming that we have somehow earned it and are personally responsible for having it. And in believing the converse, that if really nasty things are our lot in life, we have no doubt screwed up royally and deserve exactly what we got. It's the American way. That's why we can all relate so well to the anger of the prodigal son's big brother, who stayed home, worked hard, and did his filial duty only to be trampled in the rush to welcome home his little brother, who had flown in the face of all that and gone off to squander his inheritance on whores. It is simply beyond our grasp that our Father might forego decorum to fall on the neck of such a child and smother him with kisses. But such is the nature of God.

Assuming we want to follow Jesus, what then are we supposed to do with all of the cool stuff we've been accumulating, including the awards and diplomas displayed on our walls? Is it so wrong to feel good about our accomplishments? I don't really think God wants us to be dirt poor and live in shacks, although getting rid of junk *is* liberating, and we *are* called to simplify our lives. I don't think God expects you to burn the plaques you got at graduation. He's the one who made you smart, or athletic or civic-minded or cute. But I think he does want us to grow and to see past the ends of our noses. I sometimes feel as if I have about as much vision as a teenage girl who truly believes she will achieve nirvana if she can just make the cheerleading squad, not knowing that a few years after graduation no one will remember who made cheerleader, or care. I think it pleases God when we enjoy our lives, whether that means breaking rushing records or leading cheers or being chess champions. But I think he wants us to guard against permitting our ultimate aim to be acquisition of it.

I think he wants us to know we are no different in his eyes whether we drive a Beamer or a bicycle. I used to tease my mom about how, when I was a kid flagrantly coveting the cool stuff other kids had, she would promptly remind me that "rich people aren't happy" and hasten to add that there was probably something fundamentally wicked behind the acquisition of all that wealth anyway. Despite her proclamation, I continued to gaze upon the rich kids with envy and, further, discovered that some of them really were nice and seemed pretty darned happy to me. I reckoned that maybe it was a temporary, superficial sort of happiness, but some of their families had been rich for a long time and appeared to be decent, humble folks. Still, I think Mom's word of caution, despite its quaint distortion, had scriptural footing. Jesus' amusing image of a camel trying to get through the eye of a needle, as a simile for a rich man trying to get into heaven, comes to mind.

Jesus isn't saying that poverty guarantees paradise, nor is he saying it will authenticate our lives as disciples, but it just might eliminate some of the barriers that stand between the kingdom and us. I love Denise Levertov's reflection "On a Theme by Thomas Merton,"[11] in which she depicts Adam "like a child at a barbaric fairgrounds," his "confused attention to everything" ultimately resulting in his despair. What is most unsettling about this poem is her reminder that this is Adam's choice; "Adam fragments himself." When we stuff ourselves with all the empty calories of the world, there is little space left for the Lord, and we become like the inns in Bethlehem with no room for the Christ child.

We become so controlled by our power, our fame, our work, and our pleasures, to say nothing of our greed and anger and jealousy, that we refuse to let go for fear of losing what we hold so tightly in our closed fists. A most disturbing moment in the story of the rich young man's encounter with Jesus is his sorrowful refusal to do as Jesus says. But even more disturbing is Jesus' silence. God never forces himself on us—not in the Garden and not now. Of Adam, Levertov writes, "God suffers the void that is his absence." And though the contemporary understanding of the verb *to suffer* is applicable here, for surely the Lord is pained by our absence, what may be more important is the alternate meaning of the word, for to suffer is to permit.

In rare moments of genuine candor, I am able to confess my disappointment to God for not making it possible for me to have it all. Like the Jews of Jesus' time, I long for a regal messiah, one with whom I might happily align myself, one whom I would graciously serve, asking only the reward of a place in his court, a few trappings of success, a nice high seat from which I might look down on the world that rejects him. I wish the golden thread that stitches the teachings of Jesus together were something other than humility, but it's not. Jesus was all about humble, in word and deed. What masterful irony. The artistry of Scripture makes me giddy sometimes. The word *humble* is derived from a Latin word that means "ground" or "earth." The divine Jesus was characterized by the very ground on which he walked and the dust he washed off his disciples' feet, not by his earthly power and not by what he owned. It is good to remember the down and dirty nature of the incarnation. It's what makes it so rich, so infinitely and mysteriously wonderful. That our God would stoop to become so completely one of us, so very God and so very down-to-earth human all at once, strains our understanding of love so thoroughly we can hardly wrap our minds around it, though I think our hearts get it right a good deal of the time, for "the heart has its reasons that reason knows not of."[12]

God wants us. The question remains as to whether we want him. And so, once again confronted by the tension between our lust to satisfy the flesh and our mysterious longing for something more, we face the terrible freedom to decide whether we will choose the blessedness of God's high calling to be healed and holy, which will mean being broken and having our illusions of success summarily shattered, or opt instead for temporary spoils— the consolation prizes of the world—and turn our backs on the kingdom.

A pivotal moment in my spiritual journey occurred when I experienced the life-shattering phone call in which I was told I might have cancer. I hesitate to write about it because it was such a sacred experience. I fear I will diminish it in some way. But it's important, so I'll try. When the doctor discovered the mass in my breast, everyone from the radiologist to my husband thought it was malignant. My mother died of breast cancer in 1992, and my sister Linda had recently had a mastectomy.

The persona I work so hard to present to the world, proud, strong, seasoned, and capable, was instantly laid low and replaced by a frightened little girl who reluctantly called her friends and asked them to come to her rescue. They came instantly, three women—Carla, Pam, and Sunny—and gathered around me on the living room sofa, arranging themselves so that each had a hand resting somewhere on my body. And we prayed. I remember my astonishment at how brave each of them was, boldly going before God with pleas for my healing but also with uncen-

sored expressions of disappointment, even anger. They spoke to
God like kids who are confident they can speak truthfully without fear of stirring their father's ire. I had been ashamed of my
neediness, embarrassed to call and ask for help. Now I was simply in awe of these women, my friends. They were like those bold
men Mark wrote about who couldn't get through the crowd to
seek Jesus' help, so they cut a hole in the roof and lowered their
friend through it so Jesus could touch and heal him. I could
hardly speak, I was so knocked out by this show of bold love.
When all was said and done, the tumor removed and pronounced
benign, I was taken aback when, reading my Bible one morning, I came across an old familiar story and discovered it was my
story.[13] I revisited it in this poem, "There Was a Woman":

What terror must have gushed
through her, purifying, perhaps
chasing, the flush of blood shed,
she had always presumed,
drop for drop, in payment for
every single sin she had ever committed
in her youth. What dread
must have paralyzed her heart
to hear his voice, insistent, demanding
to know, "Who touched me?"
What shameless, haphazard niggle of
hope had possessed her, prompted this
brazen display of groveling, grabbing at his hem?
What humbling
confusion must have followed
to hear him say her reaching out
had healed her.[14]

I hasten to add that any physical healing that occurred that night pales in comparison to the sacred healing that was wrought in the lives of the women who gathered to pray. It turns out I was not the only one who realized she'd been in the presence of holiness. In one sense, we were bereft of spirit, yet somehow, beggars that we were, we were gutsy, a bit like those vigorous ancestors who'd paved the way for us, a bit like my mom. And we all learned that night that we were children of the kingdom, that our peace came in knowing we weren't alone, and that in reaching out to touch Christ, we actually found him.

2

Like Honey in the Comb
Compunction

I knew this was going to hurt. I didn't know it would hurt like this. I didn't know I would have chest pains, that my heart would feel as if it were about to burst, literally explode. It occurred to me that we err when we distinguish between our emotional and our physical hearts; today I was learning that the feelings I have for my children are housed in a very real, red heart, and grieving the loss of them could, in fact, end my life. I would learn later that the word Jesus used when he spoke of the pure in heart, *leb,* includes both the physical and the emotional.

Neither one of my sons had died. In fact, one of them was safe at home with friends. The other, our eldest son, Pat, we had just moments before delivered to his new digs at college. I had anticipated this day all summer, actually throughout his senior year of high school, trying to prepare for it so that I might get through it without earning his disdain. We both hoped I might escape with at least a shred of dignity. As I said, I knew it would hurt, that I'd no doubt blubber at an inopportune moment, but I did not anticipate this.

When he decided to stay in state to go to school, I thought it might mitigate the grief. Whenever I got weepy or whiny, friends hastened to console me with this reminder: "He isn't going far away, and you can see him whenever you like." But these gentle reproofs did not console me; in fact, they made me mad. Didn't these people understand that the details of his departure were insignificant, that he was leaving home—*leaving home,* for crying out loud! I began to remember the many foreshadowings of this event, captured in the video archives of my memory: the first time he toddled around a corner in the yard and I lost sight of him, his first solo bike ride when I stood and thought to myself, "Oh Lord, we've given him *wheels!* What on earth were we thinking?" The fact that we continued to give him means and motives to escape baffles me still. What *were* we thinking? We should have known these reckless acts of generosity would come back to bite us, as indeed they were doing today.

The drive up to Bellingham this August morning had been pleasant. It was as if the Skagit Valley had nestled down for a nap under a light blanket of morning fog that, assuming all things were normal, would be thrown off by noon, permitting the late summer sun to come out and warm the air. We made easy conversation as the highway unrolled before us, including the requisite joke about the fact that the Stillaguamish River was, indeed, still a guamish. It wouldn't take many such trips before Pat would put the kibosh on that meager attempt at humor, after he'd slogged down the I-5 corridor for the thousandth time. But that was yet to come. Today, everything was new.

There was not the usual bustle of incoming freshmen on campus when we arrived, because students employed by the university were required to report a week early to go through job orientation, and since Pat would be a fry cook in the student union, we were a week ahead of the crowd. The quiet of the place disturbed me. I don't know if I had hoped to garner some measure of comfort from seeing other mothers in pain, or if I was just looking for validation that I was not the only woman on the threshold of a panic attack. The place was a ghost town. The good news was that we didn't have to jostle for a spot near the dorm, a mammoth high-rise affair called Nash Hall, so that unloading the trunk and getting Pat settled into his room on the sixth floor was relatively easy. Having lived at home throughout my college career, I was unprepared for the monastic appearance of his dorm room, a small cell with two desks and two beds and something that vaguely resembled a closet emitting the residual odors of hordes of former students.

We spent the day doing what we could to transform his quarters into something warm and familiar, making up the bed with his down comforter from home, posting Darth Vader on the wall at the foot of his bed, finding a hiding place for his guitar so it wouldn't get stolen when he left his room unlocked (which we all knew he would do routinely), and hooking up a stereo whose speakers would have been better suited to the Seattle Kingdome. The final touch was suspending his bicycle from the ceiling, and we were done. The three of us piled into the car for a quick motor tour of the town, making note of music stores and beach walks within hiking distance of school, and then it was time for us to go.

Back at the dorm, I scribbled down the phone number of the pay phone nearest his room, as well as the number posted on his RA's door. It was clear that any idea I had of reaching him easily was ludicrous, and this did nothing to quell the burgeoning anxiety rising within. As he walked us to the car, he said he thought he'd take a bike ride around town later, and I suppressed the questions that leapt into my mind: "Who will know you've gone out? Who will know where you've gone and whether you've come in safely?"

I looked at his father, whose feelings I knew mirrored mine, and marveled at his composure, his stoic detachment. In fact, he cracked a joke, which caused us all to laugh, and on that note, quickly, before a more melancholy chord could be struck, we climbed into the car and eased away from the curb. When I looked back, I watched Pat, tall and lean, disappear into the bowels of that monstrous, empty dormitory, and I began to cry.

Of course I cried. His father cried too. The difference was that his father eventually stopped, whereas I seemed to have launched a ship that was never going to return to port. At first, I let the tears flow unrestrained. They were the good tears of grief. But somewhere along the road, they turned to the groans and ululation of something more, something darker and uglier. I was going down in a quagmire of remorse. The simple grief of remembering him as a child, innocent and adorable, was lost in a sea of shame that left no room for sentimentality. I wanted him back; I wanted another chance to be his mother so I could do it right this time. One after another, scenes from his young life played through my mind, as if from a home movie, shining the light of truth on my life as a mother.

I remembered, when he was still in foot jammies, my impatience with him for interrupting me, standing in the doorway beckoning me to come look at something with him, some phenomenon that had engaged his inquisitive little mind, like the water pipes under the kitchen sink, for instance, where he had bent his toddler body at the waist like a jackknife to peer and point, then look to me for an answer to his inquiry: "Where does the water go?" I see him at three, suffering a painful earache and longing for his own bed only to discover we had allowed movers to come while he was at Aunt Nancy's and load all of his things on a truck and take them away. Walking into the empty house, he emitted a primal scream and, before I knew it, darted past me and dashed out the front door. He was at the end of the street and around the corner before I caught and tackled him, wrestled his angry little body into submission. Another moving day two years later, I would find him sitting in an empty garage on his tricycle, a woeful look on his face, watching the movers load the truck again. This time he would make a vain attempt to exercise a measure of control over his life by refusing to relinquish his trike, the last thing to be loaded into the van. Asked what he was feeling, he announced that he was confused, described a totem pole lodged in his middle where all of his feelings were fighting to see who got to be on top.

I try to stop the tape from running. I cannot bear it. But I have lost control of this situation. I remember the night I lost my temper and smacked his little brother on the behind. Pat was five. I see him, in my mind's eye, as he drapes a comforting arm around Michael's baby shoulders and escorts him down the hall, returning moments later to stand in front of me, feet spread apart, hands on hips: "You asked God for babies and that's what he gave you! If you wanted grown-ups, you should have asked God for grown-ups!" And I see him kneeling on our king-size bed at six, having awakened from another round of night terrors, refusing to allow me to hold or comfort him, telling me I had hurt him when he was little. I cannot believe that this did not prevent me from ever hurting him again, but continuing scenes reveal that it did not.

I am rolling my eyes and sighing sighs of grave disappointment when he tells me he's forgotten to do his science project for school, or worse, I'm in his face, spewing venomous reprimands over another lost library book. A library book, for crying out loud. I would rather be flogged than remember any more.

Mercifully, relief comes when I remember the night I asked him to forgive me. He was fourteen, all signs of child vanishing from view. Wretched with shame for sins committed against my kids and newly aware of the manifestations of sinfulness in my marriage, I asked Pat to sit with me and hear my confession. I was touched by his willingness to do so and overwhelmed by his beauty. That he was merciful and forgiving did not surprise me. And though, despite the desire of my heart, I would discover I was not through sinning against him yet, rarely would it be with the reckless sinfulness of the past. That night proved to be a milestone in our relationship, a relationship in which each forgives the other unfailingly, though not always as promptly as we should and not without the accompanying pain that one learns to expect when shattered pride is involved, as it always is when grace is called for. Little did we know then how many times each of us would be called upon to forgive the other.

I believe that all of this occurring as it did at the onset of Pat's adolescent years was a great gift to our family, perhaps because it was marked by an unmistakable posture of penitence and sorrow and the generous outpouring of grace and forgiveness that accompanies repentance. Because God set our feet on a new path

that night, we survived Pat's teen years. Oh, they were punctuated with the usual jots and tittles of adolescent angst, but all was
covered in grace, a grace that would take us through that shad-
owy time a few years later with his brother. We discovered the
healing that rises out of genuine remorse. And on this harbinger
day, having delivered our firstborn into the world, I was discovering the properties of undiluted grief, a compound made up of
certain loss and unattenuated remorse. Truth stood before me, feet
spread apart, hands on hips, and I wept.

*Blessed are those who mourn,
for they will be comforted.*

I don't like a lot of contemporary Christian music. Actually, I'm
ambivalent about it. I like the way the drums and the amplified
instruments permit me to pretend I'm Linda Ronstadt and belt
out songs without any danger of actually being heard. Furthermore, some of the music draws me into worship in a way the old
Wesley hymns do not, perhaps because I'm pretty kinesthetic and
many of these new songs evoke a sort of rocking and rolling that
allows me to get out of my head, where I am all too frequently
held prisoner. I'm not sure about any of this, but I am sure of one
thing—when I get to heaven and I'm no longer in danger of
being "caught" dancing and subsequently ridiculed by my big
brothers and their friends, I plan to move back the furniture and
boogie my way through at least half of eternity. But I digress. I'm
still sorting on this one, but I think much of contemporary Christian music is just too sweet, too sentimental and gooey, like
caramel. It tastes good at first, but then it gets stuck in my teeth
and starts to make me feel sort of nauseated. Comparing contemporary praise choruses with the old standards is a bit like

comparing Hallmark greeting card verses to John Donne's holy sonnets.

All that crooning about being in love with God seems to lack decorum, though I don't want to wag, like Michal, King David's wife, at people who unashamedly throw themselves body and soul into worship. It just feels sometimes as though we're all getting way too familiar with the Lord. And by familiar, I don't mean intimate; I mean cozy, like teenagers at a beach party. I love the idea of Jesus' being my friend, but I'm not keen on the idea of his being my sweetheart. I can't think of him as my brother and my lover simultaneously. It's too incestuous.

But all of this is probably more a matter of taste than anything. You say potayto and I say potahto. Or perhaps it's a matter of choosing the appropriate music for particular occasions, as suggested by Paul when he encouraged the Ephesians to meet together often and sing psalms *and* hymns *and* spiritual songs,[1] implying there is a difference between these genres and all are acceptable. The point is to worship God in song. But worship services that feature only contemporary, soft-rock lyrics tend to make me uneasy for another reason. A steady diet of these praise choruses, or at least too many at one sitting, actually causes me to feel like an ersatz Christian, like everyone around me is a finely cut diamond and I'm a first-class cubic zirconia. Folks around me seem to be experiencing some level of spiritual ecstasy which I, feet firmly planted on the ground, cannot seem to achieve. On particularly bad days, if I'm going to be really honest, I find their ecstasy highly suspect. I'm sure this says way more about me than it does about these songs or the people singing them, and the truth be known, I've actually experienced a little ecstasy from time to time in this worship context. But such occasions are rare, and it's far more likely I'll end up feeling crummy. And though this may be a manifestation of some neurosis peculiar to me, I know I'm not entirely alone with these feelings. I look around the sanctuary and am pretty sure I detect others fidgeting, wondering what's wrong, why they're not caught up in the rapture that seems to have ignited virtually every worshiper in the place while we frauds spark and sputter in their midst like dud pop-bottle rockets on the Fourth of July. Spiritual squibs.

It brings back, with stark clarity, the night I was saved. I'd been attending vacation Bible school at the little Southern Baptist church in my hometown. My aunt and uncle, in a gesture of evangelical love, took me as their guest. For two weeks, I enjoyed standard VBS fare: the songs and stories, a bit of time at the craft table, a trip outside for a game of Father May I (a pre-PC revisionist version of Mother May I designed to reflect God's goodness). Following glue and games, there was, at last, our reward— Kool-Aid and cookies. To this day, nibbling cookies and sipping fruit juice transports me right back to the basement of our old church. That's where I met Brother George. He was the pastor, and we were all encouraged to refer to him in this quaint and familiar way. I was far more interested in his son, Billy, a typical PK who terrorized the Sunday school teachers and VBS volunteers as expected of preachers' kids everywhere, but Brother George was okay too, and besides, getting to know him couldn't hurt my chances of getting closer to his errant offspring.

Anyway, as VBS wound down this particular summer, Brother George came to visit our sixth-grade class to invite us to take Jesus into our hearts. It seems so simple when I look back on it. But it was anything but simple then. For some reason, he asked me to stay when the other kids were dismissed. I remember we sat in the back pew of the sanctuary; it was a beautiful day, and I was eager to leave. But it was clear Brother George had something important to say. He got straight to the point. In a very loving way, Brother George urged me to get saved. There was nothing mean or malicious in his endeavor, nothing sinister. Not even when he warned me that if I let even one more day go by, I might spend eternity in hell. I could, he said, say no to Jesus this morning and be hit by a truck on my way home, and what a sad and sorry thing that would be. Why on earth I did not jump at this offer is beyond me, but I declined. I said I would think about it, and the truth is, I thought of little else between then and the following weekend.

Sunday night service found me at the back of the church once more, this time standing for the altar call. For three days and three nights I had thought about the things Brother George had told me, carefully crossing streets as I mused. My restraint in accepting Jesus was not about willful stupidity, I now realize, but about a feeling I was waiting to have. I had watched others "go forward" during altar calls before, and it was clear that they were undergoing some sort of miraculous, life-changing thing, a thing required of one looking to be saved. And I had yet to experience whatever it was. On this night, though, no doubt weary from all that curbside vigilance, I decided to go for it. I think I thought the feeling would maybe come as I made my way to the front of the church.

But it didn't. Heart nearly bursting, I stepped into the aisle and began to move forward. The tears came quickly, and I was vaguely aware of people to the right and left of me smiling and nodding. "Oh Lord," I groaned inwardly, "what am I doing?" But it was too late to turn back, and so onward I went. Brother

George was pretty happy to see me coming. He wore a great big smile and welcomed me with a hug, asking me if I was there to accept Jesus into my heart. I was sobbing by this time, dying to tell him the truth: "No, no . . . I'm sorry. I don't know what I'm doing. I thought I should come forward but *the feeling* never came and this is all a big fat lie and I'd really like to just quietly go away now and never come back." Instead, I nodded a jerky, tearful assent. Placing his hands on my shoulders, he proudly turned me to face the congregation, which obviously perceived my anguish as that of a repentant sinner, and beamed at my quivering, wretched little display of remorse. Little did they know. Sister Lou Dell, the organist, struck the last resounding note of the hymn, the lights came up, and Brother George presented me to the body. I will never forget my shame as one after another came up to hug me or pump my hand, heaping blessings on me, blessings that could find no place to light for the burden of falsehood that I bore in having told this awful lie.

All that remained now, the pastor informed me, was to make plans for my baptism. Brother George told me he would be calling my mother later in the week, and I went home. When I got there, I went straight to my room. I suppose my aunt and uncle told my mother the good news, though I really don't know. I threw myself in a heap and continued to sob. In my sleep I must have managed to dissociate from the entire affair, because I awoke in a comfortable state of denial. I think I decided it must have been some other dumb girl who had made such a fool of herself the night before. This little trick would come in handy over time. I don't remember much of what happened until the phone rang a couple of nights later and I heard my mother consenting to my baptism over the phone. When she hung up, the tears began to gush again. All I remember about the exchange between the two of us is my inarticulate pleading and Mother's look of complete bewilderment, followed by her promise to call the preacher and postpone my baptism until further notice. I didn't know much about what was going on, but something in me decided that the lie I'd told at the time of that altar call was nothing compared with the lie I'd be telling if I went through with that baptism.

The end of this story will disappoint you. It's painfully anti-climactic. Here's what happened. My two older sisters, Linda and Nancy, had been going to church with Uncle Jack and Aunt Esther during this time as well, and a few months after my salvation debacle, they went forward to announce their commitment to Jesus and their desire to get baptized. I decided to go with them. You might expect that the decision was fraught with angst, but it wasn't. In fact, in thinking on it, I have to wonder if I'd ever really been all that concerned about lying to God or just scared to wade into that baptismal tank alone with Brother George. I don't remember that any of us ever talked about any of this; in fact I'm sure we didn't, because what I do remember, vividly, is the abject loneliness I felt throughout this ordeal. Whether it is real or imagined, I don't know. I don't think my mother talked to me about it, though I suppose she may have tried. I remember feeling grateful to her for getting me off the hook the first time. She'd do the same thing for me later when the dentist said I had to have braces and I locked myself in the bathroom until Mom swore I wouldn't have to. Insofar as my baptism was concerned, I guess she presumed I would let her know when and if I decided to go through with it. I remember years later being surprised to hear that she had always been unsure of her own salvation because she, too, was waiting for the feeling that never came.

Though she was reassured in her twilight years that this feeling was not a requirement, I believe that in a small corner of her heart, she secretly doubted the validity of her conversion right up to the time of her death.

So maybe my feeling of being a fraud is genetic. All I know is I have long suffered from a vision of myself as an orphaned waif on the front porch of an antebellum mansion, peeking over the windowsill at the *real* family gathered around the table inside, and modern Christian song services tend to evoke and enlarge that mental picture. Everybody seems to be getting it right but me.

I've spent many hours thinking about the night I was saved and have determined that a big part of my problem was my inability to see myself as a sinner. The altar call at our church was always accompanied by the congregation singing every single verse of "Just As I Am" (sometimes more than once), the lyrics of which I simply could not appreciate at the ripe old age of eleven. I'd done some pretty snotty things to my brothers and sisters, but I hadn't yet smoked cigarettes or gone to a dance or made out in the Sunday school resource room—those occurrences would come later. The miserable "wretch" who wrote "Amazing Grace" had obviously done things I hadn't done yet. Perhaps it was within that wretchedness that one finally acquired the feeling I waited for the night I moved up the aisle toward salvation. At eleven, my understanding of sin was, of course, faulty, due in large part to grownups who manipulated the subject to keep kids in line, a temptation I too would face as a parent. Sins were the bad things you did: smoking, drinking, dancing, making out. Stealing and cheating were sins too, but the adults didn't seem nearly as worried about them as they did about the sins that led teens to commit the one really "big" sin that held such fascination for us and so terrified our parents, the one that landed bad girls in the Florence Crittenton Home (to which our mothers and grandmothers always added "for Wayward Girls" just in case we didn't fully grasp the shame associated with going there). One thing is sure, I wasn't prepared when I came face to face with my sinfulness a few short months after my baptism.

I have a little heart-shaped pin tucked away in a hidden compartment of my jewelry box. I've had it for forty years. A boy named Ralph handed it to me on a crisp October Saturday morning in Fort Collins, his name engraved in the center of it. Ralph lived down the street. Sheepish, he thrust his gift at me and then just stood there. I was standing as well, straddling my balloon-tire bike. I turned the pin over in my hand and sighed. It was very pretty, but Ralph was *such* a nerd. And he wasn't cute at all—an unruly shock of dirty brown hair always falling in his face. And those geek Lee (not Levi) jeans rolled up at the ankle. I remember thinking I had an uncanny knack for attracting misfits, boys none of the other girls would ever even talk to let alone "go with." It never occurred to me that I was pretty much the female equivalent of such a boy. (I actually held fast to a secret belief that *if* Elvis Presley ever came to Fort Collins and met me, he would not be able to resist my nubile charm and would swoop me away to live at Graceland.) What happened next on this Saturday morning is blurry, and I'd like to believe that the details I do remember are false, but they're not. I shrugged my shoulders, rolled my eyes, and muttered a meager "thanks." Clasping his heart in my sweaty little pubescent palm, I turned the front wheel of my bike away from Ralph, pushed off, and pedaled away, leaving him standing on my front sidewalk alone. I didn't like him, and I definitely couldn't afford to be seen standing around with him.

The next morning, I learned that Ralph was dead. "Don't you know that boy who lives on the corner?" my mother inquired as I emerged sleepy-eyed from my bedroom. "It seems he and his dad were getting ready for a hunting trip yesterday afternoon, and the boy's rifle, on the floor between his knees, pointed upward, accidentally went off." In Ralph's face. The same face that had looked expectantly into my face yesterday morning, just hours before he went home and died. The face I had shunned and turned away from. I was stunned.

I took none of the usual perverse pleasure kids take finding themselves close to a newsworthy event. There was no running around telling friends I was the dead boy's neighbor, that he, in fact, *liked* me and had talked to me just that morning, given me a present even! I carried the story of our meeting deep inside under layers of heavy quilts. For days, I walked around with a film-reel memory looping through my skull: Ralph's heart in my hand, the deep sigh escaping from my disappointed lungs, the rolling of my eyeballs, the shrug of my disdain—and that pathetic, worse-than-nothing little "thanks" I had tossed to him like a doggy treat before I rode off in search of cool.

My shame was real, palpable, and legitimate. I'd been an insufferable brat, and there was no one who could say anything to alter that fact, though I'm sure my mother tried. Now I understood sin. Ever after, when I sang of God's amazing grace, I would understand wretchedness. In an instant, I had made a choice I could never unmake, and I could not go to Ralph for forgiveness. He was gone. I kept the pin, and keep it still, to remind me that no matter how hard I try to be good, there's always a battle raging inside of me, as convoluted and tortuous as the prose the apostle Paul used when writing about it in the seventh chapter of Romans:

I do not understand what I do. For what I want to do I do not do, but what I hate I do. And if I do what I do not want to do, I agree that the law is good. As it is, it is no longer I myself who do it, but it is sin living in me. I know that nothing good lives in me, that is, in my sinful nature. For I have the desire to do what is good, but I cannot carry it out. . . . What a wretched man I am! Who will rescue me from this body of death?[2]

In the second of the Beatitudes, Jesus calls us to mourn and promises that in that mourning, we will be comforted, echoing the poetry of Joel, who called for the people of Israel to "rend your heart and not your garments. Return to the LORD your God."[3] It's a call that runs against the grain of our cultural ethos, despite trendy attempts to "get in touch with our feelings," which we secretly hope everyone will do in the soundproofed office of a licensed therapist. We have not always been so ashamed of our grief. A widow's weeds once silently reminded others of the wearer's loss; friends and neighbors anticipated the sounds of keening and wailing rising from the homes of those who had lost a loved one. As for penitent sinners, a mourners' bench was once provided in the church for those who found themselves caught in the throes of remorse, recalling, no doubt, James' imperative to grieve, mourn, and wail, to let laughter be turned to mourning and joy to gloom.[4] I wonder how many of us would be willing to publicly identify ourselves with these sinners today. The Roman Catholic confessional remains, of course, and there are times I want to haul my Protestant behind into one and cough up the sins that are burdening my heart. I am curious to know how much business these booths get in these days of moral anarchy, in a world in which the word *sin* has all but disappeared from our language.

One of the first things I've done in the confirmation class each year is tackle the cumbersome question of sin. I begin by pointing out that sin is a pretty old-fashioned word, seldom heard outside of church, and even there, softened as much as possible. Presbyterians are much gentler than some in their approach to sin, or perhaps I should say in their approach to discussions about sin. When I was a teenager, sex outside of marriage was a sin. Full stop. No one had any doubt about it. Today, sex outside of marriage is considered pretty much the norm, the only negative aspect of it being the possible contraction of an STD or an unwanted pregnancy. Adultery was a sin where I came from too. Now it seems to be, at worst, a selfish choice, unless of course your spouse is likewise engaged, in which case, no one's getting hurt, so it's no big deal. Don't ask, don't tell. By the world's standards at the dawn of the twenty-first century, we don't so much sin as make "mistakes" or "poor choices." We behave in "unhealthy" and "inappropriate" ways. Sadly, even when we do acknowledge wrongdoing, rather than feel any deep remorse about it, we tend to rationalize it by saying that we're only human and, after all, learn best from our mistakes. And if that doesn't work, we can always defend our sins by claiming our parents drove us to our errant ways. Fewer and fewer people, it seems to me, have the courage to own up to sinful behavior. That's good news for lawyers, maybe, but bad news for our hearts.

Many years ago our senior pastor, Jim Mead, accepted an invitation to come and talk with my Bible study group. The kids had some tough theological questions they wanted answered, and he graciously agreed to take them on. I remember that he defined sin as that which destroys, as opposed, he said, to creative things, things that build others up, give hope and promise to the world.

I like that. From everything I can gather about evil, it seems to be characterized by destruction. Jim's definition provides a quick check to use in tight situations. With one simple question, we can get a sense of the nature of our behavior at any given moment. Is what I'm doing creative and positive, or destructive and negative? I warn you, though, it's disturbing how frequently you find your motives and methods in question when you put them to this little test. A colleague at work comes into your office and shuts the door so the two of you can talk more freely about a cohort. The direction of that conversation, if it continues at all, will be changed by holding it up to the light of this simple question. It doesn't take long to realize how many seemingly harmless gestures and behaviors are in fact tainted by sin: gossip, overindulgence in food and wine, going into debt, flirting with the boss. If one is willing to follow these loose threads to their ends to see where they're liable to go, conviction of folly will no doubt follow.

In addition to this, I like to add a second test question. Is the thing I am engaged in likely to bring me closer to God, or lead me farther away from him? This one helps me get beyond what theologians refer to as sins of the flesh and into that deeper and darker domain—sins of the spirit, the chief of which, of course, is pride. And its inverse, shame. This two-edged sword has wreaked havoc in more lives than any other has.

I am convinced it was my father's shame that led him to kill himself. No one can be sure exactly what a suicidal person is thinking at the time of his or her death, of course, but all evidence in my father's life points to the fact that he was completely despondent when he could not seem to call a halt to his drinking. I learned recently that the word *despondent,* broken down, means something like "unwilling to keep a promise." My father's shame drove him to despair, and in a gesture that may well have been, in his mind, an act of generosity, he took himself out of our family picture, no longer able to make or keep promises. I will never forget the day it occurred to me that his shame was really a form of pride. Not the kind of pride that makes a man feel as if he is above the law or better than everyone else but its photo negative, a kind of pride that suggests that while everyone else is permitted to be imperfect, you alone are not. While everyone else in the world deserves God's forgiveness, somehow he expects more from you than the rest. It matters not whether we place ourselves above or below the throng of humanity; in either case, we deem ourselves outside of God's reach and, in doing so, are snatched up and consumed by pride.

If I could magically alter one moment in my personal history, I would go back and help my father see that his wretchedness was no worse than anyone else's, his sin no more profound. I would give him eyes to see himself as the broken child God saw, a child in need of an embrace. A child in need of love.

A few years ago when our youngest son, Michael, was studying to be an actor, he landed a part in a disturbing and thought-provoking play called *Short Eyes,* written by an ex-con named Miguel Pinero. In it, Michael played a convicted child molester, and living in this character's skin changed my son's life. I chose not to fly to Dallas to see him in it after he told me how it ended, but we talked about the play often during production. On one such occasion, he asked me why I thought people were so hateful in their response to child abusers, and I said I believe it goes much deeper than the obvious disdain we hold for such people. I remember watching the live news coverage of crowds gathered outside the Florida prison where Ted Bundy was about to be executed. In strident opposition to the candle-bearing activists who were present to protest capital punishment, there was a band of tailgate revelers wearing "Burn Bundy Burn" T-shirts and cooking hamburgers on a portable grill, at once jocular and bellicose in their celebration of Bundy's imminent demise. And though I've spent a lifetime waffling on this issue, I am confident of this: folks who take pleasure in an execution have big personal issues. It seemed pretty evident to me that these party animals were working very hard to put distance between themselves and this murderer, perhaps because they knew if they stopped making noise and stood still, they might accidentally catch a sidelong glimpse of themselves in a mirror and see Ted Bundy in the reflection.

When Jesus called us to mourn, he invited us to go deep within ourselves and realize our gargantuan capacity for sin. When we do that, when we imagine ourselves doing "the worst our kind can do," as Denise Levertov[5] put it, then we can begin to understand the measure of grace that has been poured out on us. In a recent Ash Wednesday service, we were reminded to think of all that we should have done and did not do, as well as all that we did which we should not have done. Debts and trespasses. A regular revisitation of our past, recent and distant, is vital to the Christian. As C. S. Lewis discovered in his study of pain, "A recovery of the old sense of sin is essential to Christianity."[6] To contemplate this, thoroughly and without distraction, will vex the spirit of a truthful person to the breaking point, and we, like David, will fall with our faces in the dirt of contrition to confess our sin: "For I know my transgressions, and my sin is always before me. Against you, you only, have I sinned. . . . The sacrifices of God are a broken spirit; a broken and contrite heart, O God, you will not despise."[7] Kyrie eleison.

I have witnessed a close friend anguish this week over her failure to share the love and friendship of Jesus with a young neighbor boy who died suddenly last weekend, a child precisely the same age I was when Brother George so desperately wanted me to know Jesus. I want to interfere with her pain, reassure her that she has been a Christ-model for this child in many unspoken ways, whether or not she ever talked to him directly about Jesus, and I actually believe it's true. I fear she is caught up in a web of toxic shame that comes not from God but from some misguided idea about her responsibility in the universe; I want to believe she is just being neurotic and self-absorbed. But I never know where toxic shame ends and legitimate shame kicks in, and in matters of God, I do not want to be presumptuous and possibly interfere with the work of the Holy Spirit. It's hard to keep quiet, to witness a beloved friend caught in the throes of remorse, but we are too quick, I fear, to help each other out of penitent despair. We would serve others better by sitting with them as they grieve, ever ready to deliver, once more, the message of grace and forgiveness after the fact, to remind them, as the Venerable John of the Ladder did in his writings about the divine ascent, that mourning and grief "contain joy and gladness interwoven within, like honey in the comb."[8]

I am not suggesting that we all walk around wearing hangdog expressions and heaving Eeyorian sighs. I am not suggesting that we indulge in what the ancient fathers called *accidie,* a level of despondency and listlessness that leads to faineancy, but I am suggesting that we live fully and completely; that we acknowledge pain, despair, and feelings of dejection, just as the psalmists did. I am disturbed by our collective commitment to distract ourselves and each other from pain, a commitment not unique to Americans. In seventeenth-century France, Pascal wrote:

How is it that a man who may have lost his only son a few months ago, and who is overwhelmed by lawsuits and other disputes, was not worried about them this morning and no longer gives them a thought? Don't be surprised; he is completely absorbed in trying to decide which way the game will come that his hunting dogs have been so hotly pursuing for the past six hours. That's all he needs. No matter how miserable he is, if he can be persuaded to take up some diversion, he will be happy so long as it lasts. And no matter how happy a man may be, if he lacks distraction and has no absorbing passion to keep boredom away, he will soon get depressed or unhappy. Without distraction, there is no joy; with distraction there is no sadness.[9]

We seem dedicated to taking this to new heights. I would love to know the dollar amount invested in research and production of antidepressant medications, to say nothing of the money spent each year on video games, movie rentals, and cruise ships. Most Americans simply would not relate to the teachings of the holy fathers in the Eastern Orthodox tradition, who teach us to ask for the gift of tears so that we might experience real repentance and a deep cleansing of the soul. I will never forget the looks of incredulity on the faces of workshop participants in a class I conducted many years ago at our church when I spoke of the "gift of pain," though Paul Brand and Philip Yancey have since published a book with that title. We are so thoroughly committed to easing our pain, we have forgotten that, robbed of it, we have no way of knowing we are in need of the doctor.

I was morbidly shocked recently when I read of a certain Abba Apollo of Scetis, who confessed that, as a young shepherd, he had killed a pregnant woman because he was curious about how the baby lay in her womb. Filled with remorse, he sought out the desert fathers, who assured him of his forgiveness. "So his prayer became his activity by night and day. . . . 'I have sinned against you, Lord; forgive me that I may enjoy a little peace.' And while he felt certain that God had forgiven him for the death of the woman, he continually doubted God's forgiveness for the murder of the child. When he expressed this, an old man said to him, 'God has forgiven you even the death of the child, but he leaves you in grief because that is good for your soul.'"[10] One has only to read the stories of Jacob and David and their troubled families to realize that though we are forgiven, we still may have to suffer the consequences of our actions, along with painful memories. For most of us, this will mean a measure of sorrow residing in us for the rest of our lives, no matter how hard we pray for it to go away. There is an old Russian proverb that says, "What men usually ask for when they pray to God is that two and two may not make four." But two and two do make four, and God, in his mercy, permits us to face the truth of our choices and remember our sins so that we might never again give ourselves completely over to our natural selves.

I would like to live my marriage over and eradicate all my errors, do it right this time. I want a second chance to raise my sons and never miss an opportunity to climb under the kitchen sink with them to ponder the wonders of modern plumbing; I ache for a chance to refrain from berating them over something as meaningless as a forgotten homework assignment. I want to return to the sidewalk in front of my childhood home and accept Ralph's token of love with a broad smile. I want to erase every unkind word and hateful epithet I've ever uttered, rid myself of every covetous thought. I would like whatever good works I've done to have been done out of love for God rather than out of a need to win the approval of my peers. I would like, for once and for all, to accept the grace and forgiveness of God. The litany of things I would change is endless and an exercise in futility and, most frightening of all, born in an ember of pride still alive in me, a desire to somehow be just a little better than all the other sinners who continually need the salvation of Jesus Christ. I would no doubt be farther along on my spiritual journey if I could accept my brokenness for the felix culpa that it is, a gift of self-awareness that leads me ever back to God.

It's at times like these I find comfort in the words of songwriter Pierce Pettis, a craggy voiced contemporary bard whose song "God Believes in You" (beautifully rendered by a local band of guys who, I think, don't appreciate the theological insight they revealed in naming their band Dead on Arrival) speaks eloquently of God's mercy.

> When you're so ashamed that you could die—
> God believes in you—
> and you can't do right
> even though you try—
> God believes in you.
> Blessed are the ones who grieve,
> the ones who mourn,
> the ones who bleed,
> in sorrow you sow
> but in joy you'll reap—
> God believes in you.[11]

And we pray it's true. Despite our sure knowledge that we'll fail again, that we will, over and over, require God's mercy. As

Scott Cairns wrote to me in a recent letter, "And when we fall (as we surely will), we must not be slow to return to prayer; though we are ashamed, though we are ashamed for the thousandth time, the healer wants to heal us."

I'm heading off at the end of the month to the Festival of Faith and Writing at Calvin College in Grand Rapids, Michigan, and I'm curious about one of the workshops titled "I'm So Tired of Victory: Restoring Proper Sadness to Christian Art." The truth is that though I long for Christians to get real and take the risk of being honest about their struggles, and though I long for all of us to accept melancholy and anxiety as doorways that lead to God, I am not tired of victory. And I pray that no one ever stops singing praise choruses just because I have trouble relating. I pray grace will continue to cover well-meaning pastors who speak recklessly about Mack trucks and hell in their attempts to scare the latter out of little kids. I pray that my friend will move out of the pit of remorse and into repentance for what she failed to do regarding the neighbor boy and know that despite her faulty ways, God has forgiven her, that he is using her grief to continue the work of transformation he began in her long ago. I pray that all of us will have the courage to walk into the flames of repentance knowing God will meet us there. I pray that we will see joy and sorrow mingle like watercolors to create an indescribable new hue, an utterly new spirit. I pray that we will joyfully weep today because we know that tomorrow we'll be laughing.

3

Till We Come to the End
of Pride
Dispassion

We were all young and foolish, I realize now. At the time, I thought I was young and cool, and I thought my brother, Mike, was old and sophisticated, and very, *very* cool. He had already been away for a four-year stint in the navy and was back home, married and the father of a brand-new baby girl. He was roughly twenty-five, a sage. I was not yet twenty.

I had always looked up to my big brothers—stand-ins for my missing dad, I guess—so I was thrilled when I was invited along for an evening out with Mike and Janey and their friends. I adored Mike. He was tall and lean and handsome. His indigo eyes disclosed a sensitivity he veiled effectively most of the time with caustic wit. My sisters and I flattered him regularly, and he loved it, enjoyed feigning self-deprecation as he coyly reminded us that people frequently mistook him for a tall Paul Newman. Our girlfriends all had crushes on him, and though I never confessed it for fear of going to hell for incestuous thoughts, so did I.

All my life I heard Mother and her brothers compare my brothers to Daddy, and though it was generally agreed that Bruce bore the most obvious physical likeness to him, in temperament, it was Mike's gift for spinning a tale and his proclivity for drinking and fighting in tandem that won him the spot as most like our father. I would wonder later if that was why Mother had to protect Mike from Daddy's wrath, as she said she often did. I've wondered if our father did not see himself in Mike, a sensitive, tender child who needed to get tough or die.

I thought Mike was tough, and I loved it. I clamored to hear, over and over, oft-told tales of his escapades, like the one he and his pal Jim Specht (whom I always thought was named "Speck") loved to tell about the night they "subdued the Murphy brothers back in '63." I knew full well, of course, that with each telling, embellishments and flourishes were written in to make the story better than it had been in previous tellings.

On this night, as we made our way home after a night at Clancy's, a roadhouse on U.S. 287 between Loveland and Fort Collins, I was about to witness his bravado firsthand. We had all been drinking, despite the fact that I was underage. Clancy's doorman was none too picky about whose face appeared on a photo ID. We had stopped to pick up the baby and were headed home when a great big pickup rolled to a stop beside us at a traffic light on College Avenue, and the honest-to-goodness cowboys in the cab, obviously well lit themselves, leaned forward and began trying to get Jane's and my attention with lewd remarks which, in their drunken condition, they apparently thought charming and seductive.

I was in the back seat and felt the energy in the car grow dense, saw the muscle in Mike's jaw tighten. Jane immediately moved to distract him from the situation, insisting it was nothing, gently demanding that we ignore them and go home. To his credit, Mike made an effort to comply, turning off the main drag a few blocks shy of his normal turn, leaving the pickup behind. Or so we thought. Suddenly, out of nowhere, they were beside us again, apparently made bold by Mike's avoidance of them. Both vehicles rolled to a stop at the corner of Mountain Avenue and Howes, right across from St. Joseph's Catholic Church. Again, Jane pleaded with Mike to ignore the cowboys, reminded him the baby was in the car. I think he tried. I tried to keep my eyes straight ahead, too, fighting an urge of my own to respond. My heart was pounding.

Suddenly, without a word of warning, Mike opened his door and stepped into the street. Jane groaned. I cheered, though silently; I did not want to incur my sister-in-law's wrath. We both watched as Mike walked to the passenger's side of the truck and tapped on the window. A look of drunken befuddlement appeared on the cowboy's face. I remember thinking how silly he looked as he accommodatingly cranked down the window so that Mike, with a single, short jab to his face, could knock him out cold. His head bounced off the back of the seat, his hat pitched forward, and he was out. Jane leaned to the window and begged for Mike to please get back in the car. I honestly don't remember whether I spoke aloud or to myself, but I was having the time of my life. Mike, apparently deaf to any voice other than the one that compelled him to get out and defend the honor of his wife and sister, now stepped, calm as you please, around the front of the truck. Why the driver did not run him down or at least slam the truck into gear and take off mystifies me still, but he just sat. And waited. A snootful of booze may make you brave, but it doesn't make you smart. When Mike tapped on the driver's window, the driver did exactly what his buddy had done just moments before, and like his buddy, he was out like a light after one well-placed punch. I don't think a single word was spoken by anyone outside the car, though plenty were being spoken within and would no doubt be spoken later out of my hearing. As for me, I was completely and unreservedly proud of my big brother, who wordlessly climbed back into the car.

I have no memory of what took place beyond that. I'd seen him come home bloodied and bruised before, been there the night he was home on leave and the cops came to question him about an assault on some drunk fraternity boys downtown. But this was the first time I'd ever seen him in action with my own eyes—and they were bright with energy and pride. That there was an infant in the car and Mike's actions might have resulted in catastrophe never occurred to me, or if it did, it had been handily doused by the adrenaline pumping through my veins. Like I said, a snootful of booze doesn't make you smart.

I began telling the story to friends the next morning and have told it, with little need for embellishment, hundreds of times, and I've always told it with secret, if not outright, pleasure. At the time, it seemed to me, my brother simply did what had to be done.

Blessed are the meek,
for they will inherit the earth.

I don't much care for meek. And judging by box office statistics, I'm guessing I'm in the company of most Americans, target audience for a car ad I saw recently that concludes with this parody of Scripture: "The meek shall inherit the dust." It gives me little pleasure to nestle in among the masses or to be in the company of government officials who flex their muscles from time to time in defiance of the law. I would prefer to aspire after meekness. I want to appreciate Ghandi more than I do Dirty Harry, but the latter has always given me greater satisfaction. As much as I long to distance myself from a world that is energized and entertained by brute force, I'm afraid I flow with the mainstream much of the time. I want fearless, bold, in-your-face guys running things—a few good men. When the little guy gets peed on, I want Bruce Willis, avatar of brash courage, to swing through the plate-glass window and kick butt. When I was a girl of twelve, I longed to be a boy so I could deck all the creeps who picked on all the helpless little geeks in my neighborhood.

Tracy Davis. He was known among us as the local retard— long before any of us had had lessons in political correctness. He was the kid in Everytown who serves as the receptacle for all the pubescent garbage that gets thrown around by youngsters straining to grow up. Tracy forgot how to brake his bike one day on the school playground and ran over a smart-aleck kid named Chuck. Chuck's leg was broken, and as he lay on the gravel writhing and wailing, I remember the look of wide-eyed bewilderment on Tracy's face. Every day on the bus ride home, bullies pelted him with verbal insults, and most days we were all so absorbed in our own little grievances and growing pains we hardly noticed. But there were days, despite Tracy's apparent immunity, when it just became too much for me. How I longed to be my big brother on one such day, when a chorus of puny little voices repeating an absurd little ditty over and over—something about Tracy's lack of mental acuity—finally tipped me into rage. I stood up in the aisle of the bus and whirled around. The way I choose to remember it, I said something wicked and profound in Tracy's defense. The sad truth is I think I croaked out something like, "Why don't you all just shut your stupid faces, you, you . . . stupid . . . *stupids*." It was a far cry from the well-placed punch I had hoped to administer, leaving them with their stupid heads lolling on the backs of their stupid seats. I think one of them nailed me with an apple core.

The truth is this third beatitude gives me heartburn. Every time I read that verse, I rappel away from it, as if I've just been told at the reading of my grandfather's will that he's left me the entire extended family and they're all going to live at my house. The whole thing confounds me. Let's see . . . I'm supposed to be meek instead of stick up for myself, and my reward will be the world, which I don't want and thought I was supposed to hate? It gives me vertigo—until I realize, again, that I'm mishandling the language. Maybe, I pause to consider, meek doesn't mean wussy, and the earth doesn't mean the world.

Recently, I met up with a former creative-writing student at a local tea shop. Her name is Nikki, and I love the way she plays with words. It's as if, when she sits down to write, someone has dumped a brand-new, king-size box of Tinker Toys in her lap, each stick and wheel a word. She rolls the pieces around, checks out sizes and colors, chooses one, holds it up to the light, finds a partner for it, and begins to build. I decided Nikki was the perfect candidate for the free-association experiment I had in mind as I began digging around in the soil for clues about the meaning of meekness. With just minutes left before it was time to part company, I handed her my journal and said, "Do me a favor while I go take care of the check. Write down every word you think of when you hear the word *meek* and then write down words and phrases that strike you as its opposite." Three minutes later, I was back and the page was full. And while I recognize this as a clear case of anecdotal research, I think Nikki's list is pretty reflective of the way society at large views the meek. Here are some of the words she associated with the quality of meekness (some proudly manufactured in her imagination): *scutting, tiny, hiding, peeking, small, implosion, folding, flattened, camouflaged, gray, squigid(?), forgetting, daydreaming, mink, weasel, clear, transparent, translucent.*

What interests me is the picture that emerges from her list. Her catalog of adjectives and her ear for assonance and alliteration led her to identify two wily little mammals—a weasel and a mink—and though she never actually identified a mouse, a result no doubt of having teachers who tirelessly attack writers for slipping into cliche, she offered the standard animal manifestation of meek, the mouse—a "squigid" little thing, hiding, peeking, ultimately folded and flattened. Her list echoes one dictionary entry that indicates that the word is derived from a Welsh word that means "soft."

I am curious about her inclusion of *transparent, translucent,* and *clear.* Though one might deem these undesirable qualities, especially tucked as they are within this context, they seem incongruous to me. I guess I'm inclined to ponder them in a more positive light—attributes associated with things simple and uncomplicated. A psychologist once told me that the word *simple* is derived from two Greek roots that together mean "without pleats." Could it be that despite the accepted notion we hold of meek there is something in the condition of meekness that is fundamentally good, something through which light can pour? In a world that bombards us with the convoluted and complicated, is there not, in most of us, a longing to return to simplicity?

Now that I think of it, when I conjure up a mental lineup of all the people I might describe as meek, I am aware that they are people who possess a unique sort of integrity, an integrity manifested in a perfect match between what's going on inside their hearts and heads and what's going on outside—expressed in their living, in their speech and actions. People without pleats. They are frequently somewhat laconic, able to express much in few words, and when they do speak, they seem to take great care in choosing their words, as if they are acutely aware of the power of language. Many, as it turns out, are poets, though not all write poems, and this comes as no surprise. Yet despite all this, I can't quite shake my attraction to the bold and beautiful and wonder if I'm stretching here to find something, anything, good about being meek.

Nikki's list of opposites is less predictable, more personal, I think, though still reflective of society at large. It includes *status, taking up space, boy, grand, girl, sky, heavens, expanding, rewarding, leaping, greenly, blue, expansive, loud, princess, shouting, jumping, wondermazement, soaring, believing*—all words that suggest abundant energy, a collection clearly informed by e.e. cummings' "leaping greenly spirits of trees and blue true dream of sky."[1] The list offers images of boldness and confidence, and it's hard to believe anyone would desire anything less, or that God would have us desire anything less. It seems we find ourselves snagged on the same outcropping we encountered when we explored the first of the Beatitudes. Just as being poor in spirit seems contradictory to the abundant life we are promised in Christ, so too does being meek.

And just as before, we have to examine the way in which these words and phrases have evolved through time and how they are entwined in the zeitgeist of our culture in order to get ourselves unsnagged if we hope to fully appreciate what Jesus is suggesting. Webster provides three definitions of the word *meek*. The first suggests that the meek are able to endure trials without resentment. Certainly a desirable quality. The second suggests deficiency of spirit and courage and so seems in opposition to the first, since endurance through travail requires, one would think, a strong spirit and a lot of courage. The third asserts that meekness is the absence of strength and violence. Murkiness prevails, as these two adjectives, *strength* and *violence,* are hardly synonymous; surely one can be strong without being violent.

Martin Luther King Jr. comes to mind. I was a kid in the '50s and early '60s and, to be perfectly frank, far too busy trying to survive the perils of adolescence way out west in the Rockies to give much of a rip about what was happening south of the Mason-Dixon Line. Civil rights, I thought, had little to do with me or mine. Fort Collins had, as far as I knew, one Negro family back then, the Nunallys, and they were a curiosity to me, but little else. It never occurred to me there might be people in my world who did not share all the rights and privileges of the rest of us. Not until I fell madly in love with Sammy Blanco and discovered my own family's racial prejudices would I understand that the disease of racism flourished in our community. Later, when I got a driver's license, I would discover enclaves such as Andersonville, Buckingham, and Spanish Colony, our very own ghettos inhabited by disenfranchised Chicano families, many of whom had come to Colorado as migrant workers to harvest sugar beets and decided, for one reason or another, to stay. When I did start paying attention to news from the civil rights front, I remember that I was curious about and puzzled by King's philosophy of nonviolent protest. Bringing up the rear of a rough bunch of Irish children who had had to get tough quick, I could not imagine how one might go about getting what one wanted without knocking somebody out of the way first, which always seemed like the thing to do, if not literally then at least verbally.

Actually, my earliest awareness of a character who possessed strength without violence came couched in a great story, of course, and it came at just about the same time my consciousness was being permanently altered regarding life in my hometown, just as I was about to make a break from those innocent salad days of my youth. I read Harper Lee's *To Kill a Mockingbird* and met Atticus Finch, a.k.a. Gregory Peck, whom I adopted as my fantasy father and for whom I still long on days I need a lap to crawl into. I will never forget the first time I witnessed the scene in the movie when Bob Ewell, the ignorant, pitiful antagonist, a rabid racist, spits in Atticus Finch's face while Atticus' young son looks on. The heroic restraint displayed in this scene is palpable, as Atticus, jaw clenched, slowly draws a handkerchief from his pocket, wipes the gob of spit from his cheek, and walks away. What is most fascinating to me about all this is the complete, unfettered admiration I felt for this character, despite my youthful adherence to a code of justice which called for serious poundings if necessary. I *knew* Atticus had done the right thing. So did everyone else in the audience. Because despite the intense pleasure we experience when we watch the good guy toss the bad guy through a window, we know in our hearts there is a nobler way to confront evil and ignorance. And we know that winning isn't everything, or that our idea of winning is temporal and puerile while God's idea of winning is eternal and very grown up.

I am reminded of C. S. Lewis' reflections about the laws of nature in the opening chapters of *Mere Christianity,* in which he suggests that humans possess knowledge of a standard of right and wrong that separates us from the rest of the animal kingdom, something within that enables us to feel remorse when we have done a wrong thing. It is this something that was awakened in me when I watched Atticus wipe that spit off his face. I wanted him to take this guy out the same way he had taken out the rabid dog earlier in the movie, but I knew that what he did instead was the *right* thing. And I knew that Atticus Finch wasn't a wuss. He was gentle and kind, compassionate and generous. But he was no coward. He was also a man of few words, who, when he spoke, was eloquent and incisive. Like Martin Luther King Jr. Like Moses. Like Jesus.

David Hill, in his commentary on the book of Matthew, points out that "the meek *(praeis)* of the third beatitude are the same as the poor *(ptochoi)* of the first—the humble, oppressed saints of God." He is quick to point out that the poor in spirit lack neither courage nor the Holy Spirit but are people who have long suffered economic and social distress and "have confidence only in God."[2] Meekness, it turns out, has little to do with weakness and everything to do with obedience—and knowing where strength comes from.

And though this helps us some, it still poses problems for *Die Hard* fans who are not big on authority figures or on obedience. Obedience means submission, and submission means powerlessness, and Americans are loath to relinquish power. Oh, we obey the law most of the time, but mostly we choose to cooperate because it makes sense to do so and we don't want to be bothered with the consequences of not obeying. On the other hand, if you push this issue too far, you'll run headlong into the woods and stumble across a hidden enclave of Americans dressed like

G.I. Joe who proudly take issue with the law of the land and have the provisions and artillery to carry out a full-on rebellion if it comes to that. And though we tend to think such extremists are basically wacky, we know they represent something fundamental to the American spirit. Ever since Lexington and Concord, we have thumbed our noses at authority. The very idea of acknowledging, let alone bowing to, a Lord and Master is anathema to most Americans. On a TV talk show many years ago—*Donahue,* if I'm not mistaken—I listened to a guest express grave concern over a doll that had been placed on the market. Her concern was that the doll was positioned in a posture of prayer, a posture she feared would encourage young girls to embrace the archaic Christian notion that they should submit to others, specifically opposite-sex others. From the classroom to the voting booth, we tend to be wary of giving ourselves into someone else's hands. The root of the word *authority* is, of course, author, and Americans prefer to write their own lives, thank you very much, and from all appearances, meekness does not figure into most of our scripts. We seem to embrace a collective consciousness that keeps us vigilant, ever ready to reclaim our rights as individuals should they be threatened in any way.

Assuming we actually want to be all that Christ suggests we might be, the logical place to look for examples of the sort of meekness that is pleasing to God is, of course, the Bible. The foremost example is Jesus himself, who "made Himself of no reputation, taking the form of a bondservant, and coming in the likeness of men. And being found in appearance as a man, He humbled Himself and became obedient to the point of death, even death on the cross."[3] In this and other biblical examples, we find several qualities that characterize the humble, including obedience and submission, self-awareness, sacrifice, and suffering. Hardly your typical Christmas wish list.

I was surprised to learn that Moses was described in Scripture as meek, "above all the men which were upon the face of the earth."[4] Of all the characteristics I might have chosen to describe Moses, meek would not have been one of them, but that's probably because my understanding of Moses was based entirely on Charlton Heston's cinematic interpretation of him in *The Ten Commandments*. I still have to remind myself it's not Moses making those public service announcements for the NRA. Anyway, the story in which this reference occurs is eerily contemporary in tone, as Miriam and Aaron, Moses' siblings, appear to be vexed because Moses married a foreigner, a Cushite—evidence of the long-standing presence of racism in the world. But it seems pretty obvious that what they are really ticked off about is Moses' preferential treatment as God's appointed leader. The record of their conversation reads like a typical family gripefest: "Has the LORD spoken only through Moses? . . . Hasn't he also spoken through us?"[5] Who does Moses think he is anyway? In a richly dramatic moment, God responds to Miriam and Aaron in a pillar of cloud: "When a prophet of the LORD is among you, I reveal myself to him in visions, I speak to him in dreams. But this is not true of my servant, Moses; he is faithful in all my house. With him I speak face to face, clearly and not in riddles; he sees the form of the LORD."[6] Two things are clear, especially in light of the leprous condition in which Miriam is left when the dust settles (though she is restored to health at Moses' request). First, one should never forget the holy admonition to fear the Lord. Second, God apparently likes Moses' meekness.

It may pose a problem for some readers to learn that Moses is the presumed author of the book of Numbers, creating suspicion that this is one of those perverse situations in which a proud man boasts of being humble, but an exploration of Moses' spiritual journey indicates that this is not the case.

The NIV translation of the Sermon on the Mount uses the word *humble* rather than *meek* in the third beatitude. *Humble,* as we learned earlier, is derived from a root which means "of the earth." We might say "down to earth." It is important to remember that Moses was not always so meek, that he wound up in the desert for forty years with lots of time to think after he murdered an Egyptian taskmaster who was abusing a Hebrew slave. It's tempting to vindicate Moses by making the killing of the Egyptian some sort of noble act, a sort of Metro-Goldwyn-Mayer good-guy-kills-bad-guy thing, but the way I read it, there was little of nobility in it, and probably much of pride. Moses, "glancing this way and that and seeing no one, killed the Egyptian and hid him in the sand."[7] Hardly the act of a hero, even if his actions were rooted in a desire to free his people, as suggested by the recounting of this story in Acts. The next day, when Moses attempted to exercise leadership among his brethren by intervening in a quarrel between two of them, he learned there had been witnesses to the killing and "he was afraid." Whether he fled because of his fear and the knowledge that Pharaoh was gunning for him or because he suddenly realized his time had not yet come, he took it on the lam and spent the next forty years tending sheep and raising a family.

One can only speculate on the experiences he had there and what they taught him about himself and about God. But whatever took place, it began with a breaking of Moses' spirit, a shattering of his pride, which, it seems to me, is always where humility begins. Far from the brash young man who struck down a slave driver many years before, Moses stands before the Fire of God on Mount Sinai and says, "Who am I that I should go to Pharaoh? . . . I am not eloquent, neither before nor since You have spoken to Your servant; but I am slow of speech and slow of tongue."[8] Moses has been brought low and, having been brought low, can now be of use to God. "Now therefore, go, and I will be with your mouth and teach you what you shall say."[9] That he should describe himself as meek in his recollection of the incident with Miriam and Aaron is not an act of boasting but a simple statement of fact grounded in the truth of his experience. Moses was self-aware, and his awareness irrefutably humbled him, just as it did David after Nathan confronted him about his blatant abuse of power in his sexual tryst with Bathsheba and the murdering of her husband. Both David and Moses were proud, powerful men of the world, but they were made truly mighty only after they were humbled by acknowledging their iniquity and receiving God's mercy.

Strange as it seems, I am reminded of a little book I read many years ago about a dog. The author is Phillip Keller. Not a stellar literary accomplishment, *Lessons from a Sheep Dog* is a simple story about a border collie named Lass. Keller describes their first encounter this way: "Crouched in the dirt, covered with dust, the dog glared at me. Her ears were laid back in anger. Deep, guttural, menacing growls rumbled in her throat." She was "loco," according to her owner, who was trying desperately to find a home for her. Loco and dangerous. "She was a dog 'gone wrong' . . . totally useless . . . a sad spectacle . . . almost beyond hope, beyond help."[10] Behind the vicious snarls, however, Keller saw something keenly intelligent and good, something worth saving. "Too beautiful to destroy," Lass went home with the rancher. The rest of the story is about the breaking of Lass and what her owner learned about God's insistence that we place ourselves under his benevolent authority so that we might enjoy an abundant life. This is not an easy thing. Indeed, it goes against our most primitive instincts. But like Lass, surely we can learn, and surely it is desirable to learn. Having come to this conclusion, I appreciated Barclay's commentary on the language of this beatitude all the more when I came across it. He points out that the Greek word used here, *praus,* is sometimes used to describe an "animal which has been domesticated, which has been trained to obey the word of command, which has learned to answer to the reins."[11]

As Kierkegaard suggests in this prayer: "True it is that man experiences a shudder like that of death when Thou, to become a power in him, dost take power from him—oh, but if even animal creatures understand at a subsequent moment how well it is for them that the royal coachman took the reins which in the first instance prompted them to shudder, and against which their mind rebelled—should not then a man be able promptly to understand what a benefaction it is towards a man that Thou takest away the power and givest life?"[12]

Oh that we might gladly exchange our pitiful little illusion of earthly power for eternal life, gladly call Jesus Lord, Master, Adonai.

In our attachment to heroes who are rough and tumble and slightly rebellious, we reveal ourselves to be pretty puerile. We excuse every sort of behavior on the grounds that "it's only natural," especially in these times when the culture is leaning toward yet another version of pantheism as a substitute for what it considers the pariah of organized religion. I always wince when I hear someone use the nature defense in debating social issues, as if determining that because "it occurs in nature all the time," must be okay for human beings too. Using nature as a moral plumb line is actually pretty amusing if you follow the thing to its full extension. Is it okay for women to follow the example of the black widow spider, who kills off her partners after sex? Shall we encourage young men to run in packs, like untethered dogs in search of females in heat? Whether we like it or not, and despite what you may have to say about our poor stewardship, God clearly gave mankind dominion over nature and expects us, I think, to lift our gaze when determining moral guidelines. One need only to accidentally bring up a hard-core porn site on her computer when she is innocently looking for the White House comment desk to be reminded that following our natural inclinations can be downright disgusting and hideously demeaning— and very likely to result in a truckload of grief. Despite our cultural rebellion against anything that smacks of religion, everyone seems to know that the basic tenets of the Ten Commandments are still the best rules to live by, rules dictated by a loving father.

Besides Atticus Finch and Moses and Martin Luther King Jr.—and of course, Lass—two extraordinary women come to mind when searching the vault for exemplars of meekness. The first is Mary, Jesus' mother. Even taking into account the cultural and historical factors that distinguish biblical times from modern times, that God chose an adolescent girl to be the mother of the Messiah boggles my mind. Surely there was a woman somewhere, a woman with a bit more maturity and wisdom, who might have better comprehended the magnitude of the task she was being given. But alas, God didn't consult the likes of me when making his choice.

We actually know very little about Mary. We assume she was young, and we're told she was a woman of humility and "low degree," suggesting she was not highly valued in her culture, regardless of God's view of her. According to Strong's concordance, the word *humility,* as used in Scripture, suggests modesty, lowliness, and humblemindedness, not things we urge teenage girls to aspire to today. (In a classroom full of teens last spring, not one of them knew the meaning of the word *modesty*.) The Greek word for *humility* combines two roots: *tapeinos,* which means "humble," and *phren,* which means "mind." Whatever other qualities she might have possessed, it's clear that God did not want pride, arrogance, and ego to interfere with the work of the Messiah's mother. It was Mary's selflessness, her faithfulness and submission to God, her unquestioning willingness to obey, that apparently earned her this terrible honor. No wonder some people venerate her, for who among us would respond as she did? Who among us would sing the Magnificat in Mary's situation?

As for Mother Teresa, there is probably no better example of humility in the twentieth century. Her ministry was defined by obedience to God's command to serve others. Hard work, compassion, and prayer characterized her life, and her remarkable eloquence rose not from any elaborate training in the oratorical arts but from her heart.

Every spring I am distressed anew by the pressure placed on high school students to get into "the best schools," as if anything less will result in certain disaster. And Christian parents exert as much pressure on their kids in this as anyone else, as far as I can tell, often placing much more value on their children's academic accomplishments than on their religious training. To lionize high achievers is to suggest that success as defined by the culture is the same as success in God's eyes. Would that we might pray for our children to be godly with the same verve we pray for their success at getting into Harvard.

And all the intellectual sparring about semantics and the finer points of theology in some circles creates ample strife in a community as well, to say nothing of being a significant energy drain on everyone involved. There's nothing quite like a lugubrious attack on a sermon to wear a person out. And the worst of this nonsense is it causes folks to question their capacity for understanding God, as if only the clever get the keys to the kingdom. Mind you, I think these heavy thinkers have their place in the Christian community. Where would Presbyterians be without Wittenberg? The body is, indeed, made up of many members. It's just that the brains sometimes get really snotty about the hands and feet and start thinking they're better than everyone else.

But we buy it. The "great sin" of pride prevails—unless we're fortunate enough to be blessed by a visitation and reminded that there's a difference between intelligence and wisdom, that nowhere in the litany of things cited that please the Lord do we find grade-point averages or advanced degrees. This compelling anecdote from Merton's *Wisdom of the Desert* sticks the point: "Some elders once came to Abbot Anthony, and there was with them also Abbot Joseph. Wishing to test them, Abbot Anthony brought the conversation around to the Holy Scriptures. And he began from the youngest to ask them the meaning of this or that text. Each one replied as best he could, but Abbot Anthony said to them: 'You have not got it yet.' After them all he asked Abbot Joseph: 'What about you? What do you say this text means?' Abbot Joseph replied: 'I know not!' Then Abbot Anthony said: 'Truly Abbot Joseph alone has found the way, for he replies that he knows not.'"[13]

And I love the story from *The Sayings of the Desert Fathers* about Abbot Arsenius, who was himself a highly educated man born in Rome around 360. "He was renowned for his austerity and silence and this, combined with his learning, made him somewhat forbidding to the Coptic monks." Here's the story. "Someone said to blessed Arsenius, 'How is it that we, with all our education and our wide knowledge, get nowhere, while these Egyptian peasants acquire so many virtues?' Abba Arsenius answered: 'We indeed get nothing from our secular education, but these Egyptian peasants acquire virtues by hard work.'" And in a subsequent story, after Abba Arsenius consults an old Egyptian monk and is asked by his followers, "'How is it that you, with such a good Latin and Greek education, ask this peasant about your thoughts?' Abbot Arsenius replied, 'I have indeed been taught Latin and Greek, but I do not know even the alphabet of this peasant.'"[14]

By such stories as these, we are humbled, reminded that our minds, though gifts from the creator of all good things, can become prisons from which we must be freed if we ever hope to know the real joy God wants us to have. Simone Weil, an eccentric French philosopher who sometimes felt burdened by her own active mind, wrote, "The difference between more or less intelligent men is like the difference between criminals condemned to life imprisonment in smaller or larger cells. The intelligent man who is proud of his intelligence is like a condemned man who is proud of his large cell."[15]

This is not to suggest we should board up the schoolhouse and toss a match into the library; it's a call to humbly recognize the gifts of our brothers and sisters who have not had the privilege of education. Until we come to the end of our pride, we cannot come to the beginning of meekness, a necessary place where we discover the truth—that the things that give power and status on earth have little place in the kingdom, a truth that sent the rich young man of the Gospels away in despair and may well have been at the heart of Judas Iscariot's blind betrayal.

More disturbing than the power achieved via academic prowess is that which is achieved through celebrity. I was saddened to learn about the death of Diana, Princess of Wales, but I found the sentimental stretch comparing her to Mother Teresa bizarre, no doubt a vain attempt by the media to keep their news stories marketable just a bit longer. This is not to rob the princess of her rightful place as a generous and compassionate woman, but there was little of sacrifice in her gestures of goodwill and, given what we have learned about her life, probably much that was rooted in neuroses. Indeed, Lady Di might be the first to say that she "did not know even the alphabet" of Mother Teresa. *Sacrifice* is another word we rarely hear outside of church these days. I remember reading a few years ago that President Clinton's advisers were distressed over a political gaff he made by calling on Americans to make sacrifices. His handlers apparently recommended that he immediately amend the challenge and couch it in softer terms, urging the public instead to make *contributions* to their communities. But there's a funny thing about language. Sometimes it is impossible to call a thing by another name. In the Fiftieth Psalm, God calls out, "Gather My saints together to Me, those who have made a covenant with Me by sacrifice,"[16] suggesting that our very relationship with him is grounded in sacrifice, a relinquishment of something, from rams and goats to power and prestige—indeed, life itself.

For all of my thinking and talking on the subject, I always end up back at the foot of the cross, back with Jesus meek and mild.

But certainly not soft, not weak. And certainly not ignorant. Jesus understood power, and he knew the difference between temporal power and power that comes from God. Standing before Pilate and urged to acknowledge Pilate's control over him, Christ responds, "You could have no power at all against Me unless it had been given you from above."[17] I've always been in awe of Jesus in this moment, amazed that he could be so calm, centered, and sure-footed—so utterly dispassionate. I was giddy with excitement the other day when our pastor, Jeff, shed light on this for me. He pointed out that Jesus could face the temptations in the wilderness because of what had preceded his sojourn into the desert when, rising up out of the baptismal waters of the Jordan River, Jesus heard his Father profess his deep and abiding love for him. Knowing that his Father, Abba, loved him, he could do anything, face anybody, including Pontius Pilate.

Dispassion is a curious and mysterious thing. I wasn't even sure what it meant the first time I encountered the word, though it was easy enough to guess. But I guessed wrong. I assumed it meant something like "lacking fire, without passion"—in the most negative sense. Only when I read further on the subject could I appreciate the dispassion Jesus exhibited in this situation. Dispassion is not the absence of passion. "It connotes not repression but reorientation, not inhibition but freedom; having overcome the passions [of our sinful natures], we are free to be our true selves, free to love others, free to love God. Dispassion, then, is no mere moritification of the passions but their replacement by a new and better energy."[18]

Still, moments such as these are disturbing to us, mortal sinners that we are. They cause a temblor in our hearts because they remind us that God permits the humble to be abused by the powerful at times. When the oppressed suffer at the hands of the wicked, when the brutality of it all becomes too much for us, we languish like the psalmist and wonder why God stands so far off, permitting the bad guys to prevail, just as we falter over Jesus' telling us, in no uncertain terms, that we must make the ultimate sacrifice of our egos, that we must, in fact, die in order to live. It all seems so backward and illogical that God expects us to stand naked and vulnerable in the world. And yet it appears to be true. The meek, to whom Jesus promised "the earth," are willing to suffer, and they are willing to let go, to relinquish control, to humble themselves under the mighty hand of God so they might, in his time, be lifted up.[19] We are asked to remember, as the psalmist ultimately did, that God hears "the desire of the humble" and will "do justice to the fatherless and the oppressed."[20] In *his* time. Atticus Finch was dispassionate. He knew he couldn't win the case against Tom Robinson, knew his kids would suffer the slings and arrows of persecution. He was teaching Jem and Scout about dispassion when he said that no matter what happened, they must "keep their chins up and their fists down." He could wipe Bob Ewell's spit from his face because he stood on the truth. He did the right thing regardless of sure defeat, knowing that a greater victory might be had if he did. As Keller says, reflecting on the things he learned from Lass about living under the authority of the Lord, "Let us trust Him fully. Let us follow Him fearlessly. Let us fling ourselves with glad abandon into His enterprises."[21]

And the meek shall inherit the earth, which is not, by the way, to be confused with the world and all its deceitful affectations. A wonderful memory surfaced as I researched this passage of Scripture. I learned that "the earth" as used in this context refers to the literal earth, more precisely to "arable land." The Greek word is *ge;* the Hebrew word in the Third Psalm, *'erets*. Pondering this promise of land, I remembered trips my family took back to Nebraska when I was a kid. I remembered my great-uncles, Jim, Ilef, and Raleigh, each of whom had sections of what I assume was the original Vance farm. I remembered their leathery sunburned faces and their calloused hands, hands that reflected thousands of hours of toil. I was too young then to appreciate the value of land. For me, the farm just meant emancipation and joyful abandon—hours of play, doing things like swinging from a rope out of the hayloft to fly through the air and land on a mountain of warm, scratchy hay. I remember collapsing with exhaustion at night into a big iron bed where I slept with my mother; in the morning descending the back stairs to the kitchen to find the source of the scrumptious aroma of frying bacon; finding my aunt Jesse in the early morning kitchen setting a table spread with what appeared to be breakfast for the gods: cereal (hot and cold), eggs, toast, platters of sausage and ham, hot coffee, and a giant mixing bowl full of oranges. I could not appreciate then that the survival of my mother's people had depended on the acquisition of land—real land, dirt. Soil that would accept seeds and grow crops. And the willingness of my great-grandparents and their sons and daughters and nieces and nephews to patiently and tenaciously work that land, cooperate with it, in order to live. Nor did I understand that I should be grateful. Only now, as I ponder Jesus' promise, do I fully realize the true value of my family heritage. The Vances were God-fearing people, modest and humble, hardworking and generous. They were meek, mild-mannered folks, and they were anything but weak. In the first beatitude, Jesus promised the kingdom of heaven to the poor in spirit, but here he promises land, and suddenly I am aware for the first time what the Promised Land is really all about. It's about having a place to build a home, land on which to erect a house, soil in which to plant seed; it's about understanding, fully, what the psalmist wrote in the Sixteenth Psalm: "O LORD, You are the portion of my inheritance and my cup; You maintain my lot. The lines have fallen to me in pleasant places; yes, I have a good inheritance."[22]

I do not pretend to understand how all this will work out with regard to eternity. Does it mean we will spend it here on earth, rather than in some lofty place where the streets are paved with gold? I don't know.

But I am confident that if Jesus is there as he promises to be—our companion and friend, our Lord, Adonai—it will mean there will be plenty to eat and drink, and we will be satisfied, and it will mean eternal emancipation and a thousand hours of joyful abandon.

4

Starving in the Land of Plenty
Hunger for God

Mom wasn't what you think of when you think of a church lady. You weren't likely to find her at ladies circles or potluck suppers, and she was certainly no theologian. But she intuitively knew things some religious people never understand. She knew, for instance, what it meant to set a table in the wilderness.

She knew that on a cold October night when the world was turning to slush, homing signals would be activated; folks would be dropping by, and they'd be hungry. She knew when it was time to lift dropped table leaves, light lamps, and lay a fire. And Mom knew how to throw a cheap cut of beef in a hot skillet with a mess of sweet onions and set the coffeepot to percolating, filling her house with the fragrance of goodness.

When we came to the table, she knew that an awkward grace was better than no grace at all, knew enough to ask someone to seek God's blessing for the food we were about to eat—we being her children, a motley gang of religious misfits whose genes were drenched in Irish whiskey and whose experiences had led us to various confessionals and sanctuaries over the years, many of them having little or nothing at all to do with the church.

Mom knew how to simmer a kettle of garden green beans with a ham hock and vinegar and present them with meat and potatoes and gravy and a platter of vine-ripe, sliced tomatoes on the side, somehow knew that good beats gourmet every time. And she knew how to load up a grandson's plate with the things he loved and quietly omit the things he hated and would otherwise be forced to hide. Mother understood grace. She knew exactly when to pour the coffee and cut the cake, when to laugh during the same stories she'd heard ten thousand times, and could listen to the rambling discourses of the unschooled on everything from the corruption of the government to the clear and obvious signs that we were surely in the midst of the end times.

And though the table was never quite big enough to start with, somehow there was always room for new- and late- comers. As if she were feeding the five thousand, Mother made a little food seem like plenty, and because of this plenty, we never knew till we were grown that we had grown up poor. Mother knew how to provide food and sanctuary for her children for an evening so they could face the freezing rain one more time. What she probably didn't know is that each time she fed us, she was giving us a glimpse of eternity.

"I would have lost heart had I not believed I would see the goodness of the LORD in the land of the living."[1]

Blessed are those who hunger and thirst for righteousness,
for they will be filled.

I pulled the book of poems off the shelf because of its title. I had never heard of Michael Ryan and had no idea what sorts of poems I would find, but I could not resist a volume titled *God Hunger,* maybe because I am convinced that despite our affluence in America, we are starving to death. In commenting on Ryan's poems, Robert Pinsky observed that they reflect "the unfillable craving people feel for some generosity of meaning beyond the circumstances of the self." The poems do not disappoint. In them is found the despair and the longing of the hungry, and in them, often discernible in the negative space around the words, is found this truth: satisfaction is not to be found in the things of this world.

Most Americans don't know much about physical hunger, really. We watch the news and see naked little children with bulging eyes and bloated bellies, and we know enough to know we should feel worse than we do. We've been told the bloating is a bizarre visual deceit that makes the dying children actually appear to be full, but so much is lost in the two-dimensional world of television; we cannot feel the bones under what should be thriving baby flesh; we cannot smell the stench of poverty. Most of us cannot even imagine that sort of hunger. As for hunger of a more spiritual nature, most of us are far too busy to notice any grumblings from within that might be trying to tell us we need food. Not something more but something substantial, something better than mere activity and distraction. The fact is, none of the Beatitudes thus far subjected to my meandering meditations has proved more challenging or mysterious than this one.

It has been said that confusion is a sure sign of the presence of evil in the world. If that's true, evil is alive and active in our society today when it comes to food. We are a society seemingly dissolute, committed to the indulgent life, willing to drive out of our way to find specialty shops where we pay exorbitant prices for exotic cheeses and fine wines, fresh herbs, baby vegetables, and free-range chickens, and a triple grande skinny no-whip mocha to go. We take immense pride in our discriminating tastes and wallow in our pleasures, and yet, judging by late-night infomercials, we are absolutely terrified of getting fat. Recently, surrendering to insomnia, I trudged to the living room, grabbed the TV remote, and began surfing for something that would induce sleep. Instead, I found a fitness guru flaunting his six-pack abs on the air. I was transfixed. Not in admiration but in a bizarre fascination with a body that looked for all the world like that of molded plastic, and with a face about as animated as Barbie's Ken. Further surfing turned up an array of infomercials hawking every manner of product promising the purchasers, if they act quickly, everything from faces that defy aging to perfect, unpinchable bodies. It seems that we literally want to have our cake and eat it too.

This bizarre union of decadence and discipline is perhaps most vividly manifest in eating disorders such as anorexia and bulimia. While I claim no expertise in this area, it is pretty obvious that these disorders are epidemic in the U.S. and are linked, at least to some extent, to our society's obsession with food, fitness, and physical beauty—an obsession which, when the dust clears, reveals, I think, hunger of a much deeper kind. Anorexia nervosa is an especially insidious condition because at its onset it seems like such a right thing, a healthy thing. The anorexic appears to be a model of self-discipline, counting calories, exercising regularly. Fashion models and movie stars, prima ballerinas—the idols of our daughters—often appear to be anorexic, weighing in far below what is considered normal. America's teenage girls, along with many of their moms, live to hear the envy in their friends' gushing inquiry, "How did you get so *thin?*"

Bulimia seems different to me, although I'm sure some patients have some facet of each of these disorders at work simultaneously. But bulimia seems bound up in shame from the get-go, maybe because it involves cheating. The word comes from the Greek root *bulim,* which means "hunger." A bulimic, then, is a hungry person, but there's a catch. When the bulimic is beset with hunger and begins eating, she cannot seem to achieve satiety. Because bulimics are never fully satisfied, they eat voraciously, or binge, and then, seized by fear and shame, they purge by means of laxatives or self-induced vomiting. The cycle quickly becomes compulsive. The chronic emesis results in serious health concerns, of course, and the chronic shame is devastating, emotionally and spiritually.

It is painful for me to write about this because I've been tormented and handicapped by shame about my weight since the onset of puberty. Prior to that time, I was a remarkably skinny little girl, so skinny I was teased about it by siblings and neighbor kids. I looked terminally ill, or as my chubby sister used to taunt, like a "skeleton without no bones." But one summer night between fourth and fifth grade, someone stole into my bedroom and kidnapped the skinny me, leaving behind a sorry little pubescent chunk of a girl I hardly recognized. A chunk with zits, no less. It all happened so fast, I was left hopelessly confused, a state in which I have remained to some degree my whole adult life. Inside, I still felt like the lithe little girl everyone agreed looked like Elizabeth Taylor in *National Velvet,* but whenever I passed a mirror, I spied this other wretched little pudge pretending to be me. Physically, everything sort of evened out over the next few years until in high school I was, according to the charts, just about right. Unfortunately, we didn't know much about charts back then, so the ideal weight for all adolescent girls was somewhere between 100 and 110 pounds, regardless of height. I think it was presumed we were all the same height as Sandra Dee and Annette Funicello. That meant that I, at 5′ 9″ and 145 pounds, was fat— a word I, along with virtually every American female alive, would come to loathe over time.

By now you're no doubt wondering what any of this has to do with hungering and thirsting after righteousness, but there is a connection. In fact, David Hill points out in his commentary on Matthew[2] that because Luke's account of the Sermon on the Mount does not include the phrase "after righteousness," one might presume that Jesus is calling followers to go hungry in the most literal sense of the word: "Blessed are you who hunger now, for you will be satisfied," followed by the cautionary admonition, "Woe to you who are well fed now, for you will go hungry,"[3] suggesting that Jesus expected his followers to embrace hunger literally, as fourth-century ascetics would, in fact, do, as well as many current day Lenten sojourners who choose to fast in the days leading to Easter.

In thinking on this connection, the story of Daniel comes to mind. Here was a young man whose captors recognized him as someone they might shape and hone into a servant of the Babylonian Empire. He was the cream of the Hebrew crop, the National Merit Scholar and all-around good boy of his time. To this end, the king's chief eunuch insisted that he eat food from the king's table and enjoy the indulgences of palace life. But Daniel declined. Respectfully, of course. He asked permission for him and his friends to continue their simple diets of vegetables and water and invited the eunuch's messenger to examine them at the end of ten days to see if they were not in good physical health. Reluctantly, the steward agreed. When he returned after the trial period, he found that "their features appeared better and fatter in flesh than all the young men who ate the portion of the king's delicacies. Thus the steward took away their portion of delicacies and the wine that they were to drink, and gave them vegetables." And God gave them something too: "knowledge and skill in all literature and wisdom; and Daniel had understanding in all visions and dreams."[4] It would be reckless to presume, however, based on this story, that God will bless only vegans. I think the story isn't so much about what Daniel ate, or refused to eat, as it is about his being obedient and, perhaps, wanting to distinguish himself from the ungodly, and this to demonstrate not his piousness but his confidence in God, his belief that his prosperity would come not from indulging in the fat of the land but from his relationship with God. For many Christians, the call to fast comes from a similar desire. Followers of Christ have always been concerned about the ways in which food affects our spiritual lives, as illustrated by this story from Poemen, "called the shepherd," in Benedicta Ward's collection of sayings from the desert: "The hegumen of a monastery asked Abba Poemen, 'How can I acquire the fear of God?' Abba Poemen said to him, 'How can we acquire the fear of God when our belly is full of cheese and preserved foods?'"[5]

Alexander Schmemann addresses the subject of food this way: The first time a fast was broken was in the Garden, when Adam and Eve decided that what God had provided was not sufficient. Tempted by the fruit of the forbidden tree, they succumbed. Sin, described by Schmemann as the "mutilation of life given to us by God," robs us of real life, the life God meant for us to enjoy—the life Daniel understood was his for the taking—and replaces it with dependence on things of this world. Jesus, of course, represents the new covenant, and his ministry began with his baptism and his subsequent journey into the wilderness, where he fasted. And though, during Holy Week, we may annually recite the passage of Scripture in which Jesus tells Satan that "man does not live by bread alone," we conduct our lives as if we don't buy it at all. But for some, the Lenten fast becomes much more than a token oblation through which we hope to give a repentant nod toward heaven. For some, it is a sincere effort to remember the giver of true life, a journey into hunger that reminds them of their utter dependence on God rather than on the things of this world.[6]

As we explore the connection between physical and spiritual hunger, however, it is supremely important that we heed the words of the apostle Paul in the fourteenth chapter of Romans, where he reminds us that squabbling over what we should and should not eat will only lead us out of fellowship with one another and into the sort of legalism that inevitably divides, and conquers, God's people. We must not lose sight of the ultimate objective, which is to know God. It's no wonder various sects have attempted to pursue this relationship on a purely spiritual plane, but the reality is we exist in these bodies—bodies God called good—and so are well advised to make peace with them and determine just how they figure into our relationship with God, for despite all of our efforts to separate our spiritual and physical lives, they are divinely and mysteriously interwoven.

Indeed, I've found it quite impossible to deal with spiritual matters with any sort of integrity and leave the body behind.

Even when people don't realize it, they may be using their bodies in an attempt to satisfy longings of a spiritual nature. Young women have given their bodies to men (and I suppose to other women) in exchange for what they hope is love. People have always used various substances to expand their minds, in search of ecstasy, and who among us hasn't foraged for "comfort food" when the world gets to be too much with us? It should certainly come as no surprise that adolescents use their bodies in an attempt to claim some measure of autonomy, even though, at the same time, they are crying out for help. As Frederick Buechner concludes in his remarks about anorexia, "In our sickness, stubbornness and pride, we starve ourselves for what we hunger above all else."[7]

The parents of today were the kids of the '60s, the era in which we learned that God was dead, the era in which we turned to sex, drugs, and rock 'n' roll to fill the void. It didn't work. "They are as sick that surfeit with too much as they that starve with nothing," wrote Shakespeare.[8] That we are sick with hunger is clear; the only question is to whom and to what do we turn to satisfy this hunger?

I have come to believe that our obsession with our bodies, our drive to make ourselves desirable, is rooted in our longing to be touched and held. I recently heard a Vietnam vet tell the story of his imprisonment as a POW thirty years ago. Held in solitary confinement in a small cell for over three years, he received his meager meals on a tray thrust through a space under the door. One morning someone was sweeping the walk outside his cell. Impulsively, when the prisoner saw the broom straws slip under the door, he reached down and took hold of them. The sweeper froze, then dropped to his knees and thrust an open hand underneath the door. The prisoner's voice broke as he recounted what happened next. Kneeling, he grabbed the proffered hand and held it, and wept. It was, he said, the first human touch he had experienced in three years. He was starving.

Our need for touch is elemental. Some even suggest that there is truth in old myths and legends that say a soul is kissed by God and proceeds through life remembering that kiss and measuring everything else against it. In an article in *The Catholic Northwest Progress,* Father Ron Rolheiser writes, "Inside each of us, beyond what we can name, we have a dark memory of having once been touched and caressed by hands far gentler than our own. That caress has left a permanent mark, the imprint of love so tender and good that its memory becomes a prism through which we see everything else."[9] We are scented pelargonia, a flower whose fragrance is not released until touched by a human hand.

In his book *Recovered Body,* Scott Cairns includes several prose poems in a section titled "The Recovered Midrashim of Rabbi Sab." The first time I heard Cairns read "The Entrance of Sin" from this collection, I think I emitted an audible sigh, it so thoroughly stabbed my heart:

> For sin had made its entrance long before the serpent
> spoke, long before the woman and the man had set their
> teeth to the pale, stringy flesh, which was, it turns out,
> also quite without flavor. Rather, sin had come in the
> midst of an evening stroll, when the woman had reached
> to take the man's hand and he withheld it.

And we know it to be true. We know it because we have been Eve and longed for the hand that is being withheld, and we know it because we have been Adam and withheld our hand, perhaps to punish or wound or, even more disturbing, because we have discovered a bizarre and ironic satisfaction in isolation, as suggested by the closing lines of the poem:

> The beginning of loss was this: every time some manner
> of beauty was offered and declined, the subsequent iso-
> lation each conceived was irresistible.[10]

I once advised my son Pat, then a teenager, that if he was exploring a thing for truth, to look for paradox, a sure sign that truth is at hand. Such is the case in our insatiable longing for touch and the powerful lure of isolation. It's Romans 7 all over again.

I've done my level best to keep my physical and spiritual lives separate, to pursue God with my spiritual heart and ignore the fact that my physical heart pumps real blood through a very real body. I have tried to deny the fact that I actually get hungry despite being overweight, that I am a sexual being who needs to be touched and held despite the plethora of fat jokes suggesting I should crawl under a porch somewhere until I can shed those ugly pounds (and maybe do something about unsightly facial hair while I'm under there). The whole thing is utterly humiliating. And messy. As I once expressed in a poem of my own titled "Bodies and Blood," "it's hard to treat them sacramentally, these / frail, failing malodorous bags of ourselves," and though there may still exist some believers who take issue with this, I believe we must somehow effect a reconciliation between our bodies and our spirits if we hope to fully appreciate the inheritance we are promised. It was, after all, Jesus' body that was broken, his blood that was shed. There was nothing tidy about the crucifixion. To strive for integrity means striving for wholeness;

in fact, the word is rooted in mathematics, where we learn that an integer is a whole number. To be integrated is to have all the fragmented pieces of ourselves come together to make a whole. It is a good thing, a righteous thing, to make peace with our bodies. To come before God whole.

"Let integrity and uprightness preserve me,"[11] the psalmist writes. Righteousness. Another word that has all but disappeared from our contemporary lexicon. We are about as likely to run across it in our routine reading as we are to run across *sin* or *sacrifice*. In fact, it makes people uncomfortable to talk about righteousness; I suppose because they're afraid that in our zeal, we'll try to heave our personal notions of right and wrong into their laps. Frankly, I don't think the world is much interested in being righteous as long as we're all happy, a sentiment reflected in a TV drama I watched recently in which a father, attempting to aid his son in the resolution of a moral dilemma, asks, "Isn't the only real question here, son, what will make you happy?" Indeed, it appears personal happiness has become the foundation upon which we make most of our decisions. And the fundamental problem in doing so, I believe, is that we think of the words *hunger* and *appetite* as synonyms when they are not. I have an appetite for a lot of things, many of which are not good for me, but I can't remember the last time I experienced real hunger. I'm smiling because I'm remembering a scene in the Coen brothers' movie *O Brother, Where Art Thou?* in which Ulysses Everett McGill, turning down his share of a gopher that's been roasted on a stick, says, "No thank you, Delmar. A third of a gopher'd only arouse my appetite without beddin' 'er back down." Clearly, Everett was not hungry.

Most of us never even allow ourselves to get hungry. It is our appetites we hustle to satisfy, and in this pursuit, it's pretty much every man for himself. And woman. And child, too. Any responsibility we do feel for our neighbor stems from an unwritten creed that dictates we can't step on anyone else's happiness in the pursuit of our own. It makes for some pretty sticky courtroom dramas. In a dialogue between Luci Shaw and Dallas Willard featured in *Radix* magazine, Willard posits that the loss of moral knowledge in our culture can be traced to a "rise of a kind of hedonism, along with an exaggerated individualism . . . a triumph of the will . . . the self. Everyone thinks that we ought to be able to do whatever we want to do." He goes on to suggest that admitting any sort of moral knowledge into this solipsistic equation is likely to get in the way of our doing whatever we feel like doing. Doing the right thing, it turns out, may involve not getting your way. It may even involve sacrifice. It will certainly mean altering the ways in which we measure success. As long as our happiness depends on having the right academic credentials, getting job promotions, and seeing how many figures we can add to our annual income, we are not likely to find room for righteousness as a primary criterion for decision making. As Willard observes, "Everything of value culturally, given the loss of moral knowledge, is sucked into this economic vacuum where it's chewed up and spewed out until nothing of value remains."[12]

Jesus' words here certainly suggest there is a loftier aspiration than self-gratification to consider in the designing and living out of our lives. And further, that satisfaction, indeed happiness—bliss, even—might be ours if we choose to feed on what is right, for ourselves and others, rather than gorging on what is tasty and immediately at hand.

If Moses is our role model for meekness, Abraham has to be our model for righteousness. As God was pleased later with

Moses, he was certainly pleased with his servant Abram, whom he took outside and instructed to look "toward heaven, and count the stars if you are able to number them. . . . So shall your descendants be." God promised, and Abram "believed in the LORD, and [God] accounted it to him for righteousness."[13] God reckoned Abram righteous *because* he believed. We continually make the mistake of calculating our okayness with God by adding up our good deeds, presuming they reflect our righteousness when the truth is it is our faith in God that transforms us into righteous beings. As a student in one of my classes said recently about aspiring to meekness, the defining characteristic of humility seems to be faith under duress. The word *righteousness* is derived from a verb that means "to be clear, justified." Lined up with God. Simple. Without pleats. And whole—a man or woman of integrity. When we are walking with God, he will *in*spire us, inject the Spirit into us. Indeed, he might just enflame us into models of righteousness in spite of ourselves. Faith always precedes good works.

I believe it was Augustine who said, "Love God and do as you please." It reminds me of a wonderful story from the desert. When one of the fathers asked Nisterus the Great, "What good work is there that I could do?" the father responded with a question, "Are not all actions equal? Scripture says that Abraham was hospitable and God was with him. David was humble and God was with him. Elias loved interior peace and God was with him. So do whatever you see your soul desires *according to God* and guard your heart."[14] If we genuinely love God, grace will cover the choices we make. If we are not in love with God, we lose our touchstone for distinguishing right from wrong, good from bad. We will always wonder if Jesus truly is the Christ or just another false messiah. Confronting the Jews at the temple, Jesus said, "My teaching is not my own. It comes from him who sent me. If anyone chooses to do God's will, he will find out whether my teaching comes from God or whether I speak on my own."[15] Choosing God precedes discernment. When the Lord is the light of our salvation, when the one thing we seek is to dwell in his house all the days of our lives and behold his beauty, chances are he will take delight in us, even when we stumble, and maybe, just maybe, we will recognize him when we encounter him on our Emmaus Road.

We dare not forget, though, that faith in God means something more than merely acknowledging his existence. I was not surprised recently when our associate pastor Lyn Corazin pointed out that faith, as understood by the Hebrew people, was not as cerebral a thing as it is for so many of us today, that it included the gut as much as it did the brain, that it was, in fact, an experience that involved the entire body. Faith means throwing your whole self in with God, as Abram did. It means relinquishing your rights and subjecting your life to a higher authority. And there again is the rub. Once more we are up against the wall facing this nasty business of sacrifice and self-denial, commanded to look past our immediate gratification and our rights and fix our eyes on Jesus. Faith means acknowledging our tendency to run in bad company and make selfish, sinful choices; it means asking God to protect us from our very selves, to draw us away from that which destroys and toward that which gives life. "Do not gather my soul with sinners, nor my life with bloodthirsty men, in whose hands is a sinister scheme."[16]

To be sanctified means to be set apart, made holy. It is an ongoing process that begins at the hour of one's conversion. The question is, What does righteousness look like? Does it look like a well-scrubbed family walking into church every Sunday morning? Does it look like a group of people marching outside a clinic to protest abortion? Does it look like college students staging a sit-in at the gates of a nuclear weapons plant? Or standing outside a penitentiary holding candles and praying for an inmate being strapped to a gurney inside? Maybe. Maybe. Or maybe it looks like a penitent sinner on her knees in the confessional, or a politician on the stump demanding a return to prayer in the classroom. Somehow I doubt that it's the latter, not because freedom to pray at school is a bad idea but because so many Christians, it seems to me, still take their cues from the Pharisees rather than Jesus; so many still get snagged on external behaviors and forget that what Jesus called for, indeed what he promised us if we choose to follow him, is utter transformation from the inside out. I do not think Mona spoke figuratively when, at her baptism, she said she felt the cells of her body being changed. The story of the rich young ruler comes to mind again, touching on both the subject of hunger and the subject of righteousness. The first thing that strikes me about this young man is that he is good; he's out there trying to live a righteous life. He is aware of the laws and doing his level best to keep them. But something is missing from his life, because even doing good does not satisfy the hunger we have for a relationship with God. Being good is not the same as knowing God; going to church is not the same as going before the throne of God. There is only one thing which truly satisfies, and that is a living relationship with him. And so, Jesus invites this young man to unencumber himself to walk with him. What the rich man didn't apprehend, what we fail to apprehend, is that our understanding of righteousness comes after we make that choice.

God provides ample guidance for determining how we're supposed to live. The Bible is the Word of God, and when we belong to God, it becomes the authority of our lives. In the Fifteenth Psalm, David approaches God: "Who may dwell in Your holy hill?" Eugene Peterson captures the response in contemporary language this way: "Walk straight, act right, tell the truth. Don't hurt your friend, don't blame your neighbor; despise the despicable. Keep your word even when it costs you, make an honest living, never take a bribe."[17] Seems simple enough. Not easy, though. Especially that part about despising the despicable. My sweet mother admonished me time and time again to never use the word *hate*. "Do not use that word in this house," she would say. But here I am called to despise, which derives from a Latin word that means "to look down on." Talk about paradox. In a few pages I will launch the exploration of the fifth beatitude, which calls us to be merciful, and I'm not at all sure how to do both of these things at the same time. I know that the first, despising the despicable, requires discernment and that I cannot possibly know who or what to despise without the help of God. What I'm not sure I can pull off is showing mercy at the same time I'm despising someone. And yet I am aware that God, who knows all the secrets of my heart, has managed to love me despite my despicable behavior over and over again.

When I think on my own sins and feel, again, the bite of remorse, I understand the cries of the people of Israel in the book of Micah as they sought instruction as to how to be reconciled to God: "Shall I come before Him with burnt offerings, with calves a year old? Will the LORD be pleased with thousands of rams, ten thousand rivers of oil? Shall I give my firstborn for my transgression, the fruit of my body for the sin of my soul?" To which the prophet responds, "He has shown you, O man, what is good; and what does the LORD require of you but to do justly, to love mercy, and to walk humbly with your God?"[18] All the fatted calves in the world, including hefty endowments dropped in the offering plate, or for that matter, years of loyal service to the church or in the mission field, are of little significance to God if our hearts do not belong to him. Doing justly and loving mercy are, in fact, manifestations of a life that is given humbly to God, along with the fruit of the Holy Spirit listed in Paul's letter to the Galatians: love, joy, peace, patience, kindness, goodness, faithfulness, gentleness, and self-control. These are virtues for which we strive and continually fail to achieve, or at least sustain, on our own power. Even walking closely with God, we stumble, like children toddling alongside Mom and Dad. But he is always at hand to lift us up, dust us off, and set us to walking again. It's all about companionship in the long run, all about who's walking beside you, all about to whom you look to tell you where to plant your foot next. I am utterly astounded that God wants me for a companion; there is no accounting for taste. But loving the unlovable is so like Jesus.

Curious about righteousness, I recently read through Proverbs again and decided to glean from them those imperatives that appear repeatedly throughout the book. Here's the list I came up with:

Trust God rather than yourself.
Keep his words in your heart,
and fear him.
Curb your tongue;
don't argue, speak in anger, or gossip.
Be humble and show mercy.
Seek things that

give life rather than steal it.
Honor your parents,
welcome discipline, and work hard.
Hate evil.
Choose wisdom over folly;
avoid the company of revelers.

The list of things the Lord despises likewise fascinates me: dishonest scales, duplicity, gossip and sinful talk, a perverse heart, a warped mind, and the sacrifices of the wicked. I don't know about you, but this powerfully convicts me. I realize there is ample room here for interpretation, but it seems clear to me that in our zeal to point out right and wrong to others, we often omit some things God thinks are pretty important, things like gossip and cheating and sacrifices brought to the altar when our hearts are full of wickedness. "Rend your heart and not your garments."[19] And I am led to think about our chronic eagerness to point out the failings of our brothers and sisters when what we should be doing is cleaning up our own shanty hearts and lives, a task which, for most of us, will take a lifetime of dedicated attention— along with an avalanche of grace—and will leave little time for fixing our friends and family.

One thing seems painfully clear in this discussion. People who do not accept the authority of Scripture but still want to live "good" lives have a gargantuan task in trying to determine how to do it. Even my husband, who is generally put off by most of the jeremiads issuing forth from certain corners of the Christian community, says he finds the world a scary place today because it appears to be an environment marked by moral anarchy, a society that lives by the strangely ironic code that I understand is chiseled in stone over the Sorbonne: "To forbid is forbidden."

I was a young high school teacher back in the '70s when conservative Christians stirred up a hornet's nest over classroom games that called on students to make moral decisions based on a given situation. Situational ethics, they called it. Frankly, I thought those Christians were alarmist fanatics. Hindsight and maturity reveal that there was cause for alarm, if for no other reason than the fact that such games signaled that adults were abdicating responsibility by asking children to make such decisions (even hypothetically), just as we were abdicating responsibility for raising our kids by blithely adopting a sort of Hollywood model of righteousness that defined our parental responsibilities. We looked to the fantasy world of *Kate and Allie* to see how single moms managed to do their own thing and still raise great kids. We sympathized with the *Kramer vs. Kramer* mom who "needed space" and left home in search of her happiness. All over the country, parents reversed the natural course of things and asked the kids to be the grown-ups while they went out to find themselves. *Self-actualization* became the buzzword of the '70s. A decade later I heard a comedian make an astute observation about America's collective pursuit of self-actualization. He pointed out that in the '40s the most popular magazine on the newsstand was *Life*. In the '70s, he went on, it had been narrowed down to *People,* and alas, in the '80s the hottest new magazine at the checkout counter was called *Self*.

And though some believe that a renewed interest in morality and ethics suggests a shift in this trend, we cannot deny the disturbing picture of our culture that surfaces when it comes to the question of morality. Philip Yancey addressed this issue in an article titled "Nietzsche Was Right" a few years back. "Something unprecedented in human history is brewing: a rejection of external moral sources altogether."[20] The closest we come to adhering to any outside authority, as I pointed out in the previous chapter, is to look to Mother Nature for approval, which we must do gingerly for it to work to our advantage. As a friend once said about the rationale she came up with for a selfish choice, "It's fragile, so don't mess with it."

Yancey goes on in this article to point out the irony of this "evolutionary psychology" coexisting with political correctness, which, by its very nature, presumes an absolute morality. And as if that weren't irony enough, he reminds us that though proponents of political correctness often position themselves as adversaries to the Christian church, it is the church that provides "the very underpinnings that make such a movement possible." Christianity, Yancey points out, "brought an end to slavery, and its crusading fervor also fueled the early labor movement, women's suffrage, human rights campaigns and civil rights." It seems that no matter how many times we toss our Bibles into the bonfire, the flames will not consume it. Those same Ten Commandments Moses brought down from the mountain just keep surfacing as the only reasonable baseline tenets upon which human beings must, if we are to survive, build our lives.

Despite all our lavish indulgences, it seems we are starving to death, and what we are hungry for, as suggested by the title of Ryan's collection of poems, is God. Everything else, it turns out, is a mess of empty calories that ultimately leaves us feeling as if we should be full when we are, in fact, still hungry for the stuff that nourishes our bones. "He who loves pleasure will become poor; whoever loves wine and oil will never be rich."[21] As Buechner concludes in an essay in which he examines the seven cardinal virtues, "Maybe it's only love that turns things around and makes the Seven Deadly Sins . . . look pale and unenterprising for a change. Greed, gluttony, lust, envy, pride are no more than sad efforts to fill the empty place where love belongs, and anger and sloth just two things that may happen when you find that not even all seven of them at their deadliest ever can."[22]

And who you hang out with really does matter, though your teenage children will do everything they can to convince you this is not true. Back in 1973, I was a charter faculty member of the Alternative School in Commerce City, Colorado. It was one of the first programs of its kind in the U.S., and I was proud to be a part of it. I still am. I worked with some great kids then, and I had some wonderful friends and colleagues, but I wince every time I think about the paltry standards we set for those students when it came to fundamental things, such as their language. We were young teachers, very cool, very with it. I think we actually believed that we could improve our relationships with these kids if we did away with all the civility required of them—and ourselves—in the regular school. To make a long story short, my language went to hell in a handbasket during that time. I tossed the f-word around like rice at a wedding. I am utterly mortified to remember it. I am not seeking to blame others for my idiocy. I was the grown-up. It was my job to set the standard, rather than follow the trends set by students, and I didn't. Now, a quarter of a century later, I hardly ever use the f-word, and when I do, I'm sorry.

Human beings are strangely susceptible to aping others. Everyone knows when I've spent time with one of my sisters because I begin to sound like whichever one of them I've been with. My kids would frequently walk in the door at night as I was hanging up the phone and, following a brief dialogue, inevitably say something along the lines of, "Let me guess, that was Aunt Linda you were talking to on the phone, right?" When they were young and we had the requisite discussions about which movies they were permitted to see and which CDs were banned, we used the expression "Garbage in, garbage out" to explain that the stuff you put into your head generally slips out of your mouth eventually. I thank God every time I think about the folks God put in our lives when we moved into our present home, because they're people who love good literature, good food, great music, and God and have little need for booze and debauchery—as a rule, anyway.

"Fix your eyes on Jesus," we are instructed in Hebrews. Long for him. Seek him. Keep his company. Righteousness is not the stuff we do to earn God's favor; it is the result of being in relationship with him. Hungering after it means hungering to know the Lord. "Beware," I caution my Bible students, "of those times in your life when you find you are favoring the company of the ungodly, when you find you have little interest in your Bible and no time for worship or prayer," for as Abbot Palladius once said, "The first step away from God is a distaste for learning, and lack of appetite for those things for which the soul hungers when it seeks God."[23] I fantasize sometimes about a day when one of my sons walks into the room and says, "Let me guess . . . you've been hanging out with Jesus today, haven't you?" Not because I'll be spouting Scripture to show off my knowledge of God but because I'm beginning to speak in the sure, sweet tones of Jesus. It humbles me to think about how far I've yet to go. Would that we might never lose our appetites for the goodness of the Lord. Would that we might stuff ourselves to the brim with him, for "the person who hungers and thirsts for God's sake, God will make drunk with his good things, with the wine whose inebriation never leaves those who drink it."[24]

5

Gentle Rain from a Cloudless Sky
Compassion

It all began last summer when we called a landscape artist to esti-
mate what it would cost to save our lawn, which, due to our neglect and the handiwork of some sort of insect, looked like a vacant
slum lot. After surveying the damage, he turned to my husband
and said the lawn could not possibly be saved. For somewhere
between one and two thousand dollars, he continued, he would
bring his crew in to strip everything bare and reseed the area, as
long as we understood there were no guarantees of success unless
we did our part. I didn't say it, but I wondered why we had to
have a part if we were going to pay him two grand.

Goaded by shame for my neglect, coupled with a hefty dose
of Irish pride, I decided he was mistaken and began a campaign

to restore the lawn and garden. For the remainder of the summer I labored, mostly with a small hand tool, to loosen and aerate the soil under and around patches of still-living grass, strip up yards of dead sod, and finally reseed and water. In late August, I escorted my husband outside to witness the fruits of my labor. "We're not there yet, but it's coming back," I announced, "and I *will* succeed."

The blessed rains of fall and winter saturated the thirsty soil, and in March, I learned about Tagro. My friend Carla attended the annual home and garden show at the Tacoma Dome and called to tell me I could have all the free Tagro I could haul away from the waste treatment plant out on Portland Avenue. It took a bit of cajoling to get Michael's assistance. The idea of loading his truck with fertilizer made up largely of stuff filtered out of the city's sewage system, including what he chose to call human fecal matter, did not appeal to him at first. I told him to pretend it was steer manure, but being the suburban boy that he is, that didn't serve him the same way it did the latent farm girl in me. To tell the truth, it didn't serve me all that well either, but I was determined to save that lawn, and a truckload of free fertilizer was nothing to turn your nose up at. So we tossed shovels into the truckbed, donned grubby clothes and surgical masks, which would prove to be absolutely useless, and were off.

Spending time with Michael is almost always a blessing. He's smart and fun and funny, finding humor in virtually every circumstance. After graduating from Southern Methodist University, where he studied acting at the Meadows School of the Arts, he decided to come home for a time to reflect, save up a bit of money, and lay plans for his future. When he left for college, neither his father nor I ever expected to get him back for more than a holiday, so we were thrilled to welcome him home, knowing it wouldn't be long before he'd be off on his next adventure, which, as it turned out, was a year in Belfast on a mission team working with the city's youth in a movement toward peace and reconciliation there.

But on this day in March, he was all mine, and we were on our way to load up his truck with the miracle product that would put us, once again, in good favor with our neighbors, at least the ones who lived upwind. As we came upon the Portland Avenue exit ramp, we filled the truck cab with pained laughter over our weak attempts at puerile puns. There is seldom a lingering silence in any space occupied by the two of us, though for some reason we grew quiet as we pulled up to the light at the bottom of the off-ramp, where I saw a woman sitting on a box holding a piece of tattered cardboard. On it was scrawled "Homeless Woman Needs Food for Family." She sat under a billboard advertising the *Emerald Queen,* a floating casino docked in Commencement Bay. Homeless people are not an uncommon sight in Tacoma, and though I have tried to ignore my fair share of them in my rush to get here or there, they are never invisible to me. Like so many middle-class Americans, I am flooded with ambivalence whenever I see one of them at the side of the road. Part of me wants to help, and part of me wants them to put down their signs and go get jobs washing dishes or scrubbing floors—any form of honest labor. I usually resolve the problem by averting my eyes till the light changes and gunning past them as quickly as I can, although I have been known to hand off a five-dollar bill from time to time, despite cynical admonitions about how they'll probably just go buy wine or cigarettes with my hard-earned cash. One year I drove around with a bag of canned goods in my back seat so I could hand out food, but usually I just hightail it and ask God to forgive me.

For some reason, probably because Mike was driving and we were held up at the light, I looked long at this woman, whom I decided was probably a Puyallup Indian—a small stout woman, her straight black hair pulled back and held with rubber bands. She wore a tattered parka and worn out Nikes. Suddenly, I realized I had made the fatal mistake of actually seeing her, and as we pulled away from the light, I asked Mike if he had been aware of her, though I was certain he had.

More than once while he was away at college, I had gasped in disbelief to learn that Mike had given aid to some stranger or another, and though I loved him for responding to this compunction to reach out to people in need, I was always terrified he would reach out to someone with evil intentions and I would never see or hear from him again. Of course, he said, he had noticed this woman, and he readily agreed when I suggested that we stop on our way back to the highway later and buy a bag of groceries to give to her. I'm not sure why I was inclined to reach out to this particular person more than some of the others I had seen holding similar signs. Was it something in her bearing, her posture, or was it, I wondered, because she was a woman and I was experiencing empathy? It occurred to me that some of the homeless men I had seen on the roadside frightened me, that I harbored a sort of chronic mistrust of men who couldn't hold down a job. Strange how we discover our prejudices in unexpected circumstances.

An hour later, the bed of the pickup full of Tagro, we headed for home. As we approached the highway, we spied a food mart and swung into the lot. There wasn't much to choose from, but we managed to fill a bag with a loaf of bread, a jar of peanut butter, some beans, a few cans of soup, and a jug of fruit punch.

I threw in a candy bar for good measure. Handing it off to the recipient proved to be tricky, as she had moved to a rather dangerous spot under the overpass and had her back to us as we approached, so we couldn't signal to her to come to us. We scoped out the situation as we sat at a light and decided I should hop out, hustle over to her and give her the groceries, and quickly get back to the curb so Mike could collect me without holding up traffic. Out I hopped. The roar of cars and trucks overhead was deafening, and the woman jumped when I touched her on the shoulder and held forth our meager offering. She smiled a toothless smile and thanked me vigorously, and though I knew I needed to be making haste for the truck, I hesitated, compelled to ask her name.

"Mary," she said.

And I replied, "God bless you, Mary. I will pray for you today . . . all day long." As I turned to go, she thanked me again, assuring me she needed both the groceries and the prayers.

Two minutes later I was fastened into my seat belt and we were making our way up the ramp to merge with traffic and head home. I wanted to say something, but I couldn't, not without exposing my tearful self. We sped along in silence; eventually, I spoke. "Her name is Mary," I said.

The day had been suddenly and poignantly altered by our brief encounter with this woman. I had touched her, asked and spoken her name, and suddenly everything was changed. I didn't just hand off a bag of groceries to a nameless, faceless, homeless woman; I *met* a woman, a hungry woman, and her name was Mary. For the rest of the day, with every bucket of Tagro I lugged up the stairs to the front lawn, I said a prayer for Mary, and as Mike and I raked and spread the stuff, we spoke quietly of the power in a name. Passages of Scripture came to me as I labored:

Jesus reached out his hand and touched the man.

Jesus said to her, "Mary." She turned toward him.

I was hungry and you gave me something to eat.

Then he said to the disciple, "Behold your mother!" And from that hour that disciple took her to his own home.[1]

I was discovering the reciprocity of mercy. In reaching out to Mary, I had been touched. When she cast her toothless smile at me, I had seen Christ and been seen by him, and for the rest of the day, I heard the sound of his voice in my ear, enjoyed the pleasure of his company, and experienced the disturbing conviction of the Holy Spirit insisting that I remember that of these things, faith, hope and charity, "the greatest of these is charity."[2]

Blessed are the merciful,
for they will be shown mercy.

"A pesky little bit of Scripture." That's what my husband called it when Mike cited the twenty-fifth chapter of Matthew to explain why he had driven a complete stranger home one evening. Here's the story. Invited to work at the Guthrie Theater in Minneapolis the summer between his junior and senior years of college, he packed up the bare essentials on the last day of classes in Dallas and headed north on I-35—to Lake Wobegon country. The Land of the Lutes.

One evening as he emerged from the theater, he observed a middle-aged man headed his way. The man appeared to be distressed and anxious, eager to explain that he'd had a flat out on the highway and needed a lift to get some assistance. And though Mike was fully aware he might well be the target of a street sting, he felt compelled to help. We were visiting Don's mother in Colorado at the time, and I heard about this incident by way of a long-distance call one evening. I had taken the call in the back bedroom, and I remember thinking maybe I would just conveniently forget to tell his father the story, that maybe in this situation, silence would be the better part of wisdom, but I couldn't pull it off. I walked down the hall rehearsing a version of the story I thought would be least likely to send his dad over the edge.

Lest you think his father is Scrooge reincarnate, let me hasten to add that not only had Mike come to the aid of a strange man bearing a shabby and fundamentally incredible tale of woe, but it turned out he had driven him to an ATM and punched in his own PIN in broad daylight so he could give the stranger what little money he had left in the world. *And* in his zeal to get the man delivered, he walked off and left his bank card in the machine, only to find it gone when he returned. All this he had done without telling a single soul where he was going or with whom. You can well imagine the scenarios that played out in our imaginations. I cursed every Ann Rule book I had ever read.

Twenty minutes after I had reluctantly relayed the story to his dad, Don—unable to restrain himself any longer—was on the phone to Minneapolis. He too carried the phone into the back bedroom. Though I wasn't privy to their conversation, I had a pretty good idea where it was going. When Don finally emerged, he appeared agitated as he fumbled through a book rack, where he found his mom's Bible and began flipping through the pages. By this time I had clued in the rest of the family about Michael's adventure, and though we tried to be discreet—Patrick, Mona, and Grandma and I—all eyes were on him as he perused the book of Matthew.

"What are you doing?" I inquired, though I knew good and well he was looking for loopholes.

He emitted a whooshing sigh. "I'm looking up the Bible verses that inspired Mike to drive off with a complete stranger today and give him all his money," which didn't, I hasten to add, add up to much.

"Read them out loud," I suggested.

Reluctantly, he began. "'For I was hungry and you gave Me food; I was thirsty and you gave Me drink; I was a stranger and you took Me in; I was naked and you clothed Me; I was sick and you visited Me; I was in prison and you came to Me.' And some other verse," he continued. "He couldn't remember it exactly . . . something about a man asking for your coat and you giving him your cloak too?" Snapping the book shut, he let out another long sigh.

"Well," he said with defeat, "*that's* certainly a pesky little bit of Scripture, isn't it?"

Indeed.

It seems our son was growing up, not only in the usual sense of the word, but growing up in Christ to boot. He was moving beyond the rudiments of righteous behavior, the normal, safe acts of charity, and giving God elbow room to actually change his heart, transform him into a new creature. He'd always been a good kid. He got good grades, obeyed his teachers, won leadership awards, did his chores, and seemed fully to understand the value of a dollar. But he hadn't always had a huge heart for others. A typical adolescent, he was too busy worrying about acquiring brand name shoes to notice what was going on around him all that much.

But all that began to change the summer he underwent brain surgery.

Less than two weeks before Mike left for college in 1995, the doctor ordered an MRI, hoping to get a lead on a siege of migraine headaches that had plagued Mike all summer. She didn't really expect to find anything, she said, just being cautious. The pea-size tumor they did find, ironically, had nothing to do with his headaches. They called the discovery an "incidental finding." Mercifully, I have forgotten the emotional turmoil I experienced in the days that followed, much as I have forgotten the pain of childbirth. I know that until that day, I had always sworn I would not be able to withstand hearing that sort of news about either one of my children. I learned later that one of my sisters, when she heard the news, ran from her house crying. She did what I could not permit myself to do.

I assumed Mike would cancel his plans to go to school, so we could deal with all of this without delay, and was utterly rocked to hear my husband, a physician, say, after consulting with the neurosurgeons, that he thought Mike should leave for college as planned. This was not okay with me. I was barely coping with the loss of him as it was, and the fact that he was going over two thousand miles away to college wasn't helping. My imagination went berserk. I saw him collapsing on a basketball court and lapsing into a coma while I dangled from the phone, on hold as I tried to make plane reservations; I imagined him dying while I tried to get through the security check at the airport. What were they all thinking, suggesting that I send him off to college with a brain tumor!

Looking back on it now, I am grateful that my cries were lost in the wind. I hate to think of the misery that we all would have endured had I been permitted to hover over Michael and fret over every hint of cold or flu, my perspective completely distorted by fear. The surgeons suggested we wait and watch. Mike would undergo an MRI every six months, unless he developed symptoms that demanded immediate attention. And so, that's what we did. For two years. And though he never experienced any symptoms whatsoever, a consultation with an expert at the University of Washington convinced us that it was time to get the thing out of there in the spring of '97.

Not long ago, I looked at snapshots we took the night before Mike reported for surgery. Sporting a GI haircut—a smidgen of hair on top, back and sides shaved—he posed for the camera wearing a jocular grin, pointing at the ink sketches drawn on his head and the fiducial devices that looked for all the world like peppermint Life Savers attached to his scalp. When I looked at these photographs, I felt ill and realized that God had given me the gift of dissociation during the time these things were taking place, had somehow permitted me to separate from myself so I could go through the motions of attending to business without actually registering what was happening. I remember how we laughed in the pre-op waiting room when they called Mike's name and he sauntered over to a clerk who was sitting behind a glass window like the ones at the movie theater ticket booth and said, "I'll have one for brain surgery, please." The room, filled with anxious patients, erupted in laughter. Good medicine when fear is crouching outside the door.

During the wait, I felt as if all my nerves were exposed, dangling from my body like tinsel. I flinched at every sound. When Don and our dear friend Claire became involved in a detailed discussion about something or other, I gazed at them in wonder. How could they chat like that while the surgeon was popping out a chunk of Mike's skull and laying it on a tray so he could take a scalpel to his brain? I wasn't angry with them; I just thought they were nuts, and the sound of their voices was making me jumpy. I moved to the other side of the waiting room. Four hours later, we walked alongside the gurney that carried Michael from the OR to ICU, where he would spend the night. I knew it wasn't necessary for me to stay with him, but I did and was glad when at 3:00 A.M. I heard him call quietly for me from his bed because he was about to throw up.

When the surgeon came to report that the tumor was, indeed, benign, just as they had assumed, I nearly collapsed with relief, sliding down the wall like that goop they were marketing to little kids a few years ago. Only then did I realize I had never believed the doctors who had predicted this outcome. I had gone about my business for two years expecting the worst and was exhausted from twenty-four months of playing grown-up when what I had wanted to do was collapse like a toddler into my mother's lap.

Mike's recovery from surgery was swift and uneventful. Less than a week after his Frankensteinian adventure in ICU, where he'd been attached to various and sundry monitors, he was in the yard playing catch with his dad. All was right in my world again. For now, anyway.

Occasionally we have a hot, dry spell in the Pacific Northwest, usually in July or August. Some of us don't tolerate them well. As soon as the thermometer soars into the eighties, we start whining about the heat—some of us more than others. We yearn for the sun all winter long, curse the rainy days of June, and then panic for fear the sun will warm us up too much, maybe—heaven forbid—turn us into Californians. The summer following Mike's brain surgery was typical. We were into our second week of hot and dry when, as he tells it, he made a decision that would transform his life. I remember the night. He had slipped out of the living room to go out and sit in the garden. Pat and Mona were living with us that summer, and our small house was perpetually humming with activity and conversation. The cool of the evening garden was alluring.

As he tells it, he began to pray. In order to immerse himself more thoroughly in this endeavor, he imagined Jesus sitting in the chair opposite his. He wanted to talk with him as he might talk with a good friend—informally, openly, with candor. And he did. Finally, he said, he told God he wanted something. He said he wanted to be more than just a believer, that he wanted to be like Peter and the others—a true disciple. And then he asked God for a sign. Specifically, he boldly asked God to take his hand. I hope you're not waiting with bated breath to read that he suddenly felt the Lord's hand in his. I didn't mean to set you up. What happened was this: from what appeared to be a cloudless sky, there came the soft fall of rain. It lasted only a few minutes and then it was gone. It may have been a fluke of nature, I suppose, though I'm inclined to think it was, perhaps, an annointing.

Writing about it puts me in mind of that extraordinary story in Exodus I alluded to earlier, the one in which Moses asks God to reveal his glory and God responds by saying, "'I will make all My goodness pass before you, and I will proclaim the name of the LORD before you. I will be gracious to whom I will be gracious, and I will have compassion on whom I will have compassion.' But He said, 'You cannot see My face; for no man shall see Me and live.' And the LORD said, 'Here is a place by Me, and you shall stand on the rock. So it shall be, while My glory passes by, that I will put you in the cleft of the rock, and will cover you with My hand while I pass by. Then I will take away My hand, and you shall see My back; but My face shall not be seen.'"[3]

I am not attempting to liken my son to Moses, though I have always thought God had his eye on Mike to be a preacher. He didn't much like it the first time I told him that, back in high school, but I just didn't think God gave Mike the particular gifts he gave him just for the heck of it. Any more than I think he gave Pat prophetic vision just for the heck of it. But that's not the point of this story.

The point of this story is that that night in the garden signaled a transformation of Michael's heart, a transformation that would modify all of his senses, enable him to hear and see, taste and touch things he had never experienced before. It would permit him to see the con man on the street in Minneapolis and help him out regardless of the man's motives. It would take him to the underbelly of New York City over spring break, where he would discover a love for people who are not lovely. It would move him to approach a schizophrenic in the booth at a greasy spoon in Dallas to see if there was something he could do to help. What had been, up to that time, a gradual and easygoing stride in the steps of his spiritual journey seemed to be turned up a notch, so that within two years Mike would graduate with his BFA in acting and lay plans to spend the remainder of his life serving God as a full-time professional minister.

Transformation. It's what I've come to believe the Beatitudes are really all about. As I put the finishing touches on the previous chapter, I suddenly saw something I had never noticed before. The Beatitudes seem to fall into two categories. The first four describe the character of one who is willing to relinquish his life to God in order to experience the fullness of God and gain entrance to the kingdom. An invitation to come before the King, with clear instructions regarding the protocol for doing so: emptying oneself, pouring out and discarding the old and making space for the new. Each of them, at its core, commands humility; each is about allowing God to break the stranglehold of pride that keeps us out of fellowship with each other and with him. These beatitudes impel us to repent and rely in utter dependence on God, while the last four describe the character of a person who has been transformed by surrendering his or her life to God. By humbly placing himself under the mighty hand of God, a man can be merciful. A woman can be pure of heart. They can be peacemakers. And they will be persecuted.

Few of us possess the quality of mercy—"it droppeth as the gentle rain from heaven."[4] At least not for sustained periods of time, though there are those, some Christian and some not, who have been given the gift of a merciful heart. I am thinking of people like my sis Linda, whose compassion was so stirred by seeing my mother-in-law trying to survive in a nursing home that she offered to become her caregiver, to move in with her and devote herself, full-time, to looking after her so we wouldn't have to uproot her and move her to Washington. Our friends up here can't believe that *my* sister is taking care of Don's mother.

When I think of merciful souls, I think, too, of Claire, whom I've known for over forty years. She nurses baby crows back to health while irate gardeners in the neighborhood are loading up their BB guns, and her big heart stretches to embrace humans as well as animals. I remember her telling about a mysterious man who was living in his car at the bottom of their hill. The whole neighborhood was leery, watching the stranger from a safe distance. And though Claire too was leery, when the temperature dropped uncommonly low one night, she lugged a sleeping bag down to the car and tapped on the window because she couldn't stand to think of him getting cold. But Claire's the exception. The people we know who actually look after the needy or visit prisoners are few and far between. Most of us tend rather to have flashes of generosity that motivate us to buy a few groceries to give a homeless woman at the side of the road, or to spend our Thanksgiving at the local soup kitchen. Maybe, when we finally get around to going through all the stuff in our garages and storerooms, we'll find an old chair or a box of chipped dishes to set out for one of the charitable groups which phone from time to time to see if we have anything we're willing to part with. We might even go out of our way once in a while to take a like-new L.L. Bean coat from our closet, deciding for once and for all that we will never lose enough weight to fit into it again. Who needs a perfectly good coat hanging on the rack to remind us we've become terminally hefty? Although our giving may be the result of divine conviction at times, I suspect it's usually guilt-driven as we look more to unburden ourselves than to help our fellow sojourners. Something about a closet rod bowed with the weight of too many clothes shames us. I started to use the word *almsgiving* a minute ago but chose not to since it evokes images of panhandlers. There's something about beggars that ignites our indignation, though I have noticed that smokers are always quick to shake out a handful of cigarettes to beggars looking for a nicotine fix. I know I always was; something about the comradery of addicts, I suppose. More often than not, we assuage our guilt with a check and leave the actual buying and distributing of food to some nameless person out there who actually has time to do it, or feels "called" or whatever. We have lawns to mow and decks to paint—and Christmas cards to get out, for crying out loud.

Actually, I don't think most of us really get the mercy thing. The word is used in interesting, idiomatic ways: criminals throw themselves on the mercy of the court, and occasionally young men beg beautiful girls to have mercy on them. But like other words we have encountered, this one seems to be slipping out of usage in our culture. I remember tossing an inquisitive glance toward my husband when his southern-born granny once exclaimed, "Lawdie massy me!" Interpretation: "Lord have mercy on me." Granny is long since dead, and I'm thinking that maybe hers was the last generation that routinely called on the Lord for mercy.

There are four different words that translate as "mercy" in Scripture, two of which are used most often to express God's faithfulness, tenderness, and kindness toward us, as in the Twenty-fifth Psalm, in which David asks the Lord to remember him with tender mercies and lovingkindness. Divine mercy, if you will, as opposed to the other two, which are about the mercy we are invited to show our fellow man.

And though the word used in this beatitude is the latter, I am compelled to give some attention to the question of God's mercy and its coexistence with suffering. Many people stumble over this in their faith journey, sometimes many times. When we revisit the Holocaust, for instance, or mass killings in the Sudan, when we hear about the cruelty inflicted upon prisoners of war or learn of the death of yet another child, a colateral victim of violence in the streets of Belfast, or remember little black girls dying in the bombing of a church in the middle of their Sunday school lesson back in the '60s or high school kids tormented and murdered by their peers in the school library in the '90s, who among us does not cry out to God for an explanation? We are haunted by the cries of anguish foreshadowing the cross: "O my God, I cry out by day, but you do not answer."[5]

To respond with glibness and pat answers would be an abomination. When students ask me to set this incongruity aright, I can't do it. I don't know why God does what he does. I don't know why he heals one child and lets another die an agonizing death, why my cousin's baby died and mine didn't, or why my uncle's wife had to witness the death of not one but two sons. I don't know why he did not rain terror on Haman when he ordered the massacre of the Jews or on Haman's modern-day counterpart, Adolf Hitler. I don't know why he didn't cast every lynch mob into the pit of hell or why he permitted Ted Bundy to weave across the country in his predatory rage. I don't know why the preparations for Israel's flight out of Egypt included the consumption of bitter herbs, any more than I know why the sight of a beach washed clean by twilight surf breaks my heart. With all humility, all I can do is offer this for consideration: just because we cannot apprehend a thing doesn't mean the thing isn't there. Herein lies the essential mystery of faith.

A few years ago when those stereographic art prints were all the rage, I was perpetually frustrated at my inability to apprehend the hidden images supposedly tucked within them. Without success, friends instructed me as to how I should squint just so. I simply could not see the ship or shark or whatever thing lay just beneath the gauzy geometric patterns. There were, I decided, two possibilities to explain this. Either I was visually disadvantaged in some way, or I was too lazy to stand still long enough to permit my brain to do what it had to do so that I might see. I settled on the first explanation, preferring a physical handicap to a character flaw. In either event, I could not see the image, but that didn't mean my friends were liars. I trusted that the second image was there without being able to see it.

All this set me to thinking about other situations in which we presume we have all the facts at hand when we don't. I remembered observing a youngster in the pre-op room at the hospital when we were there for Mike's surgery. She was begging her mother to make the nurses prepping her for surgery go away and leave her alone. With anguish, the mother tried to explain to her daughter that she knew it hurt, but that the doctors and nurses had to do these things so the little girl could be made well. But no amount of talk dissuaded the child from her perception that big people were hurting her and her very own mother was in collusion with them.

When Pat was in college, he came home one weekend full of enthusiasm about studies in physics that had led him to gain a further appreciation of God's greatness. We sat at the dining room table and conversed through the night, finally donning sweaters and scarves at dawn to take a walk in the fog. I will never forget him virtually dancing as he walked backward down the road so he could face me as we continued to talk.

What if, he suggested, God exists in an unknown dimension that permits him to see and know all, while we, no matter how hard we try, simply cannot see? Alluding to something he'd read recently, he went on, asking me to imagine people as mere shadows on a surface, two-dimensional. "Suddenly," he said excitedly, "someone commands us to look up, but we're puzzled because we have no understanding of the word *up*. And even if we could comprehend the meaning of the word, we would still not be able to do it, any sooner than a pig could fly having suddenly grasped the meaning of the word *fly*." What if, we pondered together, this is what real faith is about, about a God whose purposes are too grand and ways too glorious for us to grasp, a God who expects us to actually trust him when he allows us to experience pain and suffering because he knows something we don't know? Pat's questions put me in mind of another of Levertov's poems titled "Morning Mist," in which the poet reflects on our reaction to the "disappearance" of Mount Ranier on a cloudy morning, our inclination to "equate God with these absences,"[6] though the mountain is still there.

When I find myself overwhelmed by the question of pain, I return to the story of Job. I read again those final chapters in which God reminds Job of his omnipotence and power. I remember that God is God, and I pray that in my darkest hour, I will have the heart to say, as Job did, "Though He slay me, yet will I trust Him."[7]

Of the words pertaining to mercy among human beings, *racham,* as used in the second chapter of Hosea, is the origin of the Hebrew word for womb and suggests the sort of mercy we are inclined to show children or those among us who are weak and defenseless. The word suggests the deepest level of tenderness and compassion, such as what mothers and fathers feel for their own flesh and blood. *Eleeo* is the second of these, and those who are called *eleeo,* according to notes in the *Spirit Filled Life Bible,* are "showers of mercy."[8] When I first read that line, before I realized it meant show-ers, as in displayers, I read it showers, as in rain showers. The poet in me likes the wordplay. Show-ers of mercy are like rainwater to thirsty plants. Mercy restores hope, edifies, and gives life. *Eleeo* bears the connotation of action, moving to remove the distress of another. In fact, the English word *eleemosynary* means "charitable, philanthropic relief." *Philos.* The brotherhood of man.

Of all the imperatives given to followers of Christ, none appears to be more important than this. The call to mercy occurs time and time again in Scripture, as we discovered in the words of the prophet Micah, who instructed the people of Israel to love mercy. Likewise, the prophet Hosea admonishes the people with the words of the Lord, "For I desire mercy ... and the knowledge of God more than burnt offerings."[9] And from God's lips to our ears, as recorded in Luke, "Love your enemies, do good, and lend, hoping for nothing in return; and your reward will be great, and you will be sons of the Most High. For He is kind to the unthankful and evil. Therefore be merciful, just as your Father also is merciful."[10] The merciful, it turns out, will enjoy the company of the Most High. And though many of us would like to expunge all passages of Scripture that speak of hell, it seems those who withhold mercy should anticipate the day they will find themselves standing on the threshold of it. Don't get mad at me for talking about hell. I know it disturbs people to note Jesus' admonition: "Then He will also say to those on the left hand, 'Depart from Me, you cursed, into the everlasting fire prepared for the devil and his angels: for I was hungry and you gave Me no food; I was thirsty and you gave Me no drink; I was a stranger and you did not take Me in, naked and you did not clothe Me, sick and in prison and you did not visit Me.'"[11] I cannot imagine a worse destiny than being sent away by Jesus, never again to enjoy his companionship. Hell indeed.

Speaking of pesky little bits of Scripture, a close reading of that earlier passage from Luke awakens our awareness of the kinship between mercy and forgiveness, words often used synonymously because they are so closely connected, each rooted in the act of giving. Jesus tells us that the Father is "kind to the unthankful and evil," a concept that not only is beyond our scope of understanding but tends to make us downright testy with the Lord. This, of course, is the essence of the Good News when we apply it to ourselves, though it's mighty hard to accept when we apply it to others. God "makes his sun rise on the evil and on the good, and sends rain on the just and on the unjust. For if you love those who love you," Jesus asks, "what reward have you? Do not even the tax collectors do the same?"[12]

A couple of summers ago, our old family dog fell very ill. Maggie, a lovely little tricolor sheltie, was a perfect dog, and lest you think me biased, let me just say we have a cat named Jake who is, well, less than perfect, though cat lovers insist he is the embodiment of catness. (I think he's an ungrateful thug myself, though I confess I have an abiding admiration for him I can't quite explain.) Anyway, Maggie came to live with us as a puppy sixteen years ago when we lived in Colorado. You have to understand that I'm not one of those animal people. You all know who you are. People like Claire and Linda and Don and Mona. People who, in fact, value their animal friends more than their human ones, who lovingly sweep away the apparently inedible parts of mice and birds that wind up on the back porch. People who accept hairballs and dog puke as a natural part of the environment. I am not one of those people. I gag just thinking about pet vomit. Furthermore, because every dog that ever came to live with my family of origin proved to be either incorrigible or stupid—digging up gardens, chasing cars, snapping at neighbor children—I assumed all dogs were basically a pain in the ankle. Until I met Maggie and bought a little book written by a quirky English lady who swore you could train a dog to piddle on demand.

She was right. For fifteen years Maggie was the model of compliance, squatting to do her business the minute she heard the words, "Be a good dog, Muggs," expecting only a liver snap in return. Pavlov would be proud. But that's not what was wonderful about Maggie. What was wonderful about Maggie was that she was faithful and sweet even to me, the one who was frequently too busy to brush or pet her, the one who snapped at her when she got underfoot in the kitchen and let her water dish go dry from time to time. The one who, when I fell, metaphorically speaking, into the pit of hell, gingerly hopped onto the bed and nudged her way into my space, looked up at me with sad eyes, and rested her chin in my lap while I cried my eyes out for the thousandth time.

When the vet told us that her heart was enlarged, I thought, "How fitting that Maggie should die of a big heart." We thought she would die within days following this diagnosis, but thanks to the wonders of modern medicine, she lasted almost a year. Nursing her back to improved health was not easy, however. At one point, we were picking up all thirty-six pounds of her and hauling her out to the yard, where she continued, I might add, to piddle on command. When she refused to eat, I began to experiment with low-fat, low-sodium concoctions I thought might interest her, such as pureed turkey breast and scrambled Egg Beaters. I discovered she would eat junior Gerber meals if I placed the dish between her front feet while she lay on her rug in the hallway. I ground her pills with mortar and pestle and prayed over the powders as I stirred them into her turkey and vegetable medley. Interestingly, I did not ask God to keep Maggie alive; only to comfort her, to make her passing easy, and if at all possible, to please let her die at home.

All these things my husband would gladly have done for this beloved dog had he not been overwhelmed with work in the critical-care unit at the hospital. As it was, the task of primary caregiver fell to me. One night, as we lay in bed in the dark, Don thanked me for taking such good care of Muggs. I reminded him that Michael had been a great help to me, and then said something like, "Besides, it's not a challenge to extend mercy to someone like Maggie. Who wouldn't?"

Indeed, there is little challenge in loving the innocent and the loveable. If any of my friends needed food or clothing, if any of them ended up in prison, I'd be the first one on their doorstep looking for ways to help. There was no trick to loving my mother, who was one of the most beloved women in our community. As for forgiveness, most of us can easily find a way to forgive the child who has broken even a priceless objet d'art. What sort of oaf could possibly hold a grudge against an innocent?

Loving our enemies is a different thing altogether. Talk about rivers of Scripture across which you'd like to skip stones, this one takes the prize. In fact, this river is so wild and wide, I have to ease my way into it, start small, think about folks for whom I merely have no affection—strangers or generic miscreants like welfare bums and the homeless—as opposed to, say, wife-beaters, child-rapists, Nazi prison guards, and stepfathers who mistreat our mothers.

Let me tell you about Seth's mom. I don't remember her name. I met her at a graduation party when we went down to Dallas to see Mike graduate from college. We were standing at the buffet table when she introduced herself and said that her son, Seth, had enjoyed getting to know Mike. She was an attractive woman, small and round—what folks used to call "pleasingly plump" before we all sold our souls to the goddess Anorexis. Her hair was long, I think, dark brown, and I think she wore a red dress, though I may have added all these details later as I remembered her. It was her bright face, her spirit, that captured my interest. She was vibrant—and joyful. This was one happy woman. A woman full of energy she was looking to spend. Apparently I looked like a willing recipient.

It seems she was of the Pentecostal persuasion. In fact, when I heard the first words fall from her lips and detected her Texas accent, I had to fight the urge to flee, fearing I was about to be trapped behind the dining table with a Tammy Faye Bakker look alike for untold hours. I don't remember how the conversation turned to God, and I use the word *conversation* loosely—this was definitely a one-woman show. Before I could say Presbyterian, she had launched into a lengthy monologue about a young man we'll call Hugh. It seems she was a secretary in one of the administrative offices on campus where she had met Hugh, then a student at SMU. A very nice young man, she said, though sad somehow. She learned later, after he had left campus, that he was gay, and though this disturbed her, it did not alter her affection for him. If I remember correctly, one night at church she was, she said, "Sitting in a pew praying for my daughter. Actually," she explained with a hoot, "I was filled with the Holy Spirit and had rolled right *under* the pew and was praying hard for my daughter to call me and let me know she was okay." Hearing this, I began looking for a way around the other side of the table, wondering where all of my family had disappeared to, so I missed the punch line of the story. I think her daughter called her that very evening or something like that. She hadn't seemed to notice my temporary disconnect, as she had moved on to explain what all this had to do with Hugh.

The next day, she was out running errands when the Lord put Hugh on her heart. In fact, she said, God told her she needed to go see him, and since she had no idea where he lived, God provided guidance to an apartment complex. He told her she'd know she was at the right place when she saw a woman in the front yard with a rake. (About as likely, I thought, as finding Colonel Mustard in the billiard room with a lead pipe.) But as it turned out, there she was, raking autumn leaves right where God said she'd be. When Seth's mom asked her if Hugh lived there, though, she said no ... but he *had* lived there once, before he moved to San Francisco. Apparently Hugh had managed to get a step ahead of God. The rake lady had a forwarding address, which she happily procured. Seth's mother was now convinced that the Lord wanted her to contact this young man. Within a short time, she had Hugh on the phone.

He was, of course, surprised to hear from her, and for reasons she could not understand, he confided in her that he had AIDS and was not expected to live long. She asked if she could fly to San Francisco to see him. "So there I was," she laughed, "35,000 feet in the air winging my way to San Francisco! I remember thinking, 'You do *not* have the money to be doing this,' but I just didn't feel like God was giving me a choice." A curious Hugh met her at the airport with reluctant enthusiasm. He knew she was a Christian and came right out, she said, and told her in no uncertain terms that he had little use for Christians and their self-righteous attitude toward gays and lesbians. If she was here to try to convert him or lecture him on his sinful ways, she had best just return to Dallas. Not sure how to respond to this, she said the first thing that came to her, something she was certain came courtesy of the Holy Spirit. "I just want you to know that Jesus loves you, that's all," she said, and that was the last that was said on the subject. She stayed with him for the better part of a week, till her vacation time was used up, and then she flew back to Dallas. Not long after, she received a late night call saying Hugh was critically ill. The end was near. Once more, she doled out the money for an airline ticket and found herself winging her way to the West Coast.

She arrived in time to spend a few days with Hugh in the hospital, though I think she said he was unable to converse with her as he lay in a semicomatose state. As it became clear that he would not rebound, she desperately wanted to remind him that Jesus loved him, but remembering his admonition, she said nothing.

"And then," she said, "the Lord told me what to do. He said, 'Sing to him.' So I did. Mostly children's songs like 'Jesus Loves the Little Children,' 'Jesus Loves Me, This I Know' . . . just whatever song the Lord put on my heart."

"So, what happened?" I asked, assuming that the whole point of the story was leading up to a dramatic and glorious testimony: *and suddenly, Hugh looked up, and with his dying breath, gave his life to Jesus!*

"I'm not sure, really," she confessed. "All I know is that when I first got there, he looked scared and wretched, but as I sang to him, he seemed to relax a little, and just at the hour of his passing, he wore a peaceful smile."

Now it was my turn to get a talking to by the Lord, who said something like, "Shame on you for your stuffy little stereotypes and your Seattle superiority complex." Hugh was sick, and Seth's mom (I *wish* I could remember her name) visited him, probably, I decided, while I sat on someone's patio sipping a latte and verbally tearing the poor interim pastor to shreds. I only hoped God would take my groaning as a prayer of repentance. He must have, because I found myself smiling. I loved this woman! When I turned again to speak with her, she was engaged in a curious exchange with a woman at the far end of the table, who, I'd noticed, had given her the evil eye throughout the telling of her story. Turns out it was her mother, a white-haired old lady, rolling her eyes, shaking her head, and emitting a deep sigh.

"What *is* it, Mother?" asked Seth's mom.

"Oh, nothin'," she drawled. "I was just wonderin' if you was finished with your little drama down there." (She pronounced it *dra-muh,* as in rama-lama-ding-dong.)

I laughed out loud. Mothers and daughters. People. I made a beeline for my family, whom I spied hiding out on the patio. I couldn't wait to tell them about Seth's mother, and her mother, and Hugh, and all the gifts I'd just been given while I munched on Tex-Mex hors d'oeuvres at the buffet table.

Eleeios. Seth's mom—shower of mercy. She reached out to a virtual stranger because God told her to. Do I believe she was guided by God's remote-control system to find the lady with the rake and then spend her hard-earned secretarial pay on an airline ticket to the West Coast? Yeah, maybe. Yes, I think I do. Why not? Why is it so hard for us to believe that people who lay themselves open to God actually get messages from him, take their marching orders from him? Why, when we meet a person like this, do we leap to judge her as uneducated, gullible, and foolish when more apt adjectives might be *simple, malleable,* and *wise?* "For the wisdom of this world is foolishness with God."[13] Do I believe Hugh is in heaven? I would never be so bold as to say who is or is not in heaven, though I feel fairly certain we are in for some big surprises when it comes to that. I tremble to think about it. Do I think Seth's mom is a nut? Indeed I do. Lord help me be a nut too.

God does not distinguish between those who deserve mercy and forgiveness and those who don't. I remember the first time

I heard Corrie ten Boom tell her story about encountering one of her concentration camp guards just months after World War II. There she was, on the dais, the keynote speaker at some gathering or another. She had just finished recounting stories from her book *The Hiding Place* about her years in the camp and was standing in a reception line when she saw him approach. In just moments, she would be expected to reach out and shake the hand of a man she vividly remembered from the days when she and her sister had been held prisoner. If I remember the story correctly, she stood in line, mechanically shaking hands with those who came ahead of him, and silently but adamantly told God there was no way she could do it, no way she could offer this man her hand, even if he had found the Lord and repented of all his crimes. No one was more surprised than she was when she found herself extending her hand to him, the hand of mercy, of forgiveness and reconciliation. By her confession, she was transformed—and made capable of doing the impossible.

A refreshingly honest woman, Lyn Corazin, confessed to a group of confirmands last year that she felt pretty sure she was going to be miffed about some of the people she'd find in heaven when she got there. The most erudite among us, those who know what the Bible says pretty much inside and out, find themselves caught in the tension between the desire for justice and the call to mercy. Assuming I'm pretty typical, I'd have to say that we're usually far more interested in justice (at least our brand of justice) than we are in mercy.

The crimes committed against the Jews in the Holocaust are unspeakable. We want those Dachau guards to pay for their atrocities with blood. It seems only fair. In a dark corner of our hearts, we pray that Ted Bundy's last-minute conversion was, in fact, just another one of his lies; we do *not* want to sit at table with him in paradise. I'm reminded of a PBS documentary I watched several years ago detailing the work of Helen Prejean in her campaign against capital punishment. Prejean wrote the book *Dead Man Walking*, which was later made into a hit movie. The character in the movie who is eventually executed is a composite of two death-row inmates Prejean advised and counseled over the years, one of whom was a violent man named Robert Lee Willie. Willie and a companion murdered a young woman named Faith Hathaway and then went on to kidnap a teenage boy and girl in a nearby town. They brutalized both the boy and the girl and finally left the boy for dead. For three days, they raped and tormented the girl and eventually released her. Watching this *Frontline* documentary, I was certainly moved by Helen Prejean's compassion, dedication, and mercy, but the person who really moved me was this young survivor, now a grown woman, named Debbie Morris. Reading the book, Morris was, at first, incensed by what she perceived as Prejean's lopsided version of events and the nun's inexplicable sympathy for Willie. Morris was wounded by the fact that Prejean had written the book without hearing her side of the story. But unlike the bereaved parents of Faith Hathaway, who became activists in favor of the death penalty—a choice that seems perfectly logical, a choice we can readily relate to—something, or someone, bigger than the world seemed to be agitating Debbie Morris' spirit. She said she was searching for an answer as to what God expected from her in this situation. She knew there was more to Robert Lee Willie than the violent man she had been chained to for three days all those years before—and, figuratively, chained to for years. Struggling with her thoughts and feelings, she contacted Prejean. The two women met and talked and made their peace, and began an ongoing dialogue about capital punishment. The closing lines of the documentary, dubbed over a scene in which Prejean and Morris kneel together in a small church, are spoken by Debbie Morris. With remarkable candor, she says that though her views on capital punishment have been affected by her acquaintance with Helen Prejean, she has not yet arrived at a place of absolute forgiveness. "If what I am supposed to believe," she confesses, "is that Robert Lee Willie deserves a place in heaven right there next to me and Faith Hathaway and whoever else, I'm not quite there yet." Debbie Morris' story, which she ultimately wrote in a book titled *Forgiving the Dead Man Walking,* is almost unbelievable. Given the unspeakable acts of violence committed against her, that she could even come near to the place of forgiveness and mercy boggles the mind.

Consider yet another story that shakes the foundation of our understanding. A mother of a murder victim, tormented by grief and hatred, decides to visit her son's murderer in prison in an attempt to understand what in the world spurred him to kill her precious child. After a time, mother and murderer forge a relationship, and when he asks her to forgive him, she does and, in doing so, feels her gaping wounds begin to close and heal. I wept when I heard her story. And though I could not comprehend this gesture of mercy any more than the rest of the people hearing the story, I knew she had done a right thing. She had reached out and touched this young man in the same way Jesus touched the leper and the adulteress. She had permitted him to become a real person, a mother's son. To hate him would be like picking scabs off her sores, never permitting her body, or spirit, to mend.

We know she did the right thing. We tell our Sunday school kids that God loves everyone the same, "red and yellow, black and white," but when it comes right down to it, as sisters and brothers of the prodigals of the world, we wish God would make some distinction between them and us. We want God to be fair. We want everyone to get what she deserves. Or what we think she deserves. Until we get real about our own capacity for sin. If we're lucky, something will happen along the way that will make us aware that not one of us is exempt from it, sin, and that every single one of us is capable of acts as heinous as any we have ever read about. I'm sure I'm not alone when I speculate that whatever Jesus was drawing in the dirt that day the villagers gathered stones to kill the adulteress, it served as a searchlight to illumine the dark corners of these men's hearts and reveal the truth within.[14] I thank God for many things on a regular basis—my kids, my mother and brothers and sisters, the glory of my garden—but the thing for which I am most grateful is the hour of illumination in which God made me aware of my sin. Nothing has ever hurt or healed so much.

Despite everything, we tend to dance between mercy and justice like marionettes. One minute we share the view that a God of mercy is a God unjust and zealously embrace the Old Testament's insistence on eye for eye and tooth for tooth. Accused murderers seeking mercy sound like kids caught in a playground brawl, justifying their actions by proclaiming, "He hit me first." And though we winced to hear the Menendez brothers justify the murder of their mother and father by citing incidents of rape and abuse inflicted upon them by their father, we aren't sure what to do with these young men, whether we should electrocute them or hold them. When we read the litany of crimes committed by the likes of Ted Bundy or Jeffrey Dahmer, we are convinced they must suffer for their evil deeds, and then we witness the likes of Robert Lee Willie portrayed as a human being, with real feelings and needs. A heart. A man so warped by his upbringing he couldn't seem to comprehend the horror of his acts. My son Pat saw *Dead Man Walking* just a few nights after watching a movie in which the protagonist is a mother who stalks and kills her daughter's murderer. Because Pat so thoroughly sympathized with this mother, he left the first movie convinced that death was too good for rapists and murderers. After *Dead Man Walking,* he said he and Mona drove home in silence and couldn't talk about the movie for hours. When they finally did and she asked him where he now stood on the question of capital punishment, he paused for a moment and then announced with passion that he was now "firmly on the fence."

No other issue, save abortion, causes us this sort of angst. Just when I think I know exactly how I feel about either subject, something happens to shatter my resolve, though I am certain about one thing. I know I don't want to be in line on Judgment Day behind doctors who blithely performed abortions without hesitation, without prayer. Without at least considering the possibility that they were about to take the life of someone God placed in the womb at the mercy of his or her mother. But what about understanding? What about mercy? I remember a young eighth-grade girl in my class at Heath Junior High School in Greeley, Colorado. I'll call her Doreen. Though I don't make it a practice to use the classroom as a forum for discussing my political views, this was an intimate environment, a tutorial center for "at risk" students, and during one chat or another, Doreen learned that I had serious reservations about abortion. One morning, she arrived late to class looking hammered. There were dark circles under her eyes; her color was ashen. When I asked her what was wrong, she said nothing and hurried to a seat. Whenever I tried to make eye contact with her, she quickly averted her gaze. I knew that Doreen was streetwise and sophisticated, knew too that she had a steady boyfriend who had dropped out of high school. I had a pretty good idea what had happened, though I did not want to trespass. Finally, after everyone else had left for the day and she hung back, I went to her desk and sat beside her. Tearfully, she told me she'd been out of school to have an abortion. I could tell she was vigilantly scoping me out to see how I would react. I felt a stab of sadness. I told her I was sorry, and I cried. I held my arms open in invitation, and she permitted me to hold her. I felt nothing but love for this little girl, and a deep, throbbing sorrow.

Whatever your position on these controversial issues, you know that very good people sometimes do very bad things. None of us should ever presume to know the history or the heart of the person sitting next to us in church. You do not know mine. If you did, you'd no doubt get up and move, and you sure wouldn't let your kids come to my house for Bible study. I do not know your story. But I know that men in the Bible, men after God's own heart, did ugly things. You'd have to go some to top Saul's wicked ways or David's scheme to kill his lover's husband. And these were God's anointed ones. And of course there's Paul, who sanctioned the execution of Jesus' followers.

If you haven't seen *The Apostle,* you should. I don't know how Robert Duvall manages to successfully portray virtually any character, from mob boss to cattle rustler to aging Cuban dancer, but he does it. In *The Apostle,* he plays a Pentecostal preacher. Duvall produced this movie because, as I understand it, he thought the Pentecostal preacher an important figure in American culture.

I agree, and thanks to the plethora of TV evangelists, many of whom seem to cultivate exaggerated southern drawls and sport bad hairdos, most of us operate from an abiding belief that they are all deplorable frauds. Some of them probably are. In fact, I expected Sonny, the preacher in the movie, to be just another parody, a cardboard cut-out of Jimmy Swaggart. But he wasn't. He was a mess all right, but he actually loved the Lord and wanted others to know about him. This is authenticated in the opening scene of the movie when Sonny comes upon what appears to be a fatal accident and, without benefit of audience, carries his Bible to the driver's-side window where he reaches in and touches the young driver and prays for him and his young wife, inviting them, then and there, to welcome Jesus into their hearts. He tells them Jesus loves them, and he means it.

Turns out, though, that Sonny's been unfaithful to his wife—more than once—and when he learns that she is having an affair with the youth minister at their church, he gets a snootful of booze and smashes the guy in the face with a baseball bat at a Little League game. When he realizes he has seriously injured the man, he doesn't wait around for the law but runs like a rabbit, ditching his car in a nearby canal and tossing his ID into the wind as he walks away. He goes on the lam, and though we all understand him, we want him to show a little integrity and own up to his deeds, face the music. Instead, he assumes a new identity, restores a dilapidated old church, and ministers to a small community of saints while he waits for the law to catch up with him. The movie closes with Sonny working on a chain gang and, in Pentecostal rhythms, telling his fellow inmates that Jesus loves them. Many Christians I know do not like this movie. Sonny is not the role model they want to put before their children. But I want my sons to look closely at him. I want them to know that you can make mush out of your life by indulging in your sinful nature, that one afternoon of drunkenness can alter the course of a life, and I want them to know that nothing and no one is beyond God's reach, beyond redemption.

Forgiving people who have hurt you does not mean that you condone or dismiss their behavior. Extending mercy does not mean that you sanction sin. It may mean, though, that you are willing to give someone a chance to start over. Abbot Pastor, one of Merton's desert fathers, said, "Malice will never drive out malice. But if someone does evil to you, you should do good to him, so that by your good work you may destroy his malice."[15] And it certainly means that you are giving yourself a chance to be healed. God knows that mercy begets mercy, that healing cannot happen as long as we hold onto grudges and nurse wounds. Desmond Tutu has recently published a book titled *No Future without Forgiveness,* in which he gives an account of South Africa's rejection of "the Nuremberg solution," as well as unconditional amnesty for perpetrators of apartheid in his country. In lieu of these alternatives, South Africans opted for "restorative justice," whereby these criminals would receive amnesty only after they had made a full and public confession of their crimes. According to Jorge Lara-Braud's review of Tutu's book in the *Presbyterian Outlook,* the people involved in this process learned many things, including the remarkable capacity for forgiveness on the part of the victims and the "exhilarating liberation from guilt that has come to the perpetrators who have made a public confession of their crimes."[16] It has been my experience that practicing forgiveness always results in healing and is usually accompanied by the blinding light of self-awareness, the realization that I need forgiveness every bit as much as I need to forgive. I've heard folks around our church basement, participants in the Divorce Recovery Workshop, quote a slogan of sorts: "Forgive and be forgiven." We must. It is our only hope. Indeed, it is the salve that will heal us; it is our salvation. Kyrie eleison. The Publican's prayer: "Lord have mercy on me, a sinner."

As for justice, God is perfect and is, therefore, perfectly just. We are justified by faith, and in our faith, we know that God will, in his time, line things up, justify the margins, make things right. Everything will be made right. When I spoke recently of living in the tension between justice and mercy, someone pointed out that the cross stands as a symbol for both. We are able to show mercy and extend the hand of forgiveness because Jesus stood in for us and because God told us to. If we have relinquished our will to him, he will empower us to do what on our own would be utterly impossible. And we will be blessed, just as Jesus promised. Holy Father John of Kronstadt has written, "For thy mercy to the brethren, thou shalt receive mercy from God; for temporal mercy—eternal mercy; for a little mercy—infinitely great mercy. Thou shalt be worthy not only of pardon because of sins from eternal condemnation at God's judgment, but thou shalt also gain eternal blessedness."[17]

6

A Mirror in which You See Yourself Whole

Contrition

It was a dark and stormy night. It really was. We lived in Little-ton, Massachusetts, at the time, in a big, red, two-story colonial house set snugly in the New England woods. Just a few weeks before, when my husband and I had escorted the boys on their annual Halloween treat-procurement mission, we had laughed nervously at how the dry autumn leaves skittering and scraping along our country road transported us to the Sleepy Hollows of our imaginations and scared us to pieces. A couple of prairie kids in grown-ups' clothes—lost in the fairy-tale woods.

Tonight everyone was bracing for a nor'easter predicted to blow in anytime. The witch of November. The sky was starless, the moon casting eerie shadows on Patrick's bedroom wall as it slid in and out among fast-moving clouds. It was as if our house were the set of a scary movie, leafless tree branches—the witch's bony fingers—scraping at the second-story window. A good night to be in, I thought.

I sat on the edge of Pat's little faux brass bed, my back to the window that looked out over the front yard, and pulled his covers up "head and ears," as his dad liked to say. At four, Pat still demanded bedtime rituals: a little chitchat, a little prayer, a smooch, and lights out, but tonight he was uneasy. The storm energized him, made him anxious. "It's creepy in here," he protested. I considered scooping him up and taking him into bed with us but was tired and not willing to spend the night dodging his flailing arms and legs. I opted for sticking around long enough to help him identify the sources of the strange noises invading his room and the spooky shadows dancing across his ceiling. "You'll be all right," I assured him, "and Dad and I are only a dozen steps away."

"I'm fine now," he said abruptly.

"Well, good." That was easy, I thought to myself, feeling smug about my parenting skills. "I knew if you understood what all the sounds were, you wouldn't be afraid of them."

"It wasn't that that made me not afraid," he explained.

"No?"

"Uh-uh," he said, snuggling deep into the bedclothes. "It was Jesus."

I smiled. "Really?!" More smugness. "Talking to Jesus helps, all right," I said.

"It wasn't my prayers that helped," he said. "I saw him."

Pause.

"You did, huh? Jesus? You saw Jesus? Just now?" I asked, feeling little pricklies at the base of my neck.

"Mm-hmm," he said drowsily.

"Where?"

A gust of wind rattled the windows, and the old hag clawed at the shutters.

"There," he pointed, his little double-jointed finger aimed directly over my shoulder and out into the darkness.

Don't ask me why, but I was afraid to turn around. Seeing as how I was the grown-up, however, the omniscient mommy who had, moments before, cooed assurances of safety, I turned . . . slowly. To my relief, I saw nothing but the blackness of night.

"Right there, huh? Outside your window? Way up here on the second floor?"

"Yeah!" He smiled and sat up. "Right there," he pointed. "I was scared and I looked out the window and saw Jesus floating by. He looked in, and then I felt *not* scared."

Blessed are the pure in heart,
for they will see God.

I struggled to find a narrative with which to open this section of the book. Don suggested I write about Maggie, but of course, I'd already used Maggie. Besides, as much as I love her, something about using an animal to exemplify purity of heart won't gel for me. Maybe because of something I read years ago in *Mere Christianity,* I think, where Lewis observes that it's easy to say the pure of heart will see God, for only the pure of heart want to see him. I just can't quite tinker with my mind sufficiently to imagine the desire of a dog's heart beyond maybe a scratch behind the ear and a liver snap. That's when I remembered the Jesus-sighting story with which I opened this chapter, and though I was loath to commit the unforgiveable sin of cliche and use children, I concluded they are, in fact, the closest we can get to understanding purity, though they can (and do) behave wretchedly at times. Don't forget I was the youngest of six kids, and I gave as good as I got when it came to teasing and tattling. We all know how cruel children can be.

In fact, the purity we think of when we think of children is not the purity referred to in Scripture. When we speak of the purity of children, we are really talking about their innocence and sweetness, which, though wonderful and enviable, are not the same as spiritual purity, as I understand it, despite what *Roget's* says. To say that *purity* and *innocence* are synonyms is imprecise. To be innocent is to be without guile, unsullied, harmless. And though a lot of people want to believe that children are born without sin, many Christians have a different understanding. Critics of the faith love to use this as their final volley in debates, suggesting that Christians must surely be a sick lot if we think innocent little babies are tainted by sin. I guess it would be wrong of me to speak for other Christians, but here's what I think. I think children are without guile, unsullied, and harmless, but I think sin is a condition, not an act or a behavior, and we all have an innate capacity—a natural bent—for sinning. In fact, the word translated in Psalm 130 as "iniquities" derives from *'avah,* which means "to bend," and it is this essential crookedness, this condition, for which Jesus died in our stead. It doesn't take long for the condition of Cain to show its ugly self—usually about two years, which is roughly about how long it takes before parents bring home a new baby, who is clearly going to be an obstacle for the first with regard to getting his needs met. Or her. I love Annie Dillard's remembrance in *An American Childhood* of trying to drown her infant sister by pouring a glass of water in the baby's face as she lay gurgling and cooing in her bassinet. So much for purity.

There are two Greek words which translate as "pure" in Scripture. In 1 John the author writes, "Beloved, now we are children of God; and it has not yet been revealed what we shall be, but we know that when He is revealed, we shall be like Him, for we shall see Him as He is. And everyone who has this hope in Him purifies himself, just as He is pure."[1] The word here derives from *hagnos,* from the same root as *hagios,* meaning "holy," and suggests a process by which a heart is made pure, made over to be like Christ's, which was without sin. The word Jesus used in his sermon derives from *katharos,* meaning "without blemish, clean, undefiled." It describes physical cleanlinesss, ceremonial purity, and ethical purity, suggesting also a cleansing process through which sin is washed away.

In the interest of scholarship, I should point out that David Hill, in his commentary on the gospel of Matthew, says there is the possibility of a mistranslation here, that the adjective spoken by Jesus might better be translated as "contrite," as in "blessed are the broken-hearted for they shall see God."[2] It occurs to me that all of this dovetails quite nicely either way, for among the grown-ups I know, a breaking of sorts has been essential in the purification process. It puts me in mind of something I read from the Canon of Preparation for Holy Communion on the webpage for a Russian Orthodox Church in New York: "Teardrops grant me, O Christ, to cleanse my defiled heart."[3]

I suppose it is important to note a possible misunderstanding in the passage from John's letter. In saying that a man "purifies himself," John is not suggesting that purification is achieved by man's own power but that man does, indeed, have the freedom to choose whether he will subject himself to this process. Freedom is the underpinning of our relationship with God. He will never put you through the refining fires without your permission.

All that said, it is clear that the closest we come to a state of purity like the one we will one day experience through Christ is in the blissful state of early childhood, when we are able to see Jesus at the window without the shade of cynicism dropping over our eyes. The heart of a child is trusting and open, ready for love in whatever form it presents itself.

According to Strong's concordance, as noted in the *Spirit Filled Life Bible,* the heart *(leb)* includes intellect, awareness, the mind—the inner person.[4] It encompasses the physical heart as well as that place within us that houses longing and yearning. It is the heart Jesus was talking about when he referred followers to Scripture, admonishing them to "love the Lord your God with all your heart."[5]

It interested me to learn that *leb* includes the physical heart for several reasons, not the least of which is a heightened awareness of my own heart these days, having just come from the doctor, who told me it is time to start watching my lipids. I have to smile every time I think of it, because the first thing that popped into my head was the cartoon image of Don Knotts as Mr. Limpit in *The Incredible Mr. Limpit.* I knew that couldn't be right. Then I thought of those wee black creatures that suction themselves to rocks and pier pilings, but that didn't seem right either.

"It's *lip-ids,*" Don reminded me, though by that time I'd figured it out. "The gunk that clogs your arteries. In other words, fat!" I shuddered. There was that blasted f-word again.

My doctor wouldn't prescribe the wonder drugs that now exist for lowering lipid counts until I agreed to try a change of diet and exercise and attend nutrition classes at the hospital, all of which I did, albeit grudgingly. Thanks to lipid counts, degenerative joints, crumbling teeth, and perimenopausal activity (which always makes me think of para*normal* activity), I'm a little cranky these days about my aging body. It's like you turn a corner on your fiftieth birthday and run smack into an oncoming truck. But I digress. The dietician teaching the nutrition class appeared to be roughly fourteen and a half, and though I thought it was sweet of her lithe, little self to insist she knew how we were feeling about all this, I wasn't buying it any more than any of the other old codgers in the room. I loved the guy in front of me who kept groaning and muttering things like, "My poor grandma must be turning over in her grave to hear her talk about egg substitutes," making egg substitute sound like a lewd reference to dog doo. The teacher opened the class by dimming the lights and casting a graphic photo of a clogged artery onto the screen at the front of the room, a picture they could use in a Drano commercial. It triggered my gag reflex. Mission accomplished, I thought to myself; may I please be excused?

My heart is getting old and, I fear, has been sorely neglected by me, or at least thoroughly taken for granted. Not long after my encounter with the arterial slide, I had occasion to be in the company of a two-year-old, and it occurred to me that her little heart must be clean as a whistle, pink and strong, and that all the arteries leading to it must be as clean as new copper pipes. Because her young mother has carefully orchestrated this little girl's eating habits thus far, the baby's heart has not yet been defiled by all the toxins and preservatives and fat that swim around in grown-ups' food. An unblemished heart beats beneath her flawless infant skin.

No doubt her mind is essentially undefiled at this point as well. No hate-filled song lyrics, no pornographic images or visions of gun-toting heroes have been unleashed in this child's carefully controlled environment—yet. Though I daresay she may already be well on her way to a place where she will do almost anything to avoid silence, since this is something we teach our children early in life. Take me. I swore I would never use TV as a baby-sitter. My promise lasted until my first baby was less than a year old and I discovered that the sounds of Bert and Ernie bantering in their little Sesame Street apartment made him happy. What could it hurt, I thought. At least it's not reruns of *The Untouchables,* which I discovered my husband was watching in the middle of the night with our second baby whenever he took his turn at the midnight feeding. Lord only knows what impact *that* had on the child. Curiously, he's the one who's off in the mission field. So much for the horrors of television. Anyway, like it or not, ours is a noisy culture, and that's the way we like it.

A few years ago, I challenged the kids in the Bible study group to go home and find just one fifteen-minute chunk of time in the coming week when they would willingly enter into solitude. No music, no TV, no conversation. That was the deal. Find a place, a closet perhaps, that would afford the least distraction and sit still for fifteen minutes. No paper and pen, no prayers. Just silence. And no lying down. Napping didn't count. Their recollections the following week amused me, and they were very telling. Maile, who would go on to walk away with every high-school award known to man or beast, lasted about three minutes before she caved. She couldn't stop thinking about things she needed to get done. Same with hyperachiever Mike. They both thought I had suggested a subversive activity. Margaret was in anguish in her bedroom closet. It seems her older brothers and sisters, whom she loves, were all home for a visit, and she could hear them downstairs talking and laughing. She caved too. I think

Ben fell asleep, despite my warning. All of them agreed on one thing: this was the only time they could remember trying to dwell in complete silence, ever—and it was hard.

Henri Nouwen, in *The Way of the Heart,* observed that our culture is one in which words have essentially lost all meaning. Driving through Los Angeles, he said, was like driving through a dictionary; words everywhere, pelting the eye and the ear. "Wherever I looked there were words trying to take my eyes from the road. They said, 'Use me, take me, buy me, drink me, smell me, touch me, kiss me, sleep with me.' In such a world, who can maintain," he asks, "respect for words?"[6] Indeed. In such a world as this, the power of Jesus' imperative to "take, eat, remember me" is sullied and lost in the relentless drone of words. We are a culture that appears to thrive on words flung about with abandon, including those that fill the pages of rag newspapers. Dallas Willard, in *The Divine Conspiracy,* observes that we are smothered in slogans. And it is not just the noise that should trouble us but the manipulation of our minds and hearts that occurs when we recklessly forget the power of words. As Willard eloquently observes, "Commercials, catch words, political slogans, and high-flying intellectual rumors clutter our mental and spiritual space. Our minds and bodies pick them up like a dark suit picks up lint. They decorate us. We willingly emblazon messages on our shirts, caps—even the seat of our pants."[7]

Rabbi Lawrence Kushner, in the introduction to his *Book of Words,* further notes that the carelessness with which we spew forth words extends also into the world of the religious. "Spoken too often, even the holiest reality begins to sound hollow and loses its ability to create anew. Indeed, some of our most sacred words have come to feel like sawdust in our mouths, no longer able to instruct, inspire, chasten or nurture."[8] Admittedly taking poetic license in translating thirty Hebrew words, Kushner describes gossip as garbage, calling attention to these words in Exodus: "You must not eat flesh torn by beasts of the field; you shall cast it to the dogs. You must not carry false rumors."[9] I'm sure the juxtaposition of these commandments is not coincidental. Asserting that Americans are "junkies for gossip," Kushner poses this important question: "If," he asks, "you would not eat garbage from the streets, why do you tolerate auditory filth in your ears? Personal holiness," he concludes, "involves what you take into your body, visually, aurally and orally."[10]

Sometimes it seems that the very parents who are so careful about what their children take into their bodies through their mouths abruptly abdicate responsibility for monitoring what their children take in through their eyes and ears. I vividly remember my mother's expression of grief as she sent each new child off to school. She kept me, the baby, out of kindergarten intentionally, she once said, to defer my inevitable acquisition of schoolyard doggerel. I thought about her when my husband told me about his initiation into the world in the boys' bathroom at Remington Elementary School in fourth grade, where he was held hostage by upper-class thugs until he could prove he knew what the f-word meant (and I don't meant fat) and was willing to say it out loud. Rites of passage among the pure of heart.

To aspire to reclaim our childlike hearts is not about our sinlessness but about the clarity with which children see, the honesty with which they speak. It's about their elemental simplicity. They are unfettered, unsuspicious, vulnerable, and unafraid of the truth, though they learn to lie early. The popular little coffee-table book *Children's Letters to God* illustrates the guileless honesty with which children approach God. "Dear God," writes Denise, "if we come back as something, please don't let me be Jennifer Horton, because I hate her."[11] Among the many students who have attended my weekly Bible study was the daughter of one of our associate pastors. Her name is Margaret Shoop, Muggs for short . . . just like our Maggie. Her dad once told this story from the pulpit. It seems that little Margaret, age three, had been unusually difficult one summer day, so that by the time her daddy got home, her mom was ready to relinquish all parental responsibilities where Margaret was concerned. After supper and story time, when it was time for sleep, her father invited her to close her eyes to pray.

Urging her to repeat after him, he began, "Dear God . . ."

"Dear God," Margaret dutifully parroted.

"Thank you for the beautiful day . . ."

"Thank you for the beautiful day."

"And thank you for my family . . ."

"And thank you for my family."

"Please God, help me to be a better girl tomorrow . . ."

Silence.

"God, help me to be a better girl tomorrow . . ."

Nothing.

Until at last, in a wee but willful voice, "I'm not gonna pray that, Daddy."

Margaret knew better than to lie to God, for among other things, children have enough sense to fear God. They know that angry dads are a force to be reckoned with. If there were children present the day Jesus took a whip to the money changers in the temple, you can be sure they were afraid, and rightly so. In our attempt to re-create Jesus on our own terms, we forget that he got angry. I remember laughing out loud many years ago when I heard a Bible teacher say that he had done extensive research on the passages of Scripture that tell us to fear God. I laughed because he said that despite our many and varied attempts to find euphemisms for these passages—*revere* God, *honor* God, etc.—from all that he could tell, when the Bible said to fear God, it meant be afraid. "And I say to you, My friends, do not be afraid of those who kill the body, and after that have no more that they can do. But I will show you whom you should fear: Fear Him who, after He has killed, has the power to cast into hell; yes, I say to you, fear Him!"[12]

Revisionist gospel writers would have us omit these words spoken by Jesus. I admit I'd like to be included on that panel of folks I've heard rumors about who get to vote on what Jesus really said; I'd certainly vote to jettison this and all the other references to hell.

I parenthetically foreshadowed where I'm going next when I said kids learn to lie early. But you know it's true. Remember Bill Cosby on fatherhood? If you've ever wondered whether children are related to Adam and Eve, just tell them they can have whatever they want to eat in the cupboard *except* the Mallomars, to which one of them is bound to reply sheepishly, "So where *are* the Mallomars?" Our son, Michael, around age five, helped me in my understanding of why children lie, and his explanation suggests that children most assuredly have the capacity to know right from wrong. At least they know that certain behaviors are bound to reap unsavory rewards. One day, before leaving for afternoon kindergarten, Michael came in to have his lunch, which I had set on the kitchen table for him so I could get back to whatever I'd been doing in the family room. (I wish now I had sat down with him at every opportunity, but of course I was doing something terribly important like whipping up a Halloween costume that would make all the other mothers green with envy.)

After a time, Mikey called out that he was finished and wanted to play.

"Did you eat your carrot sticks?" I hollered down the hallway.

He said yes, so I told him to do whatever he liked until it was time to walk down the greenbelt to school. Imagine my surprise a few minutes later when I walked through the kitchen and spied his carrot sticks neatly lined up on his plate.

"Michael," I called. "Didn't you say you'd eaten your carrots?"

He came around the corner. "Yes," he said.

"Then what are these?" I asked.

His eyes opened wide with innocence. "I don't know," he proclaimed.

After a vain attempt to convince me that he had, indeed, eaten the original carrot sticks and that these must have been left there by someone else, he capitulated.

"Why did you lie to me?" I inquired.

"Because," he said in a tone that revealed a sort of fascination with my obtuseness, "it's just easier."

The other day I received one of those things people are always forwarding to your e-mailbox, which has become the hot new venue for comedy. I frequently delete these offerings unless they are from someone I know shares my sense of humor. I loved this one about the kid who was praying and said, "Lord, if you can't make me a better boy, don't worry about it. I'm having a real good time like I am." I'm smiling because this reminds me of a story my niece Kristin told about her little five-year-old daughter, Rebekah.

It seems Rebekah decided to turn the bathtub into a Water World fun slide and turned the bathroom into an unholy mess while she was at it. When her stepdad discovered it, he was not happy. In gruff tones, he asked, "What in the world are you doing?" Later that night, Kristin said, following Bekah's tears of remorse and reconciliation, Kristin passed by her bedroom and heard her commiserating with her dolls. "I don't know why they ask me what in the world I'm doing," she harrumphed. "I don't know what in the world I'm doing. I'm just a little girl trying to have fun!"

But some kids aren't having much fun. Headlines pelt us with the truth. Children are shooting their classmates, picking them off like ducks at a shooting gallery. Boys and girls are killing their moms and dads over beer money, kidnapping elderly women and leaving them tied to trees in the woods to die of exposure. And experts are churning out books about rage-filled boys faster than you can say Columbine High School. We can't believe what's happening, and we seem to have no idea what to do, although, based on the expedient appearance of those books in the marketplace, it would appear that we believe information on the subject is our best hope for fixing the problem.

The popular answer these days to virtually everything that ails us is education. We seem to believe that gathering facts about the origin of a problem will somehow meliorate the situation, and that teaching the children everything we know about, say, drugs will automatically result in the kids' steering clear of them. If we catch boys and girls early and teach them everything we know about sex, maybe they'll make sound, informed choices about their sexual behavior. If we insist on political correctness in the hallways and tell the kids to play nice, one day all of our base compulsions will be as dormant as a chicken's instinct to fly. But it's not working. More kids are drinking, doing drugs, smoking, and having sex than ever before, and at an earlier age. And as for the PC movement, it's been about as effective as neatly placing a Band-Aid over the mouth of Mount Saint Helens. And though well intentioned, the movement may very well end up having done more harm than good.

I was sickened when I heard what had happened to Matthew Shepard in Laramie, Wyoming, a few years ago. It was especially heartbreaking to me because it all happened back where I grew up. Laramie is less than an hour from my childhood home in northern Colorado. In fact, Shephard was taken to the same hospital in which my mother had died just a few years before. I don't pretend to know all the things that went into the horrible making of events that night, but I am convinced that one factor must surely have been the suppression of hate and anger in the hearts of those who committed this egregious crime. About the time it happened, we were engaged at school in yet another program designed to help middle schoolers get in touch with their feelings. We called it Middle School Seminar, and despite my misgivings about it, it turned out to have some merit.

One day, however, I witnessed something that came back to me the night Matthew Shepard was murdered. Each teacher in our middle school served as an advisor to ten kids, give or take a few, and every Thursday, we combined two advisory groups for seminar. On this particular day, I was teamed up with a first-year teacher, a wonderful young woman with a natural flair for teaching. She was young, pretty, and gregarious; the kids loved her. On this particular day, following the plans laid out by some expert in the field of adolescent socialization, we had the kids draw two life-size silhouettes on giant sheets of butcher paper. Sketch number 1 was labeled, "A Person I Would Like to Have as a Friend," and number 2 read, "A Person I Would Choose to Avoid." Armed with markers, the students spent ten minutes or so filling in the white space with words that aptly characterized their silhouette people. Number 1, as you might expect, was filled with words like *nice, happy, cool, smart, good-looking, funny, honest,* and so on. The other teacher and I sat back, as instructed, and permitted the kids to write whatever they chose, as long as it did not include "inappropriate language." Suddenly, I noticed that my teammate was carefully scrutinizing the words scrawled all over guy number 2. Someone had written the word *gay* right in the middle of his abdomen.

Deferring to me as resident senior, the teacher turned to ask if I didn't think we should prompt the girl who had written it to scratch it out. I was tempted. For one thing, I wasn't wild about the kid who'd written it; she was pretty much your basic incorrigible bratty little "popular" girl who took pleasure in teasing others. But I thought better of censoring her.

"No," I said. "It's not inappropriate in the way that a cuss word is. It's not PC, and though it will make some people uncomfortable, we're obliged to let it ride. We told the kids to be truthful."

What followed was a lively discussion dominated by students who expressed pity for this girl for her lack of sophistication— good kids who were merely parroting what they had been taught by well-meaning parents and teachers—and though she tried to hold her own and insist that regardless of how she was *supposed* to feel, gay people made her uneasy, she eventually receded and fell silent. The most insidious thing about the PC movement is that what appears to be a good thing, a right thing—a thing born in the hearts of well-meaning folks with righteous ideas—teaches children to lie! This is what I thought about the night I learned of Matthew Shepard's murder and the brutality with which those young men had taken his life. Did my young student's classmates actually dissuade her from her opinions about homosexuality or did they merely teach her to tamp down her feelings like gunpowder in a musket barrel, which a random spark somewhere in her future might ignite?

Good intentions notwithstanding, I fear we are utterly confusing our children. We teach kids that tolerance and political correctness are the paths to harmony in a culturally diverse world when there are things practiced in some cultures that should surely not be tolerated, things such as genital mutilation and the procurement of pubescent girls as slaves, for example. At some point, moral law must supercede cultural autonomy. Something is not permissible simply because members of a tribe or community have sanctioned it. Perhaps the most insidious thing about what's happening in the classroom these days hearkens back to Alexander Pope's warning that "a little learning is a dangerous thing." In the spirit of synchronicity, educators are accepting what amounts to sound bites of information about various cultures without bothering to do their homework and study them in depth. Thus we have elementary school children, in the name of multiculturalism, celebrating a Hindu holiday without knowing that in actual practice the celebration includes the presenting of young girls to temple priests for sexual services. We encourage them to practice various forms of animism without explaining to them that in cultures where animism is practiced, it is generally done not out of some lofty respect for the animal but out of abject fear of what the animal's spirit will do to them if they do not bow down to it.

In our attempt to tolerate everything, we have created a sort of moral anarchy that brings to mind lines from a William Yeats poem titled "The Second Coming."

> Mere anarchy is loosed upon the world,
> The blood-dimmed tide is loosed, and everywhere
> The ceremony of innocence is drowned;
> The best lack all conviction, while the worst
> Are full of passionate intensity.[13]

In *Time for Truth,* Os Guinness tells about the frightening evolution in student responses to a classic short story by Shirley Jackson, "The Lottery." When the story was first published fifty years ago, students were shocked and outraged to imagine a culture in which each year someone in the community was chosen, by the drawing of lots, to be stoned to death. It seems the current crop of students believes that no one has any right to impose their cultural values on another culture, that though we may find this practice repulsive, we have no right to try to stop it. It seems we are on the verge of conducting our lives in accordance with the prime directive of the Star Trek generation. It makes me shiver to think of it. Lurid images of the Holocaust come to mind. Ethnic cleansing. Child pornography, prostitution, slavery.

For years, the public has assaulted the medical community for treating symptoms without getting at the cause of the problem, but this is precisely what educators today are doing. We are like mechanics tinkering around with the knobs and buttons on the dashboard when we ought to be down and dirty underneath the car, draining polluted oil so new oil might be poured in. A curious image is forming in my imagination as I write this. I see Sunday school teachers and instructors at Christian schools all across the land smugly nodding their heads in confirmation. But Christians are not much better about this than secular educators.

I think of little Denise's letter to God about hating Jennifer Horton; I can just hear her Sunday school teacher saying something to her like, "Now Denise, we don't *hate* other children." (I love how teachers of morality use the royal "we" when instructing kids.) "We love other boys and girls like Jesus did, *don't* we?" I suppose we do this because we're afraid our kids might reveal that even Christians are normal people with less-than-gracious hearts. How refreshing it would be if someone took a different approach. "Wow, Denise! You're hopping mad at Jennifer, aren't you? So, what are you going to do about it?"

In 1990 I had what women in my mother's generation called a "nervous breakdown." This was no small-time anxiety attack. There was a leak in my boat and it was taking on water fast. When it sank, I was plunged beneath the surface of a stagnant lake. I tried as hard as I could to tread water for a while, to save face, running my kids around town, supervising the Logos program at our church, but my strength waned and I was on my way down for the third count. I was ready to surrender. By God's grace, I met someone who would give me a new way of looking at my life, beginning with a new name for my breakdown. "Let's call it a nervous break*through*," he suggested, and the healing began. Before I met him, however, I got a lot of advice. I don't want to belittle the folks who were advising me, because they cared about me and they meant well. But for the most part, each bit of advice was like an additional lead weight tied around my ankles in that swirling pool sucking me to the bottom of the lake. I tried hard to do what my friends urged me to do: count my blessings, look at the bright side, "let go and let God." My poor mother. I threatened to crawl through the long-distance telephone wires one night and strangle her if she didn't stop saying that. Ironically, it was, of course, precisely what I needed to do, but I needed something else first.

I needed permission to speak the truth. Not, mind you, so that I could heap my pain onto the shoulders of my dead father and thus be relieved of it, but so that I might journey past it and venture into the depths where I would glimpse hell and fully encounter my sinful self, where I would utter a kyrie from the depths of my being for the first time. I would be called there to cast off, in fact, every excuse, every occurrence, every person I had used to justify my behavior, in order to learn that God loved not the woman who "strapped it on" every morning and went out to prove to the world that somehow she was okay but the girl whose personal prime directive had always been to get her needs met no matter what it took, even though she thought she'd killed her daddy. And all this would take a lifetime. I'd spent almost forty-five years acquiring all the stuff I thought I needed to survive. Time and patience are required to pack it, load it up, and haul it away, especially given my tendency to try to reclaim sins I've grown fond of over time. I wasn't all that eager to engage in the task, of course, because in my child's knowing heart, I understood what it would mean. Years later I would read words written by the poet Pablo Neruda which would evoke a vivid memory of the experience. "They all left. The house is empty. And when you open the door, there's a mirror in which you see yourself whole. It makes you shiver."[14]

I was terrified to stand naked before God. Something had so warped my understanding of him, I was certain if he saw me without my mask, he would turn his face away from me. I misunderstood Jesus' call for us to become like little children. Like many people, I presumed that this was merely a call to exercise a childlike faith, which it is, but it is also a call to candor, a call to confession. It's about a child's willingness to march her sullied little self right up to the throne of God and confess, "I *hate* Jennifer Horton," knowing that Jesus will not shush her into falsehood. And it is *that* which brings her to the door of the kingdom.

Years after the onset of this breakthrough, I remembered that I had asked God for it. I would never have done so, of course, had I known how dreadfully it would hurt. But I remembered a day in the car, on the move up to Washington state, when I'd told God I was sick of straddling the fence between his world and *the* world. I told him I wanted to be either a real Christian or just to forget the whole thing. I was able to say this only because I could not foresee what his response would involve, and it's a good thing. I give thanks for the things he keeps in shadow.

My sister Nancy graciously provided an image for what turned out to be an excruciating experience. Having herself squared off with some very painful issues and experiences, she said that in the midst of the healing, she had felt like an old barn out on the Colorado prairie that had had heaven knows how many coats of paint slapped on it over the years until one day—at her invitation, no less—someone came along and began the tedious and torturous process of stripping off all the layers of cover-up. There are dozens of metaphors for it, really, many from Scripture. Imagine being a blob of wet clay on a potter's wheel, spinning in the potter's hands, having parts of you sliced away, and ultimately being placed in the kiln. Think of the time it takes for everything to work together just so inside an oyster to make a pearl. Grating sands, purifying fires. Some have likened the process to pulling a tree up by its roots; the longer the tree has lived in sin, the deeper the roots and the more agonizing the process by which it is pulled up so that something new, rooted in God, can grow.

But as you contemplate the pain through which you must pass in order to be purified, imagine, too, a day when you will see the face of Jesus for yourself, when you will stand before the tri-une God and be welcomed as sister, as brother, into the kingdom. All the trappings of this world will fall away like old, worn-out clothes, and everything will be right. In fact, imagine getting to the kingdom right here and now, seeing Jesus this very day. Blessed are the pure in heart, for they *will* see God.

7

He Who Loses His Life
Simplicity

It's curious how the most significant things often happen in circumstances that seem random and insignificant. I certainly would have never guessed that I would experience a vision right in the middle of down time in my seventh grade classroom. Advisory period in our middle school is the equivalent of homeroom in elementary school. Same idea, new label—something a bit more sophisticated, sounding less dependent for kids on the threshold of adolescence, who want us to know that though they may still require a bit of advice, they certainly don't need a school classroom to call home.

On this particular day, we had no pressing business, but to avoid filling the hallways with noisy activity, I asked the students to remain in my room and invited them to help me color some prints designed to simulate stained glass. I wanted to display them in the window to brighten the place up a bit. Mostly out of boredom, they agreed and set to work, but only after making sure I understood they thought coloring was for little kids and they were only doing it to help out. The hum of idle discourse soon filled the room as students, seated in groups of two and three at tables around the room, bent over their tasks. Brightly colored crayons, pencils, and markers rolled to and fro on tabletops and were being exchanged from hand to hand when suddenly the idea of coloring had enormous appeal to me. I asked two boys if I could join them.

Omar was from Saudi Arabia, and he was beautiful—hair black and shiny as crow feathers, eyes like inkwells, and a brilliant smile. Daniel was a new student from the heart of New York City. Enrolled for just one semester while his parents did some consulting work before returning to the East, he bore an air of chronic amusement as he learned the differences between life in the Big Apple and life way up and out here in the Pacific Northwest. The culture shock was an enormous adventure for him, and he was unquestionably a novelty in the eyes of his contemporaries at this small private school. He was remarkably sophisticated in the ways of the world, though not in a crude, unrefined way. It was genuine New York savvy. To hear him talk was like being transported to the set of a Neil Simon play. Daniel was Jewish— curly brown hair, dark, intelligent eyes, and an insatiable interest in anyone whose life was different from his. I sat down just in time to hear him ask Omar how come he had not taken his share of donations for a homeless shelter into the chapel on campus earlier that morning.

"I am not permitted to enter a Christian building," Omar explained.

I had to stop and think about his remark, because though Charles Wright Academy, named for the railroad baron, had been founded by Episcopalians and sported a lovely chapel on the far side of the soccer field, any commitment to anything specifically Christian had long ago been replaced with a sort of nebulous curiosity about things spiritual, and that by only a handful of folks on campus. There is, however, a large wooden cross on the chapel building, no doubt the thing that signaled Omar to place his donations on the front steps and wait outside for his classmates to emerge.

"You can never go into a church? Ever?" asked Daniel.

"No," said Omar.

"Why not?"

Omar looked to me. Though he had been in the U.S. for much of his young life, he was still timid and unsure of his use of English.

"Well . . . um . . . I don't know," he said.

"Do you mean you don't know the reason," I asked, "or you don't know how to explain it?"

He smiled broadly, sheepish. "To tell the truth," he confessed, "I really don't know. It is because my father told me, that's all. We are not permitted to do many things American students are permitted to do."

Daniel's curiosity was piqued. "Wow! How weird. Is that why you don't come to school dances?" He didn't wait for an answer. Coloring away, he went on, "I don't think there's anything like that for me, but I'm not sure." (I smiled and thought of the litany of laws I could never get all the way through in Leviticus.) "My dad is really trying to get me to understand what it means to be Jewish. He's got me reading all sorts of books, including *The Source*," he said, looking up at me.

"Wow, yourself!" I said. "That's pretty sophisticated reading for seventh grade."

"Really?" he queried, nonplussed. "It seems okay to me, not bad at all actually," he said. He was precocious but without a trace of arrogance. He reached for a blue pencil that had rolled to the edge of the table. "My father says it's time for me to understand my religion and my culture."

The three of us fell silent and concentrated on our color choices. I was struck by a couple of things as we worked. First, the ease with which this unplanned dialogue was taking place, thanks to the nature of our task. Coloring requires a minimum of creative energy and tends to free the mind and tongue. It's a bit like hoeing the garden. Working this way together, eyes cast down, seemed to eliminate barriers that might occur in a more formal, forced setting. I was also aware of the way the boys' fathers had figured into the conversation so quickly.

"Do Muslims believe in God?" Daniel inquired.

Omar laughed. "Yes, of course we do," he said. "Allah," he said shyly.

Daniel turned to me. "I guess all religions believe in God, right?"

"Well, actually, the God Omar and his family believe in is essentially the same God Jews believe in," I said. "Do you know the word *monotheism?*"

The tilt of Daniel's head suggested brainwork. "Let's see . . . you told us that *mono* means 'one,' so it has something to do with one God, maybe?"

"Exactly," I said. "The three primary monotheistic religions in the world are Islam, Judaism, and Christianity. Not all religions are monotheistic."

"You're a Christian, right?" asked Daniel.

"That's right," I answered.

"So," his eyes brightened, "all three monotheistic religions of the world are right here at this table! Pretty cool," he said, reaching for burnt sienna.

"I guess you're right, Daniel," I observed.

Omar appeared confused and curious.

"Daniel was just saying that each of us represents one of the major religions that believe in one God, the same God, actually," I explained. His brow furrowed.

"So what happened?" asked Daniel. "How did we get so far apart if we started out believing in the same God?"

I hesitated. I thought I understood the basics here, but the last thing I wanted to do was misinform. I opted to tell the truth.

"I'm not a historian, or a professional theologian," I said, "and I don't want to get any of this wrong, but it's basically like this. The father of the Jews is a man named Abraham, who had a son, Isaac, to carry on the Hebrew line. He also had a son Ishmael, with a woman who was not his wife, and it is this line that makes up the Islamic people, though the Islamic religion is considerably younger than Christianity. Muslims follow the teachings of Muhammad, right Omar?" I looked to him for a nod.

"Each religion believes it is following God's plan. Christians have their roots in Judaism. They believe that the Messiah, or Savior, promised by God came in the person of Jesus of Nazareth. Contemporary Jews do not believe Jesus was the promised Messiah and continue to wait for the Anointed One to come." I waited for questions, but none came. "That's about it, in a way-simplified version."

"So," said Daniel, "you Christians believe Jesus is the Big Kahuna, but we don't, right?"

Not wanting to insinuate Polynesian mythology into the dialogue at this late stage, I sighed and said, "Pretty much. Yeah," and picked up a Crayola. We fell silent again until I realized it was time for the kids to go.

"Hey, guys," I said, "this was fun. Thanks for letting me sit with you." The boys smiled and noisily gathered up their books and backpacks to leave. As they walked out of the room together, I realized I'd had something of an out-of-body experience in those last few minutes as we worked in silence. Momentarily, as if I had been allowed to hover over the table for a bird's eye view of the scene, I saw a middle-aged, middle-class white woman and two lovely, young, dark-skinned boys, beautiful children all, utterly and thoroughly loved by God.

"Pray for the peace of Jerusalem: May they prosper who love you."[1]

Blessed are the peacemakers,
for they will be called sons of God.

Many of us when we hear the word *peace* in the context of religion think of the Jewish word *shalom* and assume that it means "absence of strife," an inner calm. It does, but it's more expansive in its meaning. Used roughly 250 times in Scripture, it means "the absence of agitation and discord; rest, harmony, wholeness." It includes, as well, good health and prosperity. Used in greetings and departures among Jews, it is intended as a blessing, a prayer, actually, for the person being addressed. It was, of course, borrowed by flower children of the '60s, who greeted one another with an upraised hand, two fingers poised in a victory *V*, accompanied by the simple utterance of the word *peace,* and in that context, it took on the connotation of an antiwar sentiment. But *shalom* is not the only word translated as "peace" in Scripture.

The Greek word *eirene,* used in both Matthew and Luke, also refers to inner calm, a sense of perfect well being, but expands to include harmonious relations between God and men, men and men, nations and families. It is the word used to designate the role of emperors and ambassadors sent out to facilitate peace where there is conflict, which is how Jesus uses the word in this sermon.

When I first considered this, I thought of three men. First, I remembered that President Jimmy Carter was lauded as a peacemaker when he orchestrated talks between Arabs and Israelis that resulted in the Camp David Accords in 1978. And I thought of Desmond Tutu and his role in bringing about peace in South Africa through restorative justice, which, by the way, I think comes closest to reflecting the peace of Christ. The third man I thought of is my son, Michael, in Belfast to offer a message of hope and peace to the people in that city, a beautiful city with a gaping, infected wound in the body of Christ. Three men, all Christian, each doing what Jesus said to do and each blessed.

There are so many things to consider in an expansive discussion of the subject of peace. There's inner peace such as that sought by the desert fathers, whom I've quoted throughout this book. Then, of course, there's peace as it pertains to our personal relationships with spouses, children, in-laws, cranky next-door neighbors, demanding bosses, and contentious colleagues, to say nothing of unreasonable cohorts of the faith. Finally, of course, there's global peace, even intergalactic peace, if you happen to be a "trekkie" or an "X-phile." It's hard to know where to start, what's central to this particular discussion and what's peripheral.

And though Jesus' use of the word *peacemaker* is clear and particular, meaning "to bring about peace where there is contention," it seems wise, essential, and appropriate to explore the subject of inner peace in order to fully understand Jesus' remarks. Certainly there's a lot of hype in our culture these days about the desirability of inner peace. And there are loads of theories on how to do it, from a day at the spa getting dipped and wrapped in mud and herbs to a spiritual retreat whereby you can experience the monastic life without committing to it for a lifetime.

The search for inner peace has always been part of the Christian life. It was central to early monastics, some of whom assumed an eremitic life, in which they separated themselves from society altogether in order to devote their entire lives to God. In the Eastern Orthodox tradition, there's the hesychast, one who practices prayer that leads to absolute peace in Christ, instructing novices that "interior peace means to remain sitting in one's cell with fear and knowledge of God, holding far off the remembrance of wrongs suffered and pride of spirit. Such interior peace," they believe, "brings forth all virtues, preserves the monk from the burning darts of the enemy and does not allow him to be wounded by them."[2] He is able to live at peace, to experience *anapausis,* rest in God.

In exploring the subject of peace in Scripture and in related literature, I was reminded once again of a dance, in this case a circle, or a communal affair, that begins and ends with Christ. I imagined a dancer stepping into the dance with eyes fixed on Jesus and following his lead, dancing the dance of salvation among all the others who have likewise stepped into the circle. To fix your attention on a thing is, of course, an act of intentionality and concentration. Monastics take this quite literally, approaching God through contemplative prayer, which usually involves the discipline of solitude. Most of us take this call to fix our eyes on Jesus much more figuratively, hearing it more or less as a call to put God first in our lives, whatever that means. For me, that frequently becomes little more than a sort of sentimental, greeting-card theology by which I live, trying desperately to form a habit that ends up, in reality, being an eking out of a couple of minutes of "quiet time" each morning (or every other morning, or at least once a week), ultimately hoping that maybe the drive to work will count, which is what I catch myself praying as I dash out the door to grab a latte to have on the way. Would that prayer were as addictive as that latte, but then taking people prisoner doesn't seem to be God's style.

The idea of coming fully into God's presence is a little too eastern for most of us and downright suspect to many. Having tried it from time to time, however, I can attest to the fact that it does tend to lead you into a right place, a place that affords you, if only in the moment, the power to let go of some of the things that cause disharmony between you and others—no doubt because descending into prayer of this sort, despite the terror of the descent, allows you to experience atonement in an almost physical way. From there it actually seems possible to extend the hand of grace to others, including people you never dreamed you'd agree to dance with. From there, even issues of racial and cultural disparity might diminish, indeed vanish altogether, since one outcome of such prayer seems to be a stark and troubling awareness of one's own wretchedness, one's own neediness. In such a state, incredible things might occur. Imagine peace in one's marriage, with one's children, and with one's mother-in-law; peace at work; peace between city mice and country mice, black ones and white ones. Maybe even lasting peace in South Africa, the Middle East, Belfast, even the church! One might expect an even more outlandish result from being in such intimate contact with

God—the capacity to recognize anything that is not-God, in other words, evil, and turn from it. I'm not suggesting John Lennon's imaginary world, by the way, in which we suddenly discover we're all good, though I thought his song was beautiful, despite its naivete. The song has a nice beat, as they used to say on *American Bandstand,* but it's hard to dance to. Because it's hard to dance with broken bones, at least until God has breathed on them. No, I'm not imagining a universe in which we have all ascended to a state of bliss. I'm imagining something uniquely Christian, a descent that takes you into the presence of Jesus Christ, where you must face your brokenness and accept the forgiving grace and, with it, the absolute sovereignty of God. What I'm describing is life in the kingdom and, ultimately, a peace that passes all understanding—"not as the world gives," Jesus said, but "My peace."[3]

But the fact is, not only are most of us not intentional about going deep and getting quiet, most of us—aware of that terror thing—work hard to prevent ourselves from even accidentally going there, as Pascal observed so many years ago. We're no dummies. We know that going deep into prayer will hurt us, if not kill us outright. I wonder what Pascal, father of the computer, saw in his mind's eye almost four hundred years ago. I wonder if he foresaw throngs of humanity one day staring bleary-eyed at computer screens and video games. Several years ago, I was teacher-escort to a group of kids who went bowling. Entering the dark cavern of the video arcade adjacent to the bowling alley to round up stray kids gave me pause. I told someone later I felt as if I'd accidentally stumbled into the chthonic streets of hell: stale smoke, simulated gunshots and explosions, flashing lights and bells, mechanized female voices programmed to sound sultry, purring, "You have just been annihilated."

Little wonder that in recent years there has been renewed interest in the idea of simple living among possible people, particularly those sensitive to things vertiginous who feel the world listing toward manic self-destruction. The ease by which I have come by the literature of the desert is probably due to this renewed interest in the monastic life as it was practiced 1700 years ago. I fear, though, that these desert dwellers have been misunderstood, not through any intentional corruption but merely as a result of information passing through time and culture, as well as a presumption that all monks are the same, which they're not.

According to the *Apophthegmata Patrum,* as translated by Benedicta Ward, there were actually "three main types of monastic experiments" in the fourth-century desert of the East.[4] What appears to be common to these eremites is their separation from the world. These men are brought to life through the many writings of a twentieth-century monastic, Thomas Merton, including a little volume of selected translations from the "Verba Seniorum" titled *The Wisdom of the Desert.* These hermits, while they were in a sense "anarchists," as Merton points out, "were men who did not believe in letting themselves be passively guided and ruled by a decadent state," a state which, by the way, was Christian and in the minds of these men could not possibly exist free of corruption. No doubt fearing the contamination of the church by the culture, they left for the desert. They "believed there was a way of getting along without slavish dependence on accepted, conventional values." But "they did not reject society with proud contempt, as if they were superior to other men." One of the foremost misunderstandings about them is that they were antisocial. Merton explains that this was not the case. "They did not fly from human fellowship," asserts Merton, and were, in fact, "eminently social."[5] And hospitable. What is crucial to our understanding of them is that they were fleeing toward something as much as they were fleeing from something. A novice went to the desert in search of his true self, as opposed to the false self that had developed in the context of the world. It was his understanding that such could be found only through prayer and solitude.

A funny thing happened to them out there when they disappeared into their cells to pray for hours, days, weeks at a time. Sure enough, their true selves did, indeed, emerge and, as the cartoon caricature Pogo discovered, they saw the enemy and he is us. And thus began the sometimes torturous—and often tortuous—journey of dying to the ersatz self which had found its identity in society. The difference between these men and contemporary folks seeking a closer union with God is that most of us confuse the journey with the current secular pursuit of self-actualization, which is pretty much diametrically opposed in its objective. Though each may begin with a search for self, the ancient practice ultimately resulted in the diminishment and eventual death of one's ego, while the contemporary experience seems all too often to be about self-deification, about "following our bliss," as if our true selves can be trusted to lead us to holiness.

It's tough for most of us to shake off the onus of this quest as defined by our culture thoroughly enough to make even the first steps on a real spiritual journey into self, probably because we confuse peace with gratification, or at least relief. When we find ourselves anxious, nervous, or depressed, we're inclined to do something nice for ourselves, find a way to get our minds off our troubles: take in a movie, eat a pint of Ben & Jerry's, buy a motorcycle, bungee jump off a bank building, have a drink—or an affair . . . anything to shake off the feeling of dread that hovers just above our conscious minds.

When I observe the falderal of the modern evangelical church and witness the pace at which everyone is running through the corridors of the building on any given Sunday, I think the hermits' fear of corruption among the faithful may have been quite reasonable and one that should give us pause. Richard Foster expresses it this way in his discussion of megachurches: "These have burst onto the scene in recent decades with great fanfare. And they are, in their way, most impressive, with enormous budgets and masses of people and huge buildings. But they simply are not centers of substantial renewal because they have within them the seeds of perpetual superficiality. The megachurch, by its very nature, must gravitate toward an 'entertainment religion' which turns worship into a constant effort to keep people occupied and happy."[6] That is not to say they can never be "centers of substantial renewal." I know of some that defy the tocsin sounded here. But they do present an enormous challenge, one that is not even recognized by many. Many Christians are terrified of depression and secretly suspect that melancholy of any sort is a manifestation of Satan himself. It rarely dawns on most of us that we should pause to consider what drives us, what in the world is compelling us to live such frantic lives, what we think might catch up with us if we don't stay on the move.

There is an alternative to running. Occasionally, psychotherapists invite us to face our fears and anxieties for the sake of our emotional well being. I'm not sure what most psychologists and psychiatrists think about a connection between their work and the work of the church. I'm not even sure what I think about the connection between things psychological and spiritual, between emotional and spiritual healing. I guess I think it's all spiritual when you get to the bottom of it, but it makes me nervous when people start substituting psychotherapy for religion, or more precisely for God, just as modernists erred in trying to substitute art for religion, as if to suggest a poet is more capable of finding and eloquently expressing the truth than, say, a fisherman. But I digress. I can only assume that some professional shrinks see no connection at all between mind and spirit, while others give a token nod to the spiritual aspects of healing, and a rare few see it all as an intricate weaving.

Bryan Van Dragt, a clinical psychologist, writes, "Anxiety is inescapable. This is true because anxiety is not something that one has, but is rather a reflection of what one is. It is, in effect, a message signaling that one is out of step with one's own being and with one's purpose in life. Perhaps nowhere is this purpose more clearly expressed," he goes on, "than in St. Augustine's contemplation of the Divine—'Thou has made us for Thyself, and our hearts are restless until they find their rest in Thee.' Not until this purpose is fulfilled does anxiety relinquish its hold." Van Dragt, who believes that all of us share a common quest rooted in a longing to be loved, goes on to discuss our tendency to turn away from our anxiety when we should turn and face it, allow it to take us where we need to go. Instead, we seek escape from it by attaching ourselves to whatever might fill the emptiness inside. These attachments turn out to be nothing more than temporary scaffolding for most of us, though, and ultimately collapse, pitching us headlong into despair, what Christian mystics called the dark night of the soul.[7] But what if this was seen not as standing at the edge of a life-threatening abyss? What if, instead, it was seen as life giving, as standing on the threshold of the monk's cell wherein we might go to meet God? Regardless of how you view it, this much is true: no one can make you step into the cell, or into the dance, unless you choose to do so. Cajole, maybe. Manipulate, perhaps. Maybe even provide a gentle shove, but though we will all be changed by life and its circumstances, it appears to be up to each of us as to whether we actually venture into a life with God.

When I was seventeen, I was a big fan of John Steinbeck. I read most of his books and loved him for his earthiness, the courage and stark clarity with which he saw and wrote about humanity. I would learn later that his novel *East of Eden,* a contemporary treatment of the Cain and Abel story, did not receive the critical acclaim of his other works, but I loved it, and in fact it altered the course of my spiritual journey. In it, a Chinese houseman working for the protagonist's father spends his days off meeting with local scholars, who are exploring the book of Genesis. For many nights, they struggle to come to some sort of agreement about the meaning of a Hebrew word *timshel* used in the fourth chapter, when God speaks to Cain: "Why are you angry? And why has your countenance fallen? If you do well," God explains, "will you not be accepted? And if you do not do well, sin lies at the door. And its desire is for you, but you should rule over him."[8] In the old King James, the last phrase reads "thou shalt rule over him," and in the NIV it reads "you must master it." The characters in Steinbeck's novel agree that the King James translation is close but not precise. As the main plot of the story moves steadily toward resolution, they finally agree that the best translation of *timshel* is "mayest." "[Sin's] desire is for you, but thou mayest rule over it." I remember reading the passage over and over, then rummaging through our old family Bible to examine the text for myself, making a presumptuous leap from this passage to the Ten Commandments and right out of the comfort of Southern Baptist legalism into an exhilarating yet terrifying free fall. I virtually shouted the words . . . "thou mayest!" I was like a panhandler who had dipped his tin pan into the river and found gold. I tried writing about it for thirty years without success until one day in the garden, as I was reading from a little pocket edition of Merton's book, the poem at the front of this book finally emerged.

And though by now you are surely wondering what in the world all this has to do with Jesus' call for us to be peacemakers, I think there is, in fact, a vital connection. There's a great bluegrass band known as the Dry Branch Fire Squad that makes its way around the festival circuit every year. My husband and I look forward to hearing them every February when downtown Tacoma is transformed into an unlikely venue for old-timey jam sessions and shows. Ron Thomason is the point man for Dry Branch and tells long, tangential stories between numbers. His tales wind so far afield that it often seems as if he will never return to his point or get back to his mandolin, but he finally makes his way round, and with a boyish grin he says, "Well . . . I told you all that to tell you this . . ."

Well, I told you all that to tell you this: I believe that peace, and ultimately peacemaking, begins with a choice to engage in some serious introspection, and chances are it won't be pretty. It begins with an aspiration for uncompromising self-awareness, though if you're anything like me, you'll try to renege on the deal many times after you've begun, and it will, if it's genuine, strip you of everything you own and leave you poverty stricken. *Blessed are the poor in spirit.* And you might expect also from this endeavor a fair amount of anguish and loss as you pry your fingers from the things to which you've been holding fast for a long time. *Blessed are those who mourn.* It will bring you to your knees in utter humility before God. *Blessed are the meek.* And when you start to recover, you'll realize what you've been so hungry for all this time. *Blessed are those who hunger and thirst for righteousness.*

Certainly something as precious as this, more precious than silver, is going to cost. Indeed. Peace of the God-variety invariably means a period of turmoil first, and it's not going to look like the kind of peace you get at the spa. Not if John the Baptist, introduced to us in Luke as a messenger of peace *(eirene),* got it right. One of the most colorful characters in the Bible, John strikes discord from the moment he makes his entrance. The absolute embodiment of paradox, he certainly does not appear to be even marginally associated with peace, despite the fact that he was laying the groundwork for the arrival of the very Prince of Peace himself, who would, of course, go on to radically disturb the peace even more. John, Jesus' cousin, was an agitator of the most dramatic kind, a first-rate rabble-rouser! He boldly disrupted the status quo in the name of truth. In his confrontations with Herod and Herodias, he was anything but politic. In today's culture, John might not have ended up with his head on a platter at the king's banquet, but he would no doubt be spuriously scorned by late-night comedians, who seem to derive immense pleasure from making fun of anyone who dares to challenge the moral behavior of our contemporary Herods.

The manner in which most Americans have elevated entertainers to guru status, sanctioning them as our spokesmen regarding our values and morals, fascinates me. I think it all started when we turned Ali McGraw's deathbed aphorism from the movie *Love Story* into a theological apothegm. You remember it: "Love is never having to say you're sorry." Now there's a choice bit of popular theology to live by. Anyone who's been married very long has to be laughing out loud to think of it. Ever since that poignant utterance, we seem to have turned our attention to Hollywood in search for truth.

If you think I'm kidding about its making its way into the moral mix of our times, let me tell you a story. A few years ago I had the pleasure of working with a brilliant young student, who, during a period of extreme scholastic pressure, committed an honor code infraction that I was compelled to deal with. Following a painful confrontation, the student came clean and set about immediately to make amends. Among other things, she wrote the faculty a letter in which she asked their forgiveness. I applauded this gesture, as did many others, though one faculty member expressed deep sadness that the student felt she must humiliate herself in this way. "Who among us," he asked, "has not made a mistake?" What appeared to be an act of compassionate generosity on his part was, in my mind, an insult to the student and to the rest of us. Here was a young woman who clearly understood that she had done something wrong, that she had breached the trust that existed with her teachers. Here was a student who wanted to confess so the healing could begin. Restorative justice. Whether she realized it or not, she was doing precisely what Jesus said we should do when we have sinned. The problem is we've all become so jittery about the question of right and wrong, some of us aren't at all sure how to respond to an act of genuine repentance.

John the Baptist was the foreshadowing of peace, but a peace born in truth, not in moral relativism or in polite denial. The word *polite* derives, of course, from the same root as *politics,* and some have suggested that the political correctness movement is nothing more than a New Age version of Victorianism borne not so much out of prudishness as a commitment never to offend anyone. Frankly, I'm pretty amazed sometimes at what we do in the name of politeness. It reminds me of something that grabbed my attention on the back cover of a book titled *Bold Love:* "Bold love is anything but passive. It is unpredictable, cunning and creative. It is a violation of the natural order of things. In many cases it will unnerve, offend, disturb, or even hurt those who are being loved. But in the end, it will also compel them to deal with the internal disease that is robbing them (and others) of true beauty."[9]

In much the same way that we have turned love into something sentimental and saccharine, we have turned peace into something delicate and self-indulgent, something to be found in a cup of herbal tea or an afternoon with the massage therapist, as well as a philosophy of absolute tolerance. Because we are so determined to accept everything and offend no one, it never occurs to us that perhaps we should be troubled sometimes; perhaps we should be agitated, and sometimes we may even be called to be agitators.

This is as difficult for Christians as it is for unbelievers. I remember when I was putting together the curriculum for confirmation class a couple of years ago and I came to the lessons on the old and new covenants and realized I was going to have to deal with this whole business of blood sacrifice. Few of my Sunday school teachers or youth leaders had ever talked about blood, except to sing about the blood of Jesus washing me white as snow (which, I can now confess, always confused me and left a rather sticky and grotesque picture painted on my imagination).

The whole blood thing is messy and barbaric. It helped me to work through this the following year as I worked in tandem with a Vietnam vet, my friend Rob, who has a living memory of seeing blood shed in the name of freedom. Because regardless of what your position is about the Vietnam conflict, the young men who fought in those battles were doing it in the hope of keeping people free. Though we never really talked about it, just being in Rob's presence reminded me that peace may cost us and it may very well mean blood's going to be shed. In Scripture, blood reminds us that God hates sin and cannot tolerate it. In fact, he demands atonement for it, a sacrifice. And the something sacrificed has to be real, not some nebulous, abstract token of repentance.

Indeed, when animal sacrifice became meaningless in Israel—a mindless ritual—prophets were quick to warn the pious that they were missing the whole point. The ultimate issue in blood sacrifice was the attitude of the heart. To be acceptable, the sacrifice had to represent sincere devotion, and Isaiah said that God had had enough of sacrifices insincerely offered. Like it or not, we are called to accept blood sacrifice as one of the mysteries of God's holiness. But it's important that we are clear about what God was really after. David, who fully grasped the extent of God's grace, understood. In the Fifty-first Psalm, he tells us that God's delight is in a broken and contrite spirit, a spirit that recognizes who's God and who's not. Right relationship, not mere ceremony and sacrifice, is the object of God's covenant-making activity. Sacrifices without a sincere desire for relationship with God pervert the real purpose of the sacrificial system and are unacceptable to him. This is no doubt why Jesus—the final blood sacrifice—told us to keep our gifts and offerings until we have worked out our relationships with one another, because the condition of our relationships with each other reflects the condition of our relationship with the Lord.

The prophet Nahum foreshadowed the coming of the Messiah, the one who would break the yoke of Israel's oppressors and restore peace to God's people: "Behold, on the mountains the feet of him who brings good tidings, who proclaims peace!"[10] Ultimately, all peacemaking begins and ends with Jesus Christ, whose very purpose was to reconcile God and man. But *shalom* is not merely the absence of war and conflict; it is the presence and the promise of truth, with a capital *T*. It is the blessed wholeness that will come when everything is made right. God *is* love, but not love as the world defines it. God's love includes absolute justice. Justification. Things made perfect. Because we don't like pain, we try hard to cut short the process, to put on the garments of peace without putting on the garments of truth, without acknowledging the price paid by the bringer of peace. Truth must precede peace or the peace experienced will be a grainy facsimile of the real thing. To call for peace outside the bounds of truth is a puerile invitation.

We know in our hearts that this is exactly as it should be. We know when the moral law written on our hearts has been breached; we know when restitution is called for to set things right again. Despite postmodern dogma that insists everything is relative and we have no right to judge another, we are outraged to hear of atrocities both here and abroad that remind us of man's inhumanity to man. When we thumb through a *Time* magazine in the doctor's office and read about brothers going unpunished for murdering sisters who have supposedly brought disgrace on the family because of even the mere suggestion of impropriety, and read on to find that these killings are "justifiable" according to the mores of their culture, we are incensed. Indeed this is where "tolerance" as a moral code breaks apart, along with the tenants of the PC movement and everything associated with it. We all have an innate sense of right and wrong, and though we have allowed an unholy stirring of the water, we know that somewhere beneath the turbid shallows, there is the clean spring of truth that compels us to insist that people play by the rules.

I'm reminded of a story a teacher friend tells that aptly illustrates this point. At the beginning of the year, he tells his students that he has a no-hat policy in his room, explaining that, as the benevolent despot of his domain, he has the right to impose a dress code on his students. They generally agree, albeit grudgingly. Then, for fun, he extends the notion a bit further and suggests that perhaps he will give all the girls in the class A's and all the boys B's, because the girls are, well, prettier. Needless to say, the students are incensed, the girls because it makes their skin crawl and smacks of sexual favors and the boys because it is simply unfair. All of them, without thinking about it, understand the difference between power and the abuse of power. Even if they cannot articulate precisely what the difference is, they know there is a difference and demand fairness. Were the teacher actually to impose such a grading policy on his charges, the students certainly would not tolerate it, might even be willing to disrupt the peace to make things right. Regardless of our philosophy of life, and regardless of our politics, we are chagrined to learn that someone has committed a crime and no one's being held accountable for it. "It's just wrong," as one of my students is fond of saying.

For all our scrapping to get our needs met, many people will defer to righteousness even when it means a loss to themselves. I have fond memories of a young student in my seventh grade class a few years back. Yev was from Russia, studying in the U.S. so he could play hockey. He skated with the grace of a dancer, and he loved the ice. Schoolwork not so much, especially if there was a pretty girl distracting him, which seemed to be pretty much all the time. One day I found him at my door looking forlorn. He had his vocabulary test in hand and said he needed to talk to me about his grade, a C minus. In the privacy of my room, he dropped his mask a bit as he tearfully explained to me that bad grades could mean his mandatory return to Russia. I assumed he was probably overdramatizing the situation, but I chose to take him at his word.

"Would you like me to change your grade to an A?" I asked.

He opened his eyes wide. "Are you serious?" he inquired, his accent pronounced.

Now you have to remember that I am completely ambivalent about grades—have been for all my thirty years of teaching—mostly because they are rarely ever used to evaluate a student's progress and are almost always used to reflect the level of compliance exhibited by a student. Good boys and girls get A's and bad boys and girls don't. In that moment, I decided that if Yev asked me to change his grade, I would. I said, "Yes, Yev. I'm serious. If you ask me to, I'll change your C minus to an A."

"What's the catch?" he asked, smiling.

"No catch," I assured him.

I could hear the whir of wheels turning behind his lively eyes. He really wanted that A.

"So," I said, shuffling papers, "I have to get to class . . . what's your pleasure?"

Emitting a big sigh, he dropped his chin to his chest. "No," he groaned. "I don't want you to change my grade."

"No? Are you sure?" I asked.

"You're tricking me, I know," he said. "You just want to see if I'll take something I didn't earn." He smiled broadly. "Come on Mrs. Moffitt," he insisted. "Admit it."

"I really was prepared to give you the A, Yev," I said. "But I didn't think you'd let me. You're right about that. I thought you'd decide against it," I confessed, relieved.

I concluded the discussion by promising to call his foster family to work out a plan to help him improve his test-preparation skills for next time, and with that, he was on his way.

It was a small thing, really, but the story makes a reasonable parable, I think. Despite the fact that at times it seems as if all our ethics have been lost in a black hole somewhere, most people grow squeamish doing something they know is wrong.

Still, there's no shame in being conflicted about all this. It's pretty unreasonable, really, to imagine welcoming discomfort for the sake of righteousness. It goes against our survival instincts, even when we know it's right. I guess that's what distinguishes us from the animals, though the distinction may seem slight. Still, when we think of peace, we think of a warm fire, comfort, and ease, and the words of Jesus are bound to confuse and disturb us: "Do not think that I came to bring peace on earth. I did not come to bring peace but a sword. For I have come to 'set a man against his father, a daughter against her mother, and a daughter-in-law against her mother-in-law'; and 'a man's enemies will be those of his own household.' He who loves father or mother more than Me is not worthy of Me. And he who loves son or daughter more than Me is not worthy of Me. And he who does not take his cross and follow after Me is not worthy of Me. He who finds his life will lose it, and he who loses his life for My sake will find it."[11]

Talk about pesky passages of Scripture. Not only does it seem to defy nature, it appears to be contradicted elsewhere in passages which fervently admonish us to honor our mothers and fathers, unless we consider the possibility that Jesus is simply telling us we are not to put even our dear fathers and precious mothers or our beloved sons and daughters before the Lord.

Syrupy renditions of Jesus, meek and mild, dissolve like sugar in the rain when we witness his rage as he curses the hypocrisy of the religious leaders of his time. "Woe to you, scribes and Pharisees, hypocrites!" He calls them "serpents, brood of vipers!" and challenges them with this question: "How can you escape the condemnation of hell?"[12] And in the same sermon in which we find the Beatitudes, he warns of impending judgment *(krisis)*, meaning a separating, a process of culling out the righteous from the unrighteous, a process resulting in the casting of the ungodly into Gehenna, or the Valley of Hinnom—a ravine near Jerusalem where refuse was burned. Human beings . . . tossed on the slag heap!

We want so much to repackage Jesus as some sort of Disney character, a Good Witch Glenda who flits around sprinkling fairy dust on everybody so they'll feel better. We long to make metaphors of all this unsavory stuff about heaven and hell. And though the peace of which Jesus speaks will ultimately lead to inner peace, it simply will not come cheap. The world is never fond of truth-bearers, because truth almost always means some measure of pain. And even when we own up to our wrongdoing, we want a quick fix, like a kid who's taken a nasty spill on his bike and wants a Band-Aid applied without having the dirt and rocks cleaned out, the wound debrided. I'm afraid peace cannot be obtained via the revisionist theology some of my modern-day spiritualist friends are practicing. Peace is not about escapism or even the serenity or tranquility normally associated with Eastern philosophies, though these too have been largely misunderstood, I suspect. I know very little about them, but what little I have read suggests that they too call for a relinquishing of the "I," a sort of death of self. I suppose what finally separates them from the Christian understanding of this death of self is that followers of Jesus, people who call themselves Christians, do not merely release their egos into the universe but in fact yield everything to God in Jesus' name. "He who finds his life will lose it, and he who loses his life for My sake will find it."[13]

This is a sticky wicket for those who prefer to either leave Jesus out of it altogether or at least obscure his name and face just enough—homogenize him, if you will, turn even him into a metaphor that can be poured smoothly into any religion— rather than deal with a real flesh-and-blood savior whose body was broken and who bled out on the cross. There is a story about the novelist Flannery O'Connor in which she reportedly responded to a remark suggesting that the Holy Ghost was merely a symbol by saying, "Well, if it's a symbol, to hell with it."[14] She could just as well have said the same thing of the resurrection. When Jesus becomes mere metaphor, it renders the whole religion ridiculous. There is no reconciliation between God and man if Jesus didn't die and live again. A Jesus rewritten to please the world is like a political candidate who's been airbrushed and redesigned by spin doctors—hardly worth the price of admission.

Painful as it is, though, people still keep coming back to him, because the world will not, indeed cannot, give us the peace we ultimately desire, just as Jesus said in the hours before his agony on the cross. A peace not of this world. A peace borne out of righteousness and holiness, a peace that, when found, makes right everything that was ever wrong—between mothers and daughters, husbands and wives, nations and nations. The kind of peace about which Jesus speaks is the kind that comes through absolute surrender to the Father and an acknowledgment that Jesus himself was the sacrificial lamb who would justify everything and make us right with God.

If I'm even half right about all this, it's clear that the call to be peacemakers is, at some level, a call to evangelism, and I do not mean proselytism. It is not a call to convert people to a different doctrine, to rustle folks from one fold and sign them up for another, but a call to point to the healing and redemptive powers of Jesus Christ as revealed in the Gospels, to invite individuals to experience the balm of salvation. I'm convinced that the effectiveness of the AA movement in this country is rooted in the fact that it calls for surrender to a higher power, and I'm equally convinced that the concurrent movement to debunk AA, albeit a relatively quiet one, is rooted in pride, the sort of pride that made America great, the sort that cannot abide the idea of surrendering to anything. It is yet another example, I think, of the inherent conflict between things of God and things of the world. And though AA intentionally does not specify Christ as the higher power and holds as one of its sacred tenets that it does not solicit members, it functions evangelistically in the purest sense of the word because it's all about redemption and transformation. Indeed, it has the mark of Jesus, the Redeemer, all over it. AA, along with all the other A-groups (Al-Anon, Alateen, etc.), is devoted to bringing about peace in families that have been devastated by addiction. And like the monk in his cell, the very first thing an addict must do is descend into the pit of hell and look at himself or herself honestly.

According to Os Guinness in *Time for Truth,* the word Jesus used when he spoke of hypocrites is the Greek word for *actor.*[15] Families in the grip of alcoholism are among the best actors in the world, and though Jesus gave the word the "distinctive twist of moral deception" reserved for religious leaders and people in power, it's clear that falseness and deception of any kind are most offensive to God. A person must approach the throne naked and unmasked if he hopes to experience the depth of healing God wants him to experience. The wounds must be cleaned before the balm is applied. The first of the twelve celebrated steps is to get real; it is the only hope for the drunk, the spouse, the children, and all the others impacted by addiction.

When we do what we can to help people find peace, within and without, we are pointing to Christ, the great reconciler. We are taking friends and loved ones by the shoulders and helping them to turn and fix their eyes on the loving, outreaching arms of Jesus, some for the first time. I recently experienced what I'll call a misreading that turned out to have great meaning for me. I was grazing in a recent issue of *Books and Culture* in which Timothy Jones had written an extensive review of Merton's journals. The article made me remember how important Merton has been in my spiritual life; it also made me realize how little of his work I've actually read. As I said, I was grazing, not reading carefully, when I saw these words written, I thought, about Gethsemane, the garden. Merton called it "the center of America . . . the axle around which the whole country blindly turns. I was wondering," he goes on to say, "what was holding this country together, what has been keeping the universe from cracking in pieces and falling apart."[16] As you can imagine, this gave me pause, and then I realized that he was speaking not of the garden where Jesus prayed but of Gethsemani, a Trappist monastery in the Kentucky hills! I really must stop trying to read without my glasses. But in that brief interim between what I thought I'd read and what I'd actually read, though puzzled, I was mysteriously comforted by a vision of Christ in the garden as he made preparations to take my shame upon himself. This is the Christ I long for my friends and family to know, this one, who made everything right for me, this Jesus, "the axle around which the whole country [and indeed the whole world] blindly turns."

Though the peace of which Jesus speaks on the mountain is often mistaken as a call to pacifism, it's clear that the accurate interpretation of the word is one that suggests we are to be bringers of peace to a wounded world, to invite others into the presence of the Lord, to open the circle and extend the hand of invitation to join in the dance. I've recently been especially appreciative of the less celebrated of the disciples, Philip and Andrew in particular. They never got the press Peter and James and John got, but they consistently did one essential thing: they brought people to meet Jesus, because they understood that it's only through contact with the Messiah that a person can find peace and subsequently help others to find peace. The dance begins and ends with Jesus, and only through him will God's ultimate plan be fulfilled, a kingdom of absolute peace, where lions will lie down with lambs and swords will be transformed into ploughshares.

What an honor to serve the purpose of peace at any level, to apply the balm of God's love to every situation in which we may find ourselves, even if it means telling the painful truth. For surely, that is what we are called to do, to meet people with the same love and compassion and honesty with which Jesus met them and offer them forgiveness, love, and hope. And as we study our Bibles, whether we encounter *shalom* or *eirene,* it's clear that we're dealing with a God who will stop at nothing to bring about righteous reconciliation between himself and his chosen people, which as it turns out is everybody.

8

Life on the Edge
Overcoming Sloth

Every time I heard people get up in church and talk about how their lives were changed by mission trips, I came home determined to talk my husband into signing up with me for the next one. But he was never interested, which worked well for me because then I could fault him for the fact that our lives were uneventful and boring without ever having to leave the comfort of my brand-new Italian leather recliner. One Sunday, though, I made a fatal error. After crying all the way through a sermon preached by Enrique Romero, a Mexican pastor with whom our church has worked on numerous occasions, building houses and spiffing up his church building near Tijuana, I told Harlan Shoop, our associate pastor, that I'd like to go on a mission trip sometime. A few weeks later, he called and asked me to pray about being the facilitator for a group of mission volunteers who would be conducting VBS in Metlakatla, Alaska, among the Tsimshian Indians there.

By that time, though, my impassioned heart was safely back to normal, and though I agreed to pray about it, it was a no-brainer. Token prayers. There was no way I was going to facilitate a group on a trip like this when I'd never even been on one before. I mentioned it to Don and to a few other folks, and everyone seemed to accept my reasoning without reservation. Then suddenly one night as I drove across the Narrows Bridge, I heard myself say out loud, "I need to call Harlan and tell him I'll go to Alaska." I looked over my shoulder to see who had stowed away in the car. I was genuinely baffled and couldn't even remember what I'd been thinking about that prompted such an outlandish remark. I looked at the driver of the car next to me to see if he was watching me lose my mind. He was on the phone. I drove the rest of the way home in silence, and by the time I got there, I'd decided to just go to Alaska and worry about the voices later.

The next morning, I arranged to meet with Harlan and find out the details. Have I told you yet that I'm afraid to fly? I do it when I have to, and never without putting my affairs in order before I go, and never if there is a reasonable alternative. (I also never set foot on a plane until I've recited the number painted on the fuselage to God so he doesn't get confused about which plane I've boarded.) So when Harlan said we'd be flying first to Ketchikan, my tummy turned over. Then when he said we would fly from there to Annette Island—in a floatplane—I began to stammer and made a move to stand up. Horribly ashamed of being neurotic (and Christian), I began to try to weasel my way out of the trip. But the more he talked, the less I was able effectively to weasel. All my old survival tricks were failing me. I wound up committed. And then some serious praying began.

I'm not sure when, in all the weeks of preparation, the fear left, but it did. One day Don asked me how I was doing wrestling with it, and I realized I wasn't. I looked around for it, but it appeared to have up and gone. Not one to be caught unawares, however, I figured it would return, and I'd be ready for it, armed with valium or whatever it took, but in the meantime, I would enjoy its absence and pretend to be a normal, healthy person.

It turned out this would be just the first surprise in a series of them. The next came when Don decided he'd go along. Some might call this one a miracle, actually. It's not that Don doesn't like to travel. He does. And it's not that he's against mission trips. He's not. Exactly. He's not big on evangelism, what with all the confusion between it and proselytism. He just balks at the idea of nosing around in other people's spiritual lives, but he is all for doing good works. Ours has been a sometimes uneasy relationship when it comes to God and the church, for a lot of reasons that have no place in this book. At the same time, though, I'm uneasy about a lot of the same things he's uneasy about when it comes to church, the institution, and certainly when it comes to sectarianism. On the other hand, I find it hard to figure how Christians, regardless of sect, get around the Great Commission, Jesus' parting shot to go tell people the Good News. Maybe it all comes down to how we go about it. I certainly applaud the current trend in missionary training, which emphasizes building relationships with people in an open, accepting way as opposed to trivializing and stifling their culture. After all, when you build relationships based on mutual respect, it's highly unlikely you won't get into dialogue about God when the time's right, affording you plenty of opportunity to talk about Jesus. Anyway, for reasons I didn't fully understand, not only did Don agree to come with me, even after he heard we probably wouldn't have access to showers (surprise number 3), he agreed to help out by being the storyteller for VBS (number 4). And wear a bathrobe for a costume (number 5). When Harlan suggested that we take the Alaska ferry up, I was all for it. It would mean a scenic trip up the Inside Passage as far as Ketchikan and one less airplane number for me to memorize.

The ferry trip was great, despite the fact that we slept on the floor in the observation lounge and our personal hygiene regimen was reduced to what we could do with a handful of baby wipes in the public john. We got into the adventure and even reminisced a bit about those wild and crazy days of the '60s: weekend woodsies up the Poudre Canyon; skinny-dipping out at Lake No. 4 in Wellington. It was fun—the doing and the remembering. When we stepped into the streets of Ketchikan to walk the short distance from the ferry to the floatplane dock, I saw a Native American man who looked like he should have starred in *Dances with Wolves*. He was gorgeous. Don mistook my momentary preoccupation for a return of the fear of flying, but no, I reassured him, sheepish. I was just fine.

I did hyperventilate a little when we checked in for our flight, however, but not because I was afraid. It happened when the clerk, a woman, taking down the information needed for our tickets asked, in a bold voice, how much I weighed. It had never occurred to me that I would have to disclose my weight, and since our very lives depended on my telling the truth (as opposed to the whole driver's license gig in which everyone expects you to pare off as many pounds as you can without causing the clerk to laugh out loud), I leaned across the counter and whispered a figure that was as close to the truth as I could come without collapsing in shame. Then I went to the waiting area and prayed that we wouldn't all plunge into the drink because I'd lied.

In no time at all, it was time to go. Don looked at me with concern.

"Are you okay?" he asked.

"Yeah," I answered. "Go figure. I'm fine. In fact I'm looking forward to it."

Ten minutes later we were cruising over the island, which was draped in veils of morning fog, and I felt like a kid on a carnival ride. I'd spent many pleasant moments since we'd moved up to the Northwest watching seaplanes come and go in various harbors, never dreaming I would actually ride in one myself. I loved watching them take off and especially land, creating plumes of sea foam when their floats touched the water. It was especially fascinating to be entering a world in which these planes are as commonplace as taxicabs. The flight was far too short, but after roughly forty hours of travel all told, we were in Metlakatla, guests of the Tsimshian nation.

We arrived just in time for services. The interim pastor, Dick Cochran, ushered us to our seats with our cohorts, who had flown into Ketchikan the day before. The pianist was out sick, so we sang *a cappella,* all forty or so of us. Fritz, who played an old-timey hymn on his harmonica, provided special music during the offering. The culture shock was immediate, profound, and lovely, coming as we had from our large suburban church in Tacoma, where four services are held every Sunday, each with a different kind of music and ambiance—something for everybody.

Surprise number 6 came at the potluck luncheon that followed. Well, 6 and 7. We were starving for the taste of home cooking after two days of ferry food. I was scarfing down a bowlful of green salad when I bit into something crunchy and sweet and unfamiliar. The woman seated across from me smiled when she saw my inquisitive visage and said, "Halibut eggs." Now don't think I'm a hick or something; I'm not afraid to try the occasional exotic yuppie delight, but I prefer knowing I'm doing it in advance. My tablemates enjoyed a good laugh over my gulpish response to this bit of information. Most of them anyway. Surprise number 7 was learning right off the bat that not everyone in Metlakatla thought we were the cat's meow for coming up to minister to them. The woman sitting next to me didn't laugh about the fish eggs, nor did she join in the conversation that ensued about our plans for the coming week. It was a foreshadowing.

Aside from facilitating the adults and leading mealtime devotions, I was assigned to teach the older girls in VBS, meaning the fifth, sixth, and seventh graders. It meant just nine girls total, so I thought it would be "cake," as the kids say, short for "piece of cake." The women from our church who had laid out the plans for the week were geniuses of organization. Each of us had our supplies packaged, notes to follow, games to use as fillers when we found we had extra time, and crafts that rivaled Martha Stewart's. Monday after lunch, we all gathered in the hall next to the sanctuary and waited for Don (in his bathrobe) and Kathy, our young pianist, to give us our musical cue to march in for storytime. Aside from the littlest tykes becoming momentarily disoriented and heading out the back door, it all went as smooth as latte. Don's story was great, the children were adorable, and despite the fact that I was wearing a costume, which made me feel like a dork, all was well. In short order, we were off to our classrooms.

I wouldn't say my girls were unfriendly, exactly. Some were shy. All were aloof, and a couple looked like they could be trouble. But that was nothing new; I taught seventh graders back home. Everything was pretty much par for the course, except I had only five days to do what I had come to do, whatever that was. Oh yeah, the Great Commission, and it was fairly evident that these girls were probably coming to VBS out of boredom, to fill a couple of hours in their idle summer days, and weren't at all sure they were going to cooperate with me.

Suddenly I realized there was some significant giggling and whispering going on at the corner of the table.

"What's up?" I asked.

"Nothing," said one of the trouble girls, with a pout.

"Okay then. How many of you know who the Israelites were?"

Silence.

"Did you know there were tribes of Israelites, not unlike clans within your Tsimshian nation?"

"You say that funny," said Christie.

"What?"

"Tsimshian."

"Do I?" I asked, realizing I was being tested. "Say it for me."

She did. It sounded the same to me, so I said, "I can't hear what I'm doing wrong."

"Forget it," she said with a wave of her hand, an indignant dismissal.

I looked around the classroom, decked out, as are Sunday school classrooms everywhere, with pictures of Jesus interacting with little kids. But sitting before me were a handful of young women who had seemingly little interest in hearing about the tribes of Israel, though they had shown a flicker of interest in the props I'd spread before them for today's lesson, and they were interested in my costume—probably because it wasn't a bathrobe. It was a colorful Nigerian dress given to me by friends who had worked in Lagos years before, and I'd grabbed it from my closet on my way out the door back home when I'd grudgingly remembered the costume requirement thing.

"You like my dress?" I asked.

"It's cool," said Danielle.

I confessed that I felt silly wearing costumes, and she said, giggling, that she'd wear it if I didn't want to.

"It's a deal," I said. "Tomorrow you wear the dress." God is good.

"Hey," shot Heather. "No fair. How's come she gets to wear it and I don't?"

"You can wear it too. Any of you who wants to can wear it," I said. "We'll work out a schedule."

And we did. As the week rolled out, the girls who wanted to wear it took turns, though the more sophisticated among them insisted that it was silly. It was a sweet amusement to me, this discussion about playing dress-up, a symbol, I guess, of the passage in which these girls found themselves—on the threshold of adolescence, eager to leave their dolls and playthings behind, but with lingering little-girl fantasies. On another level, I was pleased that it had occurred also because it had served to shatter the formality of the situation and initiated real interaction among us.

The next morning, I asked the girls to tell me about the four clans of the Tsimshian nation: Eagles, Wolves, Ravens, and Killer Whales. I didn't know how I was going to work it into the lesson, or if I'd be able to at all. We had only five days to cover the life, death, and resurrection of Jesus, but I was determined to make a connection with these girls before I left. They explained that anyone living in Metlakatla was connected in some way to one of the four clans, through either their mother's line or their father's. They also explained that these connections always traced back to mothers rather than fathers. So even if you were in a clan because of your dad, he was identified by his mom's clan, and she with her mother, and so on . . . back and back and back.

"So each of you is either a Raven, an Eagle, a Killer Whale, or a Wolf?"

They nodded, muttering affirmative noises.

"What's that make me?" I asked.

Annaliese's eyes opened wide, and the girls burst into giggles and snorts.

"I mean, I know I'm an outsider, a visitor. I just wondered if there is a name for me."

More snorts and giggles.

"Oh," I sighed, "I know why you're laughing. I heard somebody yesterday say a word about outsiders. It sounded sort of like they were saying 'gumption.'"

"Gum-what?" asked Christie with a furrowed brow and the absolute disdain only a preteen can intone.

"Gumption." I repeated. "It's an old-fashioned Anglo word. It means, let's see . . . guts, I guess. Courage."

The girls couldn't stop giggling. Even little Shyra, who'd sat shyly in the corner without uttering a peep until now, buried her face in her arms and tried to stifle her laughter.

Christie spoke up. "You heard somebody say 'um-shey-wa,'" she explained. Explosions of embarrassed snuffles ensued.

Naturally, when I tried saying it, the snuffles grew into full-blown guffaws. It was contagious. I too was laughing.

"What?" I inquired. "What's so funny about . . . umshwa?"

"It's um-shey-wa," insisted Christie, "and you don't want to know what it means."

"No . . . yes, yes I do," I protested. "What does it mean?"

I looked around the table. More heads were buried, eyes averted.

Heather chimed in. "Really, you don't want to know, Miss Moffitt," she insisted, and I realized that all my begging and cajoling weren't going to work, so I gave up, determined to find out before our next meeting. I had a pretty good idea, of course, but I intended to come armed with information the next day. Meanwhile, Annaliese spoke up. "You're a butterfly."

"I beg your pardon," I said, forgetting what had ignited the explosives earlier.

"A butterfly. If you're not part of the Tsimshians, if you're a visitor, you're a butterfly . . . something that flies from place to place. If you go to see them dance at the lodge, the dancers will explain it to you."

A butterfly. That was nice. I liked the idea and looked forward to attending the ceremony the next day. Meanwhile, I dismissed class and went looking for Kelly, a local high school girl I was sure would give me the dope on um-shey-wa.

She smiled when I told her about my morning with the girls. "It's nothing, really," she explained. "Well, it can be I guess. It just means like 'whitey,' you know?"

As I'd suspected, it was the Tsimshian equivalent of honkie, howlie, gringo.

She went on, "I guess it all depends on how their brothers and fathers use it at home. If they have a lot of angry feelings about white people, they probably say it like a really bad cuss word. That's why the girls were embarrassed."

Yes. Clearly, most of these girls had brothers and fathers and uncles who had very angry feelings toward whitey. But that was okay. At least now I knew what I was dealing with. The truth had set me free.

Following Wednesday's stories and songs, we marched into our room and gathered round the table.

"You'll all be happy to know I've learned what umschwa means," I said, wearing my best schoolmarmy face.

"Um-shey-wa!" said Christie, irritated, stretching the word out, no doubt hoping that maybe, before I left town, I might at least be able to say it right.

"Yes, well . . . whatever," I mumbled. "I know what it means and I'm very flattered."

Jaws dropped.

"What?" asked Heather, hesitant but dying of curiosity.

"It means," I announced proudly, pausing for effect, "beautiful, middle-aged white lady from Tacoma!" I smiled broadly and leaned back in my chair.

They roared. Chairs scraped across the linoleum. Bodies crumpled to the floor in heaps of laughter. Christie, who had been the one most leery of me from the beginning, smiled broadly and looked directly at me. I winked.

I'd done it . . . and I don't deny it, I was proud. There was no question that I was an outsider, either a butterfly or um-shey-wa, depending on who you asked, but I was in, at least for now, with these nine girls. We had bridged the racial gap between red and white, and we'd done it with laughter, of which there was plenty more to come in the next four days, especially each time I took a picture and commanded them to "say um-shey-wa!"

Having made that vital connection, we spoke more honestly about the things I had come to talk with them about. They were able to tell me that some of their cousins and brothers and sisters who had gone away to college returned angry, vocalizing their resentment of Christians like Reverend William Duncan, who in the 1800s had come to Alaska to "save" the Indians and was credited with bringing many to Christ but was accused, like so many missionaries, of doing so at the expense of tribal stories and rituals. It made it easier for me to talk about Jesus, as opposed to a belief system, to describe him to these girls, to tell about his acceptance of all people, his love for everybody, "even um-shey-wa," I said, looking to Christie for her nod of approval. "Even silly old white ladies like me."

*Blessed are those who are persecuted because of righteousness,
for theirs is the kingdom of heaven.*

My experience as um-shey-wa was a fleabite of persecution, a mere interlude of mild discomfort compared with that experienced by many Christians. The human capacity for bitterness and enmity is immense and innate. It seems our default posture is a hostile one as we seek to snuff out virtually anyone who threatens our way of thinking, our lifestyle, and our identity.

It's hard to believe that the apostle Paul sanctioned the brutal murder of Stephen, an innocent young man whose only crime was telling people about the risen Jesus. When we hear the horror stories about the persecuted church today, it's hard to believe that someone like Saul is standing by out there somewhere, holding the coats of Christians lined up before a firing squad. And it's very hard to believe that the Jesus who would transform this man into the greatest evangelical preacher in history promised blessings—bliss, mind you—to those who would suffer and even die for his name's sake.

Actually, Jesus drove home this blessing not once but twice: "Blessed are those who are persecuted for righteousness' sake, for theirs is the kingdom of heaven. Blessed are you when they revile and persecute you, and say all kinds of evil against you falsely for My sake. Rejoice and be exceedingly glad, for great is your reward in heaven, for so they persecuted the prophets who were before you."[1]

If you had trouble before trying to wedge the Beatitudes into the cultural values of the twenty-first century, I wish you all the best trying to work this one in. About the most you can hope for is that you'll be in the company of the prophets, but in the eyes of the world, of course, they're about as credible as those guys who stand on the street corner at Pike Place Market in Seattle mumbling about the end of the world.

To bring all this into the context of contemporary life, two things might get you at worst killed and at best shunned: doing the right thing, and doing it in Jesus' name. There is abundant historical perspective to back this up, and many of the most egregious acts of persecution were done within the family of God. Consider Jezebel, who had prophets massacred because she wanted to replace Jehovah with a couple of gods more tolerant of her lifestyle. Or Manasseh, who so hated prophets that he had them tortured regularly. Though it's not in the Bible, reliable tradition has it that he had Isaiah sawn in half. (It was this story that led to Michael's first intentional turn toward God. Upon hearing Billy Graham speak of Manasseh's repentance and God's subsequent and unqualified forgiveness, he turned to me with tears in his ten-year-old eyes and said, "Man, if God can forgive that guy, he can forgive anybody.") Jeremiah, of course, was dropped into a muddy cistern, which brings to mind the malevolence of

Joseph's brothers, who were consumed by jealousy and wanted to throw him into a well and leave him for dead. It would appear that anyone who gets in the way of powerful people procuring whatever it is they're after is in grave danger.

There are two words in Scripture used to discuss persecution. The first is a Hebrew word, *radap,* and the second is Greek, *dioko/diogmos.* Each of these words denotes pursuit and pressure. The word *tribulation,* used by Jesus when he warned his disciples to expect it, is a similar word, from the Greek *thlipsis,* which means "to press or oppress." Actually, it is a graphic word that suggests pressing as in a wine or garlic press. In other words, it hurts.

Persecution can be inflicted in a variety of ways, four of which are discussed in *Baker's Evangelical Dictionary of Biblical Theology.* First, they point out, there is physical persecution, which may include neglect, torture, and/or death. "Social persecution (sometimes called discrimination) consists of making individuals of a group outcasts." Mental persecution includes anything that causes anxiety or fear, and finally, spiritual persecution involves a threat directly associated with practicing one's religion, as when Peter and John were admonished to stop preaching the gospel in Acts 5.[2]

Lest we begin to think too exclusively and develop a sense of pride about all this, it's important to note that many people, from many religions and walks of life and for myriad reasons, have been the objects of persecution. I am reminded of the early civil rights workers in the South who routinely put their lives in jeopardy, or the hundreds of people in Europe (Christians and non-Christians) who suffered and died to protect Jews from the horrors of the Third Reich. And while we're at it, let's not forget that Adolf Hitler claimed to be doing what he was doing in Christ's name, just as members of the KKK believe they are ambassadors for the Lord. It's a messy business sometimes, trying to figure out who's who in this landscape. And yet, when we return to the person of Jesus, it's not so hard, really. As Pastor Mead reminded us: if it's about love and grace and mercy, and if it's creative energy, it's probably of God; if it's about hate and destruction, it's probably coming from some other source.

I remember the first time one of our kids took a social hit in the name of righteousness. It was Michael, and interestingly, it came shortly after his introduction to Manasseh. It seemed like a small deal at the time, even to Mike. He'd been invited to a sleep-over with two of his sixth-grade buddies, and in the course of the evening, one of them suggested they do something that Mike thought they shouldn't do. (None of us can remember what it was now.) Mike held out, and though his pals gave him a bad time, he thought it was all behind him, until he returned to school on Monday morning to find he was the object of some ugly ridicule. One of the boys decided Mike was very uncool, what we would have called a square back in my day, and since this young man was a popular kid, he had a lot of social clout. What began as a little teasing soon grew into full-blown harassment, and because this was prior to the days when students would be urged to lodge official complaints, Mike had to stand his ground alone for roughly six weeks, until school let out for the summer. It was a long six weeks, and it left a nasty scar. Though we counseled Mike to handle it without being ugly and trying to get even, it wasn't easy. His dad was almost beyond restraint one night after he learned that Mike had been physically sick over the events that had occurred on the playground that afternoon. He'd had about all he could stand, he said, and was going to tell Mike to forget doing the right thing and just clean the kid's clock. I asked him to wait, but inside I wanted to clean the kid's clock myself. Actually, what I really wanted was a whack at his dad, who had come to our house when we first moved in to "check out" our family before letting his son sleep over, just to make sure ours was a good home. He hoped I wasn't offended, he said, but they were Christians, and you just couldn't be too careful. I wanted to deposit his bratty little kid on his front stoop in a burlap bag. But I didn't. And neither did his dad, nor did his big brother, nor did Mike. At long last I spoke with the teachers and counselors and alerted them to what was going on when they weren't looking, explaining that Mike was trying to handle it without violence or further ugliness but that significant damage had been done. I've never seen Mike happier than he was on the last day of school that year. I wouldn't know until years later that the experience affected him throughout high school and even in college, where he often went to great lengths to avoid situations that might result in his being the object of rejection or ridicule.

Having grown up in a household in which teasing and sarcasm were all part of the rites of passage into adulthood, I was all grown up before I realized how brutal verbal abuse can be. The word *sarcasm* is, in fact, derived from two Greek words that, combined, mean "flesh ripping." During those spring weeks in 1989, I saw firsthand how brutally persecuted a kid can be merely for doing what he thinks is right.

Being cool is far more important to most Americans than being right, and though the need to be accepted by the in-crowd peaks during adolescence, it stays with us for a long time, maybe till we die. Here's how I know. Even now, at age 53, as I'm working on this book, I'm timid about professing my beliefs in the workplace. Oh, I wear my cross pendant and folks know I go to church, and I'm pretty comfortable talking about God if the occasion arises, despite the apparent aversion to anything overtly religious. I'm certainly cautious about throwing Jesus' name around, though. Given this aversion, I guess I'm afraid folks will write me off and quit listening to what I have to say altogether. My cohorts are respectful of me as a rule, though it takes very little to make me squeamish. Consider the afternoon that one of my colleagues, a man whom I've come to love, actually, angrily blurted out what he'd like to do to all those blankety blank anti-environmental Christians out there. He spoke about them as if each one bore a personal hatred for all things natural, harboring a particular animosity for the salmon, demigod of the Pacific Northwest. I was stung, though apparently I maintained an unaffected air. As the day and evening wore on, however, integrity demanded that I find a way to tell him that he'd hurt my feelings. The next day, I called him over and did so. I told him I'd felt as though he had stereotyped, lumped, sealed, and stamped all Christians and tossed the lot of us into the dumpster. I restrained myself from a tirade. I wanted to ask him how he'd feel if he heard me make a hateful generalization implying that all Jews are greedy and all Indians drunks. I wanted to ask him if he really thought all Christians sought ways to wreak havoc on the environment. I wanted to rant and unload all of my pent-up feelings about what it's like to live as a Christian in this culture, but I didn't. And I'm glad I didn't. He was genuinely remorseful for having wounded me. I figured he would be. He's a great guy. But here's the deal; I had chest pains when I called him over to talk to me. My heart hurt because I still want the popular kids to like me. I still want everyone to like me, and being a Jesus Freak doesn't usually get you into the high-school hall of fame.

Religious people have always been the objects of ridicule, but, at the risk of sounding consumed by a persecution complex, I have to say that it seems there is a special brand of persecution reserved especially for Christians at this time in history. And I think there are plenty of people who would agree, though many would be quick to point out that a lot of Christians—or people using Christianity as a platform for their personal agendas—have earned the bad press, especially when they have been allies of power-hungry governments. I mean, it's pretty hard to justify things like the Inquisition. And hard to hear the stories about the Salem witch trials, to say nothing of the Klan. Hard, too, to get past abortion-clinic bombings and "God Hates Homosexuals" webpages. I think it was Ghandi who once said something like, "I like your Christ, but I don't much like your Christians." Still, taking all of that into account, it seems that Christians take way too much heat. As one political analyst—a Democrat, even—pointed out in the 2000 presidential race, Joseph Lieberman got away with God-talk that the public would have never tolerated from a Christian.

Christians have done far more right than they've done wrong, what with their strong participation in various human rights affairs, to say nothing of the fact they've always been active in providing food, clothing, education, and medical care to the impoverished. You'd think the activities of Mother Teresa alone would mitigate the popular perception of Christians. Few people realize that the people who fought for the prohibition of alcohol did so in the name of protecting children, and that these same people provided the underpinning for what came to be known as the PTA. Martin Luther King Jr. was a preacher, and he stood firmly on the teachings of Jesus Christ. You'd think that all that good would help Christians attain the approval of the world, but it never seems to work out that way.

In an edition of *Parish Life,* Victor Potapov of the Russian Orthodox Church poses this question: "Why does the world persecute true faith, piety, righteousness, which are so beneficial for the world itself? The word of God answers us: '. . . [the] world lieth in wickedness' (1 John 5:19). Men, according to the word of King David, loved evil more than goodness (Psalm 51:3), and the prince of this world, the devil, acting through evil men, hates righteousness and persecutes it, since it serves as a denunciation of unrighteousness."[3] The apostle Paul wrote, "All that live godly in Christ shall suffer persecution."

I have a theory. I've had it for a long time, but I've never talked about it much because of the disquieting reaction it receives. Potapov's observation encourages me to go public. I've always wondered why, in this age of diversity, multiculturalism, and tolerance, Christians are essentially excluded and left unprotected. I finally concluded that it's because the only real threat to Satan is Jesus Christ. Other religions and belief systems don't worry the prince of this world because they don't threaten his reign over the hearts of the people. Only Jesus. Jesus he's scared of, and so he should be, just as I feel certain Pilate was when Jesus reminded him who was really in charge.

The world is bathed in sin, but like pigs in a pen, we don't even know it. A neighbor of ours when we first moved to Tacoma, Richard Overman, was a professor at the University of Puget Sound for many years. I once heard him discuss the seven deadly sins, and his remarks clarified something for me that had always been confusing—about sloth. I had no trouble seeing how lust, anger, envy, and even gluttony made the list. But despite the adage that insists cleanliness is next to godliness, and despite my family's uncompromising work ethic, I just couldn't see sloth as that big of a deal. Dr. Overman said something to the effect that it was essentially about things that clutter the path between oneself and God, and suddenly it made perfect sense. Each of the seven sins is about self-indulgence, about trying to fill ourselves up with everything but God, and sloth, in particular, is about permitting things to pile up and completely obscure our vision of God, indeed, clutter the very path that will lead us to God.

It reminds me of a comedy routine by George Carlin, in which he speaks of our preoccupation with stuff, getting stuff and then getting more stuff and then having to buy something to help us store all our stuff. My husband and I live in a small-ish house, at least by American standards. It's about 1600 square feet—less actually. When the boys were still home, it was a little snug at times, though complaining about it shames me when I think of the way millions of people on the planet live. Anyway, what with Don's professional stuff and mine, especially books and papers, and all the other stuff we've accumulated along the way, there are days when I feel like renting a frontloader and somehow driving it through the house, removing everything that isn't nailed down. This urge comes over me because to take a more measured approach tends to leave me paralyzed. I stand in the middle of the room and look around without a clue as to where I should start. I think that's what sloth is like. It's like lying around eating pizza and drinking beer and letting garbage pile up all around you, and when you finally decide to haul your lazy buns off the couch and tidy up a bit, you just stand there and look dumb. You can't find your starting place, so you give up—and order more pizza.

In *Mere Christianity*, C. S. Lewis writes eloquently about the chasm between our natural selves and our spiritual selves. "The natural life in each of us is something self-centred, something that wants to be petted and admired, to take advantage of other lives, to exploit the whole universe. And especially it wants to be left to itself: to keep well away from anything better or stronger or higher than it, anything that might make it feel small. It is afraid of the light and air of the spiritual world, just as people who have been brought up to be dirty are afraid of a bath."[4]

It's humiliating to imagine coming before the throne of God in need of a bath. And the world is perfectly happy if you stay dirty, because you blend in nicely with everyone and everything else.

I have said before that the world at the present time seems to be especially dissolute despite the obvious contradictions. Were an alien sent to study our culture, his report might read something like this: this is a people defined by conflicting values. They want to do whatever makes them feel good, to eat well, drink lots of beer, and have sex whenever they want with whomever they want. Under something they call the First Amendment, they insist on the right to say whatever they like, and they want the freedom to indiscriminately consume pornography, though it would appear they loathe perpetrators of sex crimes and cannot figure out what fuels their imaginations. Every year they pay tribute to a black man for his nonviolent efforts to end racial discrimination, but their favorite movie heroes are men and women who win their battles by kicking, scratching, bombing, and blasting their adversaries to smithereens. They wonder why their children carry guns. Their television shows and videos would suggest they are amused by the recreational use of drugs, though they spend billions of tax dollars on something called a "drug war." They claim to love and respect nature, though the landscape bears hideous scars left by the greedy. Finally, most of them can't seem to decide how they feel about life and death, existing in a state of perpetual debate over such things as abortion, euthanasia, and something they call the death penalty.

Conflicted though we may be, when push comes to shove, society seems content to remain comfortably unwashed, because to be washed is to be set apart—in other words, sanctified—which seems to be, at the very least, an annoyance and, in many instances, a serious threat to the status quo, what pastor and author John Alexander referred to as FIRE, the four values for which Americans will fight to the death: freedom, individualism, rights, and equality. Among many interesting things Alexander has to say on this subject is this: that the whole notion of personal rights is a relatively new idea perpetrated by philosophers of the Enlightenment. "There's not even a word for rights in Hebrew, Greek or Latin," he points out.[5] What interests me about his observation is the anarchistic nature of this set of values and the inherent conflicts that are bound to prevail. It's hard to grant you your freedom if it gets in the way of mine, or my rights. No wonder young adults seem terminally confused on the subject of courtship and marriage.

Christians who have truly relinquished themselves and all their rights—surrendered themselves to God for transformation—are going to find they do not fit in the world, just as Jesus said they wouldn't. Further, they will find that they are victims of persecution, whether it comes in the form of discrimination and ridicule, such as that experienced by high school and college students who have made vows of celibacy, or in the forms of terrorism, torture, or death.

Attempting to live as a nominal Christian, a Christian who is accepted in the church and in the world, can be done, but it takes a fancy bit of footwork to stay on that tightrope—a frightening proposition and, to some extent, the equivalent of performing without a net, because at some point, according to Jesus, you're going to have to account for it. The graphic description of the Laodicean church in the third chapter of Revelation troubles the discerning soul: "I know your works, that you are neither cold nor hot. I could wish you were cold or hot. So then, because you are lukewarm, and neither cold nor hot, I will vomit you out of My mouth. Because you say 'I am rich, have become wealthy, and have need of nothing'—and do not know that you are wretched, miserable, poor, blind, and naked—I counsel you to buy from Me gold refined in the fire, that you may be rich; and white garments that you may be clothed, that the shame of your nakedness may not be revealed; and anoint your eyes with eye salve, that you may see."[6]

And then he says something we must never forget. It comes right before the famous stand-at-the-door-and-knock passage, which is usually taken out of context and used as an invitation to unbelievers, when it was, in fact, addressed to members of the church! Like so many other passages, the troubling ones, this set-up verse is often skipped: "As many as I love, I rebuke and chasten. Therefore be zealous and repent. Behold, I stand at the door and knock. If anyone hears My voice and opens the door, I will come in to him and dine with him and he with Me."[7] This is a call for believers to repent of their marginal commitment to the Lord! If we choose to walk in the easement between Christ and the world, we can expect to be vomited up like tepid water; if we go for broke in Jesus' name, he will join us at table, though, alas, we may not get invited to the prom.

By contrast, hear what he said to the church at Smyrna, a poor church located in a city of wealth with a large Jewish population: "I know your works, tribulation, and poverty (but you are rich); and I know the blasphemy of those who say they are Jews and are not, but are a synagogue of Satan. Do not fear any of those things which you are about to suffer. Indeed, the devil is about to throw some of you into prison, that you may be tested, and you will have tribulation ten days. Be faithful until death, and I will give you the crown of life."[8]

Now, if you're anything like me, you're asking yourself a series of questions that goes something like this: so does that mean that unless storm troopers are at my door threatening to throw me in jail, I must be doing something wrong? If I'm not Smyrna, does that make me Laodicea? Certainly there have been believers throughout history who behaved as if that's what they believed. Simone Weil went out of her way to suffer for Christ, choosing to be imprisoned and live an impoverished life, dying a martyr. Does that make her better than me? Maybe. Or maybe it makes her slightly nuts, like Seth's mom in Dallas. Or maybe it just makes her Simone Weil, and it makes me Sharon Moffitt, and what I am called to do is be Sharon Moffitt, fully and passionately in line with all that God intends me to be, today and tomorrow and until it has all been said and done. I suppose it could mean jail time somewhere along the line, though it seems unlikely. Then again, it seemed highly unlikely I'd fly to Metlakatla on a floatplane. Maybe it will mean publishing a book that earns harsh criticism, or maybe it'll just mean living outside the edge of the in-crowd, in Jesus' name. Maybe all that matters is that I report for duty and leave the rest to the Lord.

The real challenge is that we are told by James to count it all joy when we fall into various trials. Jesus himself, according to Matthew, said to rejoice. It's not enough that we endure the persecution; we're supposed to be happy about it. This makes me nervous. Not scared, really, just leery of people I know who have persecution complexes grounded in denial: the drug addict who maintains that she can't get a fair chance because no one will extend her credit, or the AIDS victim who can't figure out why he's afflicted, despite leading a life of rampant promiscuity. And what about Christians who think they're being persecuted for their faith when they're really being shunned because they're obnoxious and sanctimonious? Some people seem to wallow in their persecution as if it were a cloak of nobility. Are these folks being persecuted, or are they experiencing the logical consequences of their actions? Unquestionably, they should be treated with compassion and mercy, but their sense of persecution often seems irrational and self-serving.

And then there are the media-hungry, self-appointed martyrs. I'm having flashbacks of videotape footage of David Koresh, who apparently relished the persecutorial attention he received because it confirmed for him that his work was, indeed, God's work. I remember watching those tapes, seeing him walk among his followers, his Bible open in his palm, quoting Scripture that supposedly lent credence to his teachings. Likewise Jim Jones, who knew his Bible thoroughly and used it, channeled through his charismatic personality, to entice thousands to a remote forest in South America, where he ordered them to commit suicide. In Jesus' name. John wrote, "I have no greater joy than to hear that my children are walking in the truth."[9] But how do we know who's telling the truth? It behooves all of us to look beyond the superficial in our understanding of men like Koresh and Jones. Even Satan quoted Scripture. A close look at these cult leaders reveals men who lusted after power, exploited women and children, psychologically and sexually, and lied, cheated, and stole from their followers. These men were not prophets any more than the snake in Eden was really a snake. In this age of sound bites and news clips, it is more important than it has ever been for Christians to pray for discernment—to go deep and go long and not be ensnared by the sweet siren songs of false prophets.

You'd think, given the guarantee of persecution, that Christians would be better about coming together and supporting each other. More evidence of Satan, I presume. Anyway, if I were Satan, I'd sure as heck send in the troops to divide and conquer. And I'm not just talking about the cosmic schisms, or even regional splits such as the one in Belfast. I'm talking about the way we all seem to revert to theological snobbery when it comes to how we're supposed to practice our faith. We always have, of course, which is how we came to have most of Paul's letters, evidence that he had to use tons of energy just to help people stay on task regarding the work of the church and not spend all their time quibbling over potaytoes and potahtoes. Seems the battle between the natural and the spiritual man keeps going and going and going, like the Energizer Bunny.

When I was a kid, there were two buildings in my hometown of Fort Collins that I was afraid to go into: the Masonic Temple and St. Joseph's Roman Catholic Church. I'm still afraid to go into the former. When we were kids roaming the summer streets of our little prairie town, we often entertained ourselves by playing Truth or Dare. Among the most popular dares was the one that the kid in question had to ascend the imposing steps that led to the front door of the temple, pass between huge stone pillars, push open the twelve-foot-high oaken doors, and race as fast as she could down the long, unlit hallway that led to a throne that rivaled the queen of England's. The dare wasn't fulfilled unless the runner sat on the chair (all-the-way sat) and returned to the light of day without getting snatched up by the head mason, who, rumor had it, carried small children into the bowels of the catacombs under the streets of the city and did heaven knows what to them.

Silly as this little Boo Radley drama sounds, I was reminded of it when Michael reported that in Belfast he'd observed a wee Catholic lad burst through the peace line on Workman Avenue to throw stones at all things Protestant. And I remembered that though we didn't suspect the members of St. Joe's of the heinous crimes we were certain the Masons were committing, we did wonder just what those priests and nuns were up to in there and what powerful potentate had ordered all the Roman Catholic moms to wear lace hankies on their heads before entering the building. The only thing we knew for sure, because our parents said so, is that the whole place was full of idols.

Children take all that they hear and embellish it with the vivid colors of their imaginations until they have designed the most colorful and frightening demons and dragons. It is little wonder, if nothing is ever done to challenge these creations, that these same kids grow up to live in fear.

It gets worse. With every new fissure in the family of God comes a new level of snobbish superiority. Baptists mistrust Presbyterians. Presbyterians mistrust Methodists. Southern Baptists mistrust American Baptists, if they acknowledge them at all. Methodists (at least United ones) look down their noses at anything Pentecostal, and nobody this side of the Atlantic, except for poets and artists, has even heard of Greek Orthodox Christians. About the only thing anyone can even come close to agreeing on is that most (but not all) televangelists are highly suspect. And the nicest people participate in the game. People like me. Just about the time I'm feeling huffy toward a friend who's making fun of folks who punctuate their prayers with the word "just" for no known reason, I catch myself snuffling with incredulity to learn that laypeople—in my very own denomination (which I frequently threaten to abandon)—are not allowed to administer communion under any circumstances. And what about that closed communion business that some churches practice? How arrogant is that? And there it is. The beat goes on.

Old Screwtape is as happy as a well-fed cat without a worry in the world that Christians will ever put away their personal agendas and remember it was supposed to be simple: go into all the nations and preach the gospel, Jesus said. Just go. Every time I hear people sitting around and bad-mouthing other Christians for their theology, I want to say something like, "Why don't we go find some people to feed or some prisoners to visit?" But I don't. Because I want these people to like me. I want everyone to like me. Besides, if I really feel that way, I could just quietly get up and go feed somebody all by myself without saying a word. It takes a lot less energy, though, and it's a lot more satisfying to whale on my brothers and sisters in Christ. Sometimes I don't know how God stands any of us.

I like hanging out with old Christians; they seem so ready to tell the truth about themselves, so aware that their lives have been covered in grace all along, even if they hadn't been able to appreciate it when they were young. When we first moved to Tacoma,

God sent a neighbor to my door who would change my life. Actually he sent two. The first came bearing lefse, a sort of potato pancake that changed my life only by helping me realize I didn't care much for lefse. The second woman to come by was Phyllis. She invited me to a neighborhood Bible study, where it turned out I was the youngest person in attendance. That alone was enough to make me go back, as it was becoming a rare occasion for me to be the youngest person in attendance anywhere. Ultimately, though, I went primarily to be in the company of these women, women whose lives had been buffeted and battered by all sorts of storms and they had lived to tell about it—and to discover they were still works in progress, still messing up, still returning to God for forgiveness and help. I remember smiling when Phyllis told us once that when someone approaches her and asks if she's been saved, she says, "Yes . . . many times." I met with these ladies every week for seven years, these modern-day Job-women. And when they all showed up at Patrick's wedding, I took a picture of them and wrote this caption under it: "The women who prayed Pat and Mona to the altar."

I realize there are a number of young people out there thinking to themselves, "Poor thing. She's talking about these old women as if she's not one of them." And I guess I am old now, though, like the rest of you, I don't feel any older, and I'm frequently surprised and frustrated by my body's defiance of the real me. This incongruity between the body and spirit is one of my key arguments in support of the existence of God, or at least the existence of something that transcends this mortal life. The older I get, the clearer it gets: there is a part of me, the essence of me, that is ageless. The first time this occurred to me, I think I'd just traversed the crest of a hill, both figurative and literal. It was shortly after my fortieth birthday, and I was taking a walk, looking at my feet. I thought to myself, these are the same feet that walked through the halls of Fort Collins High School and ran around the neighborhood on long summer nights when I was a child, the same feet that walked down the aisle at my wedding, the same feet on which I hobbled into toddlerhood, except now they're forty years old and one of them has a bunion that's killing me. My feet are getting old and I feel achy when I get out of a chair, but the real me is inside here somewhere and essentially unchanged in a vital, elemental way. Some days I feel as if my body is a runaway truck and my spirit is running after it, flailing its arms and hollering for it to slow down before it goes over the side of the pass. And it saddens me to say that it's a rare day when I experience any sort of integration, a harmonious union of body and spirit. Sorry, but hopeful. I read once that the form of the Greek word for sanctification is *hagiasmos,* which confirms my suspicion that sanctification does not happen suddenly but is, in fact, a process. If the word is a blending of *hagia,* which means "holy," and *osmos,* which means "thrust," an interesting image is wrought, one of being thrust into holiness, an image which suggests a great power behind the process. There is a curious sexual suggestion in the image as well, but all my Southern Baptist shields are slamming into place so fast I can barely consider it long enough even to dismiss it as pure flummery. Suffice it to say that God might even like it if we could appreciate the deep and abiding connection between our sexuality and our spirituality. I won't say any more for fear the same people who tried to censor *The Last Temptation of Christ* will come after me. Never mind that I was one of them. I told you sanctification is a process. I've grown since then. Maybe one day, I'll be as humble as my old friends.

Perhaps, in the spirit of control, or at least for the sake of halfway decent writing, I should rein in this wild-horse tangent and find a way to connect all this to persecution. I believe it began when I used the image of the world bathed in sin. The point is this. We live in a world that is so caught up in greed and hedonism; it is little wonder that we have difficulty living godly lives in it. To take a stand for righteousness and morality is to invite at least some measure of persecution from some corner of the world. And while lust for pleasure and a misguided sense of our right to pursue it regardless of the cost are central to the American way of life, these pale in comparison to the sins of the spirit, all rooted in pride, that seem to be thrusting us anywhere but toward holiness.

When C. S. Lewis writes about "the great sin," he reminds us that sins of the flesh, though sometimes unruly and likely to get us into a lot of trouble, are nothing compared with pride. Pride—which, he says, "comes direct from Hell"—"is purely spiritual: consequently it is far more subtle and deadly."[10] We are not happy, he says, being pretty. We need to be prettier. We are not satisfied with being rich but are driven to be richer than the next person, or smarter, or—and this is where the insidious nature of the beast is clearly evident—holier and more humble as well. It all comes down to power, really, and brings us full circle back to those first beatitudes, the ones in which Jesus promised that blessings would be poured not on the man who ends up with the most toys, or the woman with the most lovers, but on the man and woman who recognize their poverty and lowliness. In a world that has glorified self-actualization, those who suggest a life that leads to the gradual diminishment of one's ego—the very death of self—as an alternative are not likely to be appreciated.

To be a Christian is to be countercultural. There's no getting around it, and church leaders and teachers need to be very careful about trying to ameliorate Christianity so that it looks good next to the pleasures of the world. First because it sullies the very image of Christ, and second because it gives newcomers, especially young people, a false message: that we are just as cool as our competitors. To compete with the world is to silently agree that the world is where it's at. When I read youth group announcements that sound like spin-offs from MTV, I get very nervous. When we sell out to the image gods, we are in danger of losing our way, in danger of becoming all show and no substance. Popularity should never be the aim of the church. The message to our kids should never be that we are just as cool as the world. We're not. We're cooler. Because, as my pal Carla once pointed out, the innest of all in-crowds, the Holy Trinity, has invited us to be part of their crowd, along with anyone else who'd like to come along. And there's much joy and laughter and dancing to be had. But it won't always be fun, and the road gets narrow at times. Living in the truth is what will keep us in step with God, and when we're walking beside him, there will be times when we suffer for it. Jesus never lied to the disciples about that; he never lied to us. "Most assuredly," Jesus said to Peter, a member of the in-crowd if ever there was one, "I say to you, when you were younger, you girded yourself and walked where you wished; but when you are old, you will stretch out your hands, and another will gird you and carry you where you do not wish."[11] This was, of course, a prophecy of Peter's life, and death, as a disciple of Christ, and those of us who choose to follow Jesus know that it is ours to pick up the cross of Christ and walk where Peter walked.

And though we do not know what will be asked of us along the way, we do know that we will be living in and headed for the kingdom as we go. It is an exercise in futility to try to imagine what will be asked of us. It wastes time, and what we think our response will be is hardly ever what it in fact turns out to be. The Lord knew it would do no good and would probably result in a titanic mess to let me know when Michael was a baby that he would one day be diagnosed with a brain tumor a few days before he left for college. I love Corrie ten Boom's story about her trips to Amsterdam with her father when she was a little girl. Despite her whining and pleading, her father withheld her train ticket from her until they were on the platform, assuring her that he would give her what she needed when she needed it and not before. This memory sustained her during her days in the concentration camp when she thought she could not go on. It pays to be existential in our life with God, to trust him to give us our ticket when we need it, to know he will empower us to make the right choice at the right time—just as the train is pulling into the station—and not one moment before.

When Mike first began making noises about shifting his career plans and pursuing professional ministry, my husband struggled against the idea. Finally, after honestly and courageously traipsing through all of the stuff that was cluttering the path, he reluctantly gave his blessing. I smile now to think of it. He said to Mike, "I guess it's okay, as long as you don't think you have to become a missionary or something and go off to some dangerous assignment somewhere." Mike's response broadens my smile. "I don't think you have to worry about it, Dad. I have little interest in being a missionary in a dangerous place." The ticket to Belfast could wait.

Transformation

We've been enjoying the xanthic days of autumn in South Puget Sound lately, a warm contrast to those midwinter mornings soon to come when we will raise the shades and momentarily think we've been trapped in a black and white photograph. A soggy, wet black and white photograph. Some people say we have only two seasons up here, fall and spring. That's pretty much true, which makes the onset of each one a big deal. Right now, we're basking in the golden glow caused by the sun reflecting off changing foliage, as if a wash of gamboge were laid under the more cyanic ones that define the sky this morning. The leathery green leaves of late summer have lost their vernal suppleness, and the sweet-pea vines look apologetic for waning. The air is laced with cryptic messages that signal transformation. Spread before me on my front porch are garnet offerings left by the Virginia creeper, which hangs from the roof and appears to be staging one final burst of glory before succumbing to winter.

Recently I walked along the boardwalk in the wildlife preserve at Nisqually Delta and felt a deep, primal pang of sorrow when I spied bronze pears suspended high in untended, nearly leafless trees. The vision evoked a memory of feeling suspended myself somewhere between joy and sorrow during the final days of summer in the Colorado high country, where the extended family had gathered for a rare reunion. One early morning, Mona excitedly roused us from sleep so we could go out and watch five young bull elk grazing in the field across from our cabin. Just yards in front of us, two of them locked horns, the prelude, I presume, for fall mating rituals to come, heralded by the eerie sound of their bugling in September. It's a sound I've yet to hear but which I understand is beautiful and haunting. Certainly there was something mysterious and lovely in the sound of this predawn engagement. The collision of antlers produces a deep resonant sound one hears more with the gut than the ear. Oddly enough, it had a similar effect on me as the tones made by the Indonesian wind chimes hanging in my garden, the mellow clacking of thick bamboo reeds and coconut shells jostled by breezes. And though the behavior of these young elk was clearly combative and evoked melancholy, it did not feel threatening. It felt altogether right and somehow reassuring.

Perhaps the sorrow I feel now is a mere byproduct of being in the midst of things dying and changing, the signposts of passing time. It's certainly not unusual for me to grow reflective and emotionally full this time of year. But this fall is different, I realize, when I discover our cat's latest trophy decaying on the mat at the back door, a rat caught trying to invade our home. There's nothing like a dead rat to make you ill at ease, remind you of life in the underbrush. This my fifty-fourth autumn is different than any I've known before. The whole world is ill at ease. On a day not altogether unlike today, just weeks ago, the world watched in disbelief as jetliners careened off course and plowed into the World Trade Center in New York City at roughly the same time a third plane was converted into a missile of destruction and sliced into the Pentagon and a fourth carved out a fiery crater in the Pennsylvania landscape. Suddenly, the word *change* took on new meaning. No longer was it merely about the evocative fragrance of burning leaves and other sweet, predictable autumnal changes but about things brutal and shocking. And deadly. Dead beyond even what we normally think of as dead, for in this instance, virtually nothing but rubble remained. There were almost no bodies to carry out and prepare for burial. No remains. The fragrance of leaves was replaced by the stench of death, and Americans from shore to shore plodded through their days in stunned silence.

Today, ambling along the footpath in the delta, shoving words around in my head as if they were the square pieces on a Rubik's Cube, it dawns on me that I've actually been wrestling with this notion of change ever since the day last February when I mailed the final pages of this manuscript to my editor. What you are now reading is not what I sent off to him that day, of course. It simply could not be. Too much has happened. Things of such size and significance that they cannot be left out of this reflection of our world, our culture, and our spiritual condition. And God only knows how much more will change before these pages are in print.

These ruminations began on Ash Wednesday. My first earthquake. Well, my first *real* one anyway. I had experienced a small tremor a few years back when the congregants in church suddenly perked up like a herd of horses that smell fire. Ears were pricked, heads cocked, following what felt like a harsh slap administered to the south wall of the sanctuary, and then a ripple of wave action passing underneath, turning the pews into something akin to a kiddy ride at the fair. After a moment to assess the situation and collect ourselves, we gingerly returned to worship, suddenly more aware of our need for God than we had been moments before. Recovery took a bit more time on February 28, Ash Wednesday. The first day of the Lenten season, 2001.

I was at school, snugly hiding out in my little office off the library when I felt the jackhammer vibrations and thought the building was wambling from the effect of the big guns out at Fort Lewis that sometimes rattle our classroom windows and give us momentary pause. But in less than seconds, I knew this shaking was not caused by guns, and though I am embarrassed to admit how utterly cliche I can be at times, I think I actually said, out loud, "This is the big one!" Thank goodness no one heard me. What really surprised me was that I dove under my desk for cover, exactly as I had instructed students to do year after year since moving to the Pacific Northwest. In Colorado we had conducted similar duck-and-cover drills in anticipation of twisters ripping across the prairie. You need to know, given my size and age, that diving under a desk is no small accomplishment. I couldn't believe I'd managed it, but mostly I was just shocked to think I had actually followed instructions. You see, despite the fact that I'd dutifully spoon-fed these directions to students for years, deep down I never had any intention of diving anywhere that might leave me trapped under beams or other falling debris, because as much as I can appreciate the logic of ducking and covering, in the real-life game of rock-paper-scissors, my fear of being buried alive prevails over my fear of being swallowed up by the earth or carried off to Oz. So you can see why I was surprised to find myself folded up under my desk. I suppose I did it because it would have been unseemly to mow down students as I made a break for the exit on the opposite side of the library. As soon as the building stopped stuttering, however, and began speaking in more undulant tones, we were all up and on our way, beating a hasty retreat to the soccer field across the street, each of us eager to post our story among the others that would be told over and over in the next few days.

It was when the adrenaline dissipated and folks grew more reflective that I found myself thinking about change—specifically, the difference between the slow changes of, say, a glacier ice cap melting down and carving out a valley or a ravine, and the jolting, pressurized changes that occur suddenly and violently when tectonic plates under the surface of the earth press on each other until something gives.

In addition, I was becoming increasingly aware of changes occurring within my very self, physical changes. It turns out, at long last, that I was standing on the threshold of menopause. With hindsight, I am aware that I saw everything coming. In fact, and you can believe this or not, I think I may have foretold the Ash Wednesday earthquake. Girl Scout's honor. In my journal, a week before the quake, I wrote that "a tsunamic wave of depression is building up at the base of my skull." It was, I wrote, threatening to "shake my house and bring everything tumbling from the shelves."

I'm a little old to be playing hostess to the Change, actually. To tell the truth, I was beginning to think it was going to bypass me altogether, which seemed only fair given all the trouble this body's been to me over the years. Skipping menopause might, I reasoned, make up for the excessive facial hair and big girl genes (I almost wrote jeans) I'd been granted at birth. But alas, no. Perimenopausal activity suddenly shifted to all-out menopausal activity, and my world was rocked.

Mind you, it began subtly enough—a bit of unexplained dizziness and an inscrutable case of the blues I couldn't seem to shake.

There was nothing subtle about what happened next, however, as I found myself late one afternoon in the throes of an all-out anxiety attack that was so severe I phoned Carla and Sunny, who dutifully dropped whatever they were doing and drove over to sit with me until Don got home and took my blood pressure. To our surprise, it was very high and warranted a dreaded trip to the emergency room. I'm convinced that nothing serves to equalize humanity faster than an evening in the chairs at the ER, where *every*one, or so it seems, waits. Six hours and who knows how many diagnostic tests later, I was finally let go with a relatively clean bill of health but with an order to see my doctor as soon as possible. Turns out the high blood pressure was more than a mere manifestation of my anxiety and, among other things, resulted in the purchase of one of those little plastic pill dispensers to help me keep track of all the new tablets and gel caps I would now be required to take.

I thought about Satan or the devil or the Evil One or whatever you call him quite a bit last spring as I sat in my living room under a quilt with all the curtains drawn. I'm still not convinced that he wasn't lurking around the edges of this personal crisis, which came on full force, by the way, less than forty-eight hours after I dropped this manuscript into the mailbox. The coincidence still gives me pause.

Shakespeare suggested that in metaphor we give "to airy nothing a local habitation and a name." No one will ever convince me that Satan is a mere metaphor for evil. The day we trivialized evil, imagined it as nothing more than a caricature sprouting cute little horns, a trick-or-treater clothed in red satin and wielding a pretend pitchfork, we gave it tremendous power over us. Perhaps the heart of human folly is found not so much in our deliberate sinning but in our reckless and easy turning away from God, our readiness to turn instead to the world. We reject holiness in favor of human nature because someone convinced us it could be trusted, when in truth, to follow it is to abide in spiritual puerility for eternity, self-indulgent creatures whose prime directive is to satisfy our lust no matter what it takes. American pie. Like kids at the gates of the carnival, we are mesmerized by lights and noise that promise cheap thrills. We permit ourselves to be led, stupified, to the edge of a great abyss.

I'd love to tell you that I've been completely delivered from all the demons who hover around me, but the truth is, given God's insistence on granting me freedom, I permit them to assault me from time to time. Especially fear. I doubt that I will ever completely stop being afraid—afraid to fly, afraid of late-night phone calls, afraid of what people think of me. All fears that, in my imagination, have the same result: me left all alone in the dark. The first time I heard how many copies of this book would be in circulation, I had a panic attack. What if my literary mentors and spiritual directors and, worst of all, my big brothers and sisters think it's all bogus nonsense? How can I take back thousands of copies and win back everyone's approval? It'll be like trying to reclaim water spilled from a pail. But to my surprise, no sooner did I hit that panic button than I had an epiphany, a moment in which it occurred to me that God may indeed be changing me as I speak. I expressed it like this to a trusted friend: I will know I've reached a higher plane when criticism no longer affects me, and I will know I've come to high holy ground when neither praise nor criticism hold any sway over me at all.

The big test will, indeed, be my family. Maybe it's because I'm "the baby" or maybe it's just the nature of the Irish family—or any family—or maybe it's just our family and the fact that brothers became father figures for me. I don't know. What I do know is that I worry a lot about what my siblings think of me. I want and need their approval more than anyone else's. Lest you get the wrong idea, these are not mean people. I *love* these people. No, the angst I'm describing has its genesis within my wounded heart. Any power I have given them over me, I gave without any coercive activity on their part.

I've decided the human family is a microcosm of the family of God. I know I'm not the first person to make that brilliant observation, but here's what I mean. At its worst, the family is willful and disobedient. Its members can be egocentric and self-promoting, and their love is certainly not unconditional, not even the love between mothers and children. Sometimes it seems that the only thing that glues a family together is its dysfunction. And yet it is at the family gathering that one sees firsthand the effects of God's patience, his mercy and grace. Within the family, redemption is brought out of the abstract and wrestled to earth.

I thought about this the other day when I learned that my brother Bruce, famous for running rescue ops for the family, got a call from his daughter, who needed him to "come get" her. Granted, this may seem like minor request, but the thing is she was roughly a thousand miles away. Her dad dropped what he was doing and climbed into his car. He drove "straight through," as he always does, dining on 7-11 burritos and styrofoam coffee. And I thought, how very godlike this gesture was. We call, sometimes after years of being incommunicado, and God comes for us. Every time. We sing *God Bless America* and pray that he will, not because we deserve it but because we're scared and we hope he'll come and take care of us.

I thought, too, of my brother Tom and all the middle-of-the-night calls I made to him back when I was experiencing the onset of my nervous breakthrough. I thought about how the poor kid Mr. Williams had worried about back at Lincoln Junior High had grown up to become a captain in the U.S. Navy and, along the way, had an encounter with Jesus that led him to launch a forty-year prayer on behalf of his kid sisters and brothers, and how, despite our protests or insistence that we didn't need his brand of religion, somehow we all knew he was right. I thought about the fact that every time I called him when I was going under, he ended our conversation by praying for me, and how his prayers, full of grace and absent of judgment, always made me weep.

I thought about the fact that I looked up at the McCoy-McMahon reunion last August and saw Jim, my stepdad, walk in with his lady friend. He looked old. And small. It was hard to imagine him as he'd been back in the bulked-up days of his prime. His eyes were watery and seemed to register the equivalent of little electrical shorts from time to time as he struggled to remember which kid went with which family. As I watched him interact with my siblings, I realized that each one had—in his or her own manner and time—passed through the floodwaters of anger and rage and somehow found the grace to forgive him, despite vivid memories of his brutal treatment of our mother. When it was my turn to hold the newest addition to the family, I walked over to Jim and introduced the two of them—the oldest and the youngest family members at the gathering.

And I realized I was holding redemption in my arms. His name is Patrick Todd, and at the time, he was a mere three weeks old and about as heavy as a bag of rice. His cheek felt like the velvet of a puppy's ear. When I first looked at him, I felt like crying, and when I felt the wee heft of him, I did cry, and I thought of my own babies, and of Mary and the Christ child. Suddenly, this tiny infant was a living metaphor for redemption. With his father's permission, I'll tell you why.

Todd—my nephew and the baby's daddy—once sought his solace, sought joy and peace and comfort, in drugs. It began in his teens, of course, and his addiction was soon like a coal fire that needed constant feeding and stoking to keep him functioning in the world. At the age of eighteen, he made his first pass at rehabilitation, and everyone breathed a sigh of relief. But the allure of the anesthetized life was strong, and soon he was using again. We never knew. Well, there were hints we learned to recognize but quickly dismissed because we didn't want to believe it was true. Mostly we noticed his withdrawal from the family, his self-imposed isolation. But we never knew when he was high, at least I never knew.

When he was just twenty or so, he met Carol, the girl who would become his wife. They had a beautiful baby girl they named after my mother, a breathtakingly lovely child with strawberry-blonde hair and a delicate sprinkling of freckles across her nose. I fell madly in love with her the day she and the other little cousins all received gifts from a treasure box at a theme restaurant. As the other kids tore into theirs, she hopped up onto a park bench and gingerly held her treasure on her calico lap, her Mary Jane feet adorned in lacy anklets dangling in midair. I sat down beside her and asked why she wasn't opening her prize, and she told me she liked the idea of saving it for a while. She'd open it later. That was enough to make her my hero, but she sealed the deal the following winter when, after being consoled because she came in last at her skating competition, she calmly replied, "It's okay, really. I'm only in this for the ribbons and the roses." I love a girl who knows herself and is unashamed. It was clear that Todd adored his little girl and wanted to provide for and protect her, but he could not be entirely dissuaded from his quest for comfort in narcotics, until one bleak afternoon when his world fell to pieces. He was picked up by the police.

I was grief stricken when I learned what had happened, certain that Carol would feel she had no choice but to take the baby and carve out a new life. Within hours, jungle drums signaled the crisis, and the extended family collected itself and began to pray. And pray. Ultimately, we learned that Carol would stay, at least for a while, and they would begin counseling. Legal matters were put on hold while Todd began rehab again, and their little family managed, one day at a time, to remain intact.

In a family generously endowed with recovering alcoholics, I am not so naive as to say that Todd is cured or that his marriage will be able to sustain the blows it has taken. His story represents that of others in recovery. Many in our family have come to know the joy to be had in one day of sobriety, and each has done it in his own way, though all have done it by the grace of God. Many have taken their first baby steps toward wellness by picking up the phone and calling someone else in the family who's been through the fire, especially Uncle Mike, whose unique blend of humor, candor, and compassion seem to create a sense of sanctuary for people at the end of their rope. If we haven't learned anything else, we've all learned never to assume that the disease has been licked. What I will say about Todd, today, is that he has about him an aura of wellness and peace. And when I saw him, balancing his brand-new baby boy on his forearm at the family reunion, my heart turned toward God with gratitude—for giving, one more time, the blessing of a newborn child as a sign of mercy and hope and a reason for righteous living. As I watched Carol tend to her infant son, I marveled again at the love between mother and child, and later, when I learned that the word *cherish* as it is used in the New Testament means "to keep warm," I pondered the artistry of God in creating us to cherish our wee babies, as he cherishes each of us.

Because I need someone to keep me warm. I need to know that despite appearances, God has not abandoned the human race.

Change. Sometimes it comes as slow and easy as the turning of a leaf, the early bedding down of the sun. Sometimes it comes hard and at great cost. But come it does. One way or another. With our permission or without it. I'm reminded of one of my favorite Scott Cairns poems that ends with these lines:

> Even so, I am slowly learning one thing;
> of one thing I am slowly becoming
> aware: whether or not I would
> have it so, whether I sleep
> or no, I will be changed.
> I am changing as I speak. Bless you all.
> Suffer the children. Finished. Keep.[1]

———

I don't know how to live in the tension between justice and mercy. And I don't know how to see the world through Jesus' eyes. I don't know how we're supposed to live in the world and be not of it. There's so much I don't understand. I don't understand the mystery of the Eucharist, how it is that Christ is in us and we are in him. Nor do I understand the transforming power of baptism, especially when I think of some of the things I've done since I was baptized. I don't know how to reconcile the good things about the self God knit together in my mother's womb with those things about me that get me into such awful trouble—the mysterious cohabitation within this flesh of a self I love and a self I loathe. I don't understand how God removes the scales from our eyes so that we're able to see him, unplug our ears so we can hear his voice—discern what's true and what's not. I don't understand how to embrace poverty, literally or spiritually, how to let go of the drive and good deeds that I hoped would keep me in the black— both with my creditors and with God. I don't get why God says if I am identified with him, I have to suffer but will have peace that passes all understanding. I don't understand how God enables mothers of murdered sons to forgive their murderers or how murderers can be saved. And I sure don't know how to do what Jesus would do.

I don't know how to satisfy the deep and abiding hunger I feel with a God who sometimes seems so far away and otherworldly. Or how I can smugly disregard my capacity for egregious sin all the while I'm aware of malevolent images that weave their way into my dreams, into my unguarded mind. One minute I echo Augustine's prayer in the *Confessions* regarding his temperament: "A narrow house, too narrow for thee to enter. . . . Oh make it wide. It is in ruins. Oh rebuild it." And the next, I can't even imagine who in this wide world would ever willingly step into a fire, even one that promises to purify her soul, knowingly pass through the white water of truth that promises peace. I cannot imagine the person who would agree to any of this, knowing full well that it promises to lead straight to the corridors of ridicule and persecution, and possibly death. Are there contemporary Christians who say, as Esther did, "And if I perish, I perish," and really mean it?

Maybe all the talk in the Sermon on the Mount really is just rhetoric and metaphor and it's ludicrous to think that Jesus was describing a person of God when he uttered the Beatitudes, ridiculous to think that he really meant we're supposed to turn the other cheek. And if he did, how do we weave that little imperative into our right to defend ourselves against people who hate us and want to see us dead? This much seems certain: if salvation is earned by way of an attitude adjustment that reconciles all these paradoxes, eases all this tension, the people populating the kingdom of God will number very few. Even if I wanted to make such an adjustment, I wouldn't know where to begin.

Getting to work on the final pages of this manuscript was hard. Reading over the pages I'd written, I felt like one of the Three Stooges who's accidentally painted himself into a corner. While I expected the work of examining and writing about the Beatitudes to be arduous and knew the experience would convict me regarding my own spiritual life, I didn't anticipate paralysis. Paralysis borne not so much out of the challenge to live the Beatitudes, which appears to be impossible, but borne of the bigger question that percolated to the surface when I faced the impossibility of it all. I found the question in Scripture. "Now there is in Jerusalem by the Sheep Gate a pool, which is called in Hebrew, Bethesda, having five porches. In these lay a great multitude of sick people, blind, lame, paralyzed, waiting for the moving of the water. For an angel went down at a certain time into the pool and stirred up the water; then whoever stepped in first, after the stirring of the water, was made well of whatever disease he had. Now a certain man was there who had an infirmity thirty-eight years. When Jesus saw him lying there, and knew that he already had been in that condition a long time, He said to him, 'Do you want to be made well?'"[2]

If the Beatitudes are what I have suggested they are—an invitation to be transformed—then the question Jesus asked this man becomes the question he's asking each of us.

C. S. Lewis writes, "The terrible thing, the almost impossible thing, is to hand over your whole self—all your wishes and precautions—to Christ. But it is far easier," he goes on, "than what we are all trying to do instead. For what we are trying to do is to remain what we call 'ourselves,' to keep personal happiness as our great aim in life, and yet at the same time be 'good.' We are all trying to let our mind and heart go their own way—centred on money or pleasure or ambition—and hoping, in spite of this, to behave honestly and chastely and humbly."[3]

It reminds me of Augustine's remarks about Homer's *Odyssey*, which I ran across recently after seeing the film *O Brother, Where Art Thou?* a parody of the *Odyssey*: "Suppose we were wanderers who could not live in blessedness except at home, miserable in our wandering and desiring to end it and to return to our native country. We would need vehicles for land and sea which could be used to help us to reach our homeland, which is to be enjoyed. But if the amenities of the journey and the motion of the vehicles itself delighted us and we were led to enjoy those things which we should use, we should not wish to end our journey quickly, and entangled in perverse sweetness, we should be alienated from our country, whose sweetness would make us blessed."[4]

It's interesting that virtually all fairy tales seem, in the end, to be about trying to get home. It seems we come equipped with all the right longings. And yet I fear that very few of us are all that concerned anymore with getting home, with being good or chaste or humble, as long as we're having a good time out on the road.

When I read in the opening pages of Jeremiah describing Israel as a "she-camel" in heat, running about wildly in search of satisfaction,[5] I couldn't help but think about the American way of life. We are not unlike our predecessors, I fear, and I'm not just talking about unbelievers. I'm talking about children of God who seem to be in a constant state of conflict regarding the desire to live for God and the desire to please ourselves and our natural appetites.

We're utterly infatuated with all that the world has to offer, all the ways we can find pleasure and satisfaction, and we have very little interest in checking in with God to see what he thinks about any of it, let alone submitting ourselves to him for transformation. We think, I guess, that God will steal away all our pleasures if we give ourselves completely to him. Yet we are told he wants to give us the desires of our heart. Perhaps we don't really trust him to come through, though I think it's more likely that our reluctance comes from our knowing, or at least suspecting, that once transformed we will find that even the desires of our hearts have begun to change, and we're not altogether sure we want that to happen. It's a difficult and scary thing to give up the comforts and pleasure of what we know for what we do not know, and it's precisely at this point that the "leap of faith" becomes something real rather than some vague, hollow thing we say when we get saved. In reality, what many of us did when we made our way up to the altar, literal or figurative, was to accept the gift of salvation, and though we may have said we were "giving our lives to Jesus," we really had no intention of actually relinquishing anything to anyone. But no matter how you hold Scripture up to the light, it appears that real faith is defined by surrender. C. S. Lewis imagines Christ's saying to each of us, "I have not come to torment your natural self, but to kill it. No half-measures are any good. I don't want to cut off a branch here and a branch there, I want to have the whole tree down. I don't want to drill the tooth, or crown it, or stop it, but to have it out. Hand over the whole natural self, all the desires which you think innocent as well as the ones you think wicked—the whole outfit. I will give you a new self instead. In fact, I will give you Myself: my own will shall become yours."[6]

If the promise is this, that having emptied ourselves, we will be filled up with Christ, what could more blissful than that? The whole dilemma puts me in mind of those early desert fathers, who fled civilized society in search of their real selves as opposed to the self that had been formed and defined by society. The sorry truth is most of us are quite comfortable with the self that has been molded and shaped by circumstance. And who can blame us? The masks we donned early in life were designed to help us survive in a harsh world. It seems utterly foolish to give them up and put our trust in God. They represent the self that enabled us to get by, and we're not at all interested in that other self, the one who lurks around in the depths of each of us, dark and capable of every bad thing, the one God wants to get his hands on. We don't really think we need new eyes, new ears. Maybe, we concede, a murderer or a child molester—someone who has allowed his bestial self to run amok—needs a complete overhaul, but we can't imagine why we should have to submit ourselves to the brutal light of introspection, let alone the anguish of dying in order to live in Christ. Sometimes I think this is hardest of all for believers. Having acknowledged Christ as God's Son and accepted the grace of salvation with grateful hearts, they see no point in subjecting themselves to the further pain of the working-out part of salvation.

I recently encountered, for the first time, the writings of Carlo Carretto, a modern-day desert monk whose letters set me to thinking about the mystery of Nazareth, or Jesus' life before he began his public ministry. In *Letters from the Desert,* Carretto points out that Jesus lived the gospel long before he began his public life. He writes that Charles de Foucauld, founder of Les Petites Freres, a brotherhood of desert monks, after years of digging for facts about Jesus' life was most astonished to realize that the "Son of God—who, more than anyone else, was free to choose what he would—chose not only a mother and a people, but also a social position." He chose to be a poor wage earner. "Nazareth," Carretto reminds us, "was the lowest place: the place of the poor, the unknown, of those who didn't count, of the mass of workers, of men subjected to work's grim demands just for a scrap of bread.

"But there is more. Jesus is the 'Holy One of God.' But the Holy One of God realised his sanctity not in an extraordinary life, but one impregnated with ordinary things: work, family and social life, obscure human activities, simple things shared by all men. The perfection of God is cast in material which men almost despise, which they don't consider worth searching for because of its simplicity, its lack of interest, because it is common to all men."[7]

It's little wonder that we balk like mules at the threshold of this question regarding transformation. Who among us, Christian or otherwise and given a choice, would ever agree to accept the Nazareth life, let alone aspire to it? We can talk all day and pray all night about holiness. We can build churches and cathedrals of great beauty and paint magnificent paintings and compose incomparable oratorios all to the glory of God, but who among us wants to actually live as Christ lived—among the poor and the lowly? Isn't it enough that we go down there once or twice a year and serve dinner or drop off bags of clothes? And as if being poor weren't bad enough, to be identified with Christ also means being misunderstood, ridiculed, and rejected. To be identified with Christ means to suffer every sort of anguish. Who in their right mind would seek such a life?

Like it or not, we're right back to that question about whether God is calling us to be poor. I don't know whether he is. Frankly, I think all our gimcracks and gewgaws and showy affectations are the least of our worries, unless, of course, we permit them to replace God in our lives. God described the people of Israel as wicked, "in burning incense to other gods and in worshiping what their hands have made,"[8] and idolatry includes anything we're attached to that draws us away from God and pits us against each other. But when you really reduce it to its essence, it ends up being a whole lot more about our need for stuff than stuff itself. It's what the stuff represents we should be concerned about, things like celebrity, power, pride, and contentedness.

I don't think God wants to deprive us of pleasure. But I do think he wants us to guard our hearts against turning our trophies and test tubes, our plaques and paychecks, into the golden calves of the twenty-first century. Surely he knew what he was doing issuing that first, precedent-setting commandment to put no other Gods before him. He knows what we're like, and he knows what we're liable to do.

Between you and me, I think the biggest mystery of the faith is that God loves any of us at all. And that he's so patient, so willing to wait for us to figure out that life with him means more than a mere token gesture of commitment, and more than a mere walk up the aisle to the altar. That he's willing to wait while we figure out there's a big difference between spirituality and religion, for instance. It takes us a while because spirituality is cool; it suggests something ethereal and noble, tolerant and generous, while religion is not. It suggests something rigid and tight, self-righteous and exclusive. All this has to do with the way the words have evolved over time, of course. In truth, what distinguishes these words is that the latter suggests dedication and loyalty to God—and obedience—while the former simply acknowledges that there's more to us than our physical selves and maybe we should be more attentive to the business of our souls. Which is a very good idea, actually. I cannot imagine that it wouldn't eventually take one into God's presence—in much the same way that it led the star-gazing Magi to the stable. Spirituality and religion have in common also a shared defiance of that which places greater value on reason and empiricism than on those things which transcend reason. But they are not the same.

Much popular theology calls on us to look for God in two places. We are told we will find him in nature and that we will find him within. And though there's a measure of truth in this, both invitations make me squeamish, the first because I think nature as God is way more brutal than the Judeo-Christian God, and more important, it doesn't purport to love me. I'm reminded of Annie Dillard's narrative about the life of a water beetle she once observed sucking the innards out of an unwitting frog. The story gave me nightmares. Of course God is reflected in the wonders of nature, but to worship the things in nature makes about as much sense as lauding a work of art as if it created itself. Seeking God within is likewise distasteful. A god made up of the things that make up me is simply not very appealing, given what

I've learned about myself over time. On the other hand, a God who invites me to empty myself of all the sordid, unspeakable stuff that threatens to suffocate the person he intended for me to be, to make room for him because he loves me, is a God I'm interested in, even if he does scare me. Maybe because he scares me. Scripture, as I read it, invites us to do just that and, in that, to be forever set apart in our identity with Jesus Christ, to be religious in our devotion to one God, indeed, a very particular God, and to prostrate ourselves before him and worship him. This cannot be accomplished if we're preoccupied with worshiping ourselves—or trees and rocks and rivers, for that matter. The Christian religion is about redemption, devotion, and, finally, about separation from the world. Loosely woven spirituality is initially appealing, maybe, and it certainly meets contemporary standards set by pundits of politeness. It's not very demanding, which is nice, but in the end it's far too nebulous. It's like trying to hold on to a cloud or, worse, like putting your harvest hopes in what Paul describes as clouds without water.

That said, we are wise to remember what the Pharisees did to pervert religion, to remember that Christianity is not all mitzvah and no mercy. I try to remember this when I talk about my faith. It's not a belief system or an ideology but faith in Jesus—my brother, my savior, my friend, and my redeemer, who invites me to live in the tension between his gesture of arms flung wide and his admonition that walking with him will mean walking a narrow road. It's not about his teachings; it's about him. And no matter how much I may want to elasticize the truth so it can be stretched to cover a wide variety of religions, I can't. I can't because I can't get away from the sound of Jesus' voice:

If you abide in My word, you are My disciples indeed. And you shall know the truth, and the truth shall make you free.

I am the way, the truth, and the life. No one comes to the Father except through Me.

You say rightly that I am a king. For this cause I was born, and for this cause I have come into the world, that I should bear witness to the truth. Everyone who is of the truth hears My voice.[9]

It helps to remember the promise of glory. I remember the first time someone explained the physics of glory to me. It was Tim Dearborn from Seattle Pacific University. He was giving a talk at our church and explained that Jesus' ability to pass through walls after his resurrection wasn't about his being ethereal and ghostlike but about the fact that in his resurrected state, he was made heavy with glory, heavy enough to pass through substances that prove impassable to us in the flesh. Now that's a God worth worshiping.

Epiphanies are funny things. You look for them in cathedrals and in candle flames, and sometimes you find them there, but you're just as likely to find them in ordinary places. I don't even remember where I was when I had the epiphany that permitted me to finish this book. I know I wasn't at church. And it wasn't something that came to me in particularly eloquent terms. It was simply this. One day God told me that he'd given me something to do where my husband was concerned and that was to love him—and, he added, I wasn't doing a very good job of it at the moment. And suddenly I realized that's what this whole book is really about.

It turns out that's what this whole transformation business ends up being about. There's no way any of us can avoid being changed. The random twists and turns of life will change us despite our illusions of control. The question is, Are we interested in becoming holy? Are we willing to tip ourselves over and empty ourselves out to make room for Jesus, who tells us he will fill us up with himself, which means he's going to fill us up with love?

One should not be hasty in responding, I think. In encountering this possibility, it is wise to remember a few important things about the nature of God. The minute we say yes, for instance, he's ready. I don't think God cares one bit at which step in the dance we decide to enter; he is eagerly waiting to swoop us into his arms and carry us across the dance floor of sanctification. I'll never forget a nightmare I had once in which I was alone in a cabin in the woods with a man I thought I could trust when suddenly he turned into a demon that wanted to kill me. Somewhere deep in my subconscious was a memory of someone telling me that all I had to do if I was ever accosted by Satan was send him away in Jesus' name. Frantically, I called out "Jesus, save me!" and the next thing I knew, Jesus burst through the cabin door—in full VBS regalia—sent the monster into oblivion, and carried me out. I woke up thinking, "He was on the front porch the whole time!"

Once rescued, though, I think it's absolutely vital that we understand transformation as process, vital that we not lose heart when we stumble or when we take one step forward, only to take two steps back. It gives the dance texture and interest, and, one hopes, makes the mastery of it all the sweeter. Sometimes, though—I must confess—my personal journey hardly feels like a dance at all. It's more akin to the dusty sojourn of the turtle described in the opening pages of *The Grapes of Wrath,* an ancient, testudinal creature that slowly makes his way onto an Oklahoma highway only to be hit by a truck and spun onto his back like a tiddlywink, legs clawing the air until he can right himself and try again. And though such moments never cease to humiliate me, I try to remember that forty years is nothing to God. And I try to remember that mystery and magic aren't the same thing and that God doesn't turn us from frogs to princes and princesses with a kiss.

As for the question of our stuff, I think our station in life is of little interest to God. Whether we live in Trump Tower or a tar-paper shanty, all he wants to know is whether we're ready to stop dancing the jig we've been dancing all our lives and step into the high holy dance of his making. We needn't sell our treasures before we say yes, though we'd probably be wise to be prepared for it, I suppose. I suppose we'd better be ready for anything.

Ready even to stop resenting God for keeping secrets and praise him for the mystery that he is. The mystery that will make it possible for us to love people we never thought we could love, for instance. To forgive the unforgivable, beginning with ourselves. When God comes in, so comes knowing. Heart knowing, as opposed to head knowing. And to know is to forgive, and to love is to see, and once we see things and people for what and who they really are, anything can happen. When Paul wrote about charity, he did not mean the kind that can be written as a check or stuffed into a donation bag. He meant love. Love that permits us to see ourselves in the faces of every wretched sinner and be a messenger of grace to every hurting heart. Lewis says we will one day be little Christs. If he's right, we're in the process of being made into someone whose image we won't even recognize in the looking glass. Someone who is quicker to show mercy than to pass judgment; someone who looks beyond the skin to see a broken heart; someone who sees behind the mask of the jaded, cynical adult and finds a vulnerable, frightened child who's looking for exactly the same thing we're looking for. And it all begins and ends with love, which is to say it all begins and ends with Jesus, who, it turns out, really does conquer all.

God told me something else recently in a dream. He told me that there was something that needed to be said that only I could say. When I told my friend, Bryan, about it, he was reminded of a story from the Hassidic tradition that goes something like this: God created the world, and then something happened and it broke. It broke into a million pieces, each shard a unique shape and size. In order to heal the world, the story goes, God made each of us to bring a piece of the broken world to the others so the world might be made whole again. Do not stop to compare your piece with that of another. I can't tell you how many times I almost threw this manuscript away because I began to compare it with the works of C. S. Lewis or Blaise Pascal or Dallas Willard or Kathleen Norris or Anne Lamott. God made you because he needs you to accomplish his work in the world. There is something to do that only you can do. There are people who need a love that only you can give them. Be not afraid. Blessed are those who are willing to be transformed into Christ's likeness to bring his love to a wounded world.

Notes

Blessedness

1. William Barclay, *The Gospel of Matthew*, vol. 1, rev. ed. (Louisville: Westminster John Knox, 1975), 89.

2. Dallas Willard, *The Divine Conspiracy* (San Francisco: Harper San Francisco, 1998), 98–106.

3. Os Guinness, introduction to *The Mind on Fire: An Anthology of the Writings of Blaise Pascal*, by Blaise Pascal (Portland, Ore.: Multnomah, 1989), 28.

4. Scott Cairns, "My Good Luck," in *The Translation of Babel* (Athens, Ga.: University of Georgia Press, 1990), 59.

Chapter 1: When You're Little in Your Own Eyes

1. Ps. 34:18, my paraphrase.

2. Elizabeth Barrett Browning, "Grief," in *An Introduction to Poetry*, 8th ed., eds. X. J. Kennedy and Dana Gioia (New York: Harper Collins, 1994), 183.

3. Luke 6:20, 24.

4. William Barclay, *The Gospel of Matthew*, vol. 1, rev. ed. (Louisville: Westminster John Knox, 1975), 91.

5. Ps. 142:1–2 NKJV.

6. Kathleen Norris, *Amazing Grace* (New York: Riverhead, 1999), 62.

7. 1 Cor. 1:25.

8. 1 Sam. 15:17 NKJV.

9. Blaise Pascal, *The Mind on Fire: An Anthology of the Writings of Blaise Pascal* (Portland, Ore.: Multnomah, 1989), 59.

10. Luke 6:24 NKJV.

11. Denise Levertov, "On a Theme by Thomas Merton," in *Evening Train* (New York: New Directions, 1990), 113.

12. Pascal, *Mind on Fire,* 21.

13. Matt. 9:20–22.

14. Previously published in *Radix* 27, no. 3: 9. Appears here revised.

Chapter 2: Like Honey in the Comb

1. Eph. 5:19.

2. Vv. 15–24.

3. Joel 2:13.

4. James 4:9.

5. Denise Levertov, "The Mystery of the Incarnation," in *A Door in the Hive* (New York: New Directions, 198), 50.

6. C. S. Lewis, *A Mind Awake,* ed. Clyde Kilby (New York: Harvest Books, 1968), 239.

7. Ps. 51:3–4, 17.

8. Victor Potapov, "The Second Commandment of Blessedness," *Parish Life,* December 1992, quoting St. John Climacus, *The Ladder of Divine Ascent.* Posted on the website of the Russian Orthodox Cathedral of St. John the Baptist, Washington, D.C.: www.stjohndc.org/beatitud/9212.htm.

9. Blaise Pascal, *The Mind on Fire: An Anthology of the Writings of Blaise Pascal* (Portland, Ore.: Multnomah, 1989), 100.

10. Benedicta Ward, SLG, trans., *The Sayings of the Desert Fathers* (Kalamazoo, Mich.: Cistercian, 1975), 36.

11. Pierce Pettis, "God Believes in You," from *Everything Matters,* Compass Records ASIN B000007N93 (1998). Used by permission.

Chapter 3: Till We Come to the End of Pride

1. e.e. cummings, "I Thank You God," in *The American Tradition in Literature,* 7th ed., ed. George B. Perkins (New York: McGraw-Hill, 1990), 1423.

2. David Hill, *The New Century Bible Commentary on Matthew* (Grand Rapids, Mich.: Eerdmans, 1990), 110–11.

3. Phil. 2:7–8 NKJV.

4. Num. 12:3 KJV.

5. Num. 12:2.

6. Num. 12:6–8.

7. Exod. 2:12.

8. Exod. 3:11; 4:10 NKJV.

9. Exod. 4:12 NKJV.

10. Phillip Keller, *Lessons from a Sheep Dog* (Waco: Word, 1983), 18.

11. William Barclay, *The Gospel of Matthew,* vol. 1, rev. ed. (Louisville: Westminster John Knox, 1975), 96–97.

12. Perry D. LeFevre, *The Prayers of Kierkegaard* (Chicago: University of Chicago Press, 1956), 109.

13. Thomas Merton, trans., *The Wisdom of the Desert: Sayings from the Desert Fathers of the Fourth Century* (New York: New Directions, 1970), 52.

14. Benedicta Ward, SLG, trans., *The Sayings of the Desert Fathers* (Kalamazoo, Mich.: Cistercian, 1975), 10.

15. Simone Weil, "Human Personality," in *Selected Essays, 1934–43* (London: Oxford University Press, 1962), 26.

16. Ps. 5:5 NKJV.

17. John 19:11 NKJV.

18. Kallistos Ware, introduction to *John Climacus: The Ladder of Divine Ascent,* Colm Luibheid and Norman Russell, trans. (Mahwah, N.J.: Paulist, 1982), 32.

19. 1 Peter 5:6.

20. Ps. 10:17–18 NKJV.

21. Keller, *Lessons from a Sheep Dog,* 121.

22. Vv. 5–6 NKJV.

Chapter 4: Starving in the Land of Plenty

1. Ps. 27:13, my paraphrase.

2. David Hill, *The New Century Bible Commentary on Matthew* (Grand Rapids, Mich.: Eerdmans, 1990), 112.

3. Luke 6:21, 25.

4. Dan. 1:15–17 NKJV.

5. Benedicta Ward, SLG, trans., *The Sayings of the Desert Fathers* (Kalamazoo, Mich.: Cistercian, 1975), 192.

6. Alexander Schmemann, *Great Lent: Journey to Pascha* (Crestwood, N.Y.: St. Vladimir's Seminary Press, 1969), 93–99.

7. Frederick Buechner, *Whistling in the Dark* (San Francisco: Harper San Francisco, 1993), 10.

8. William Shakespeare, *The Merchant of Venice*, act 1, sc. 2, in *The Complete Works of Wm. Shakespeare* (New York: Doubleday, 1936), 449.

9. Father Ron Rolheiser, OM, "Dark Memory," *Catholic Northwest Progress,* October 1997: 9.

10. Scott Cairns, "The Entrance of Sin," in *Recovered Body* (New York: Braziller, 1998), 40. Used by permission.

11. Ps. 25:21.

12. "Spiritual Disciplines in a Postmodern World: Luci Shaw Talks with Dallas Willard," *Radix* 27, no. 3: 4.

13. Gen. 15:5–6 NKJV.

14. Ward, *Sayings of the Desert Fathers,* 154, italics mine.

15. John 7:16–17.

16. Ps. 26:9–10 NKJV.

17. Ps. 15:2–5 MESSAGE.

18. Mic. 6:6–8 NKJV.

19. Joel 2:13.

20. Philip Yancey, "Nietzsche Was Right," *Books and Culture,* January-February 1998, 14–17.

21. Prov. 21:17.

22. Buechner, *Whistling in the Dark,* 124.

23. Thomas Merton, trans., *The Wisdom of the Desert: Sayings from the Desert Fathers of the Fourth Century* (New York: New Directions, 1970), 44.

24. *Daily Readings with Isaac of Syria* (London: Templegate, 1989), 24.

Chapter 5: Gentle Rain from a Cloudless Sky

1. Luke 5:13; John 20:16; Matt. 25:35; John 19:27 NKJV.

2. 1 Cor. 13:13 KJV.

3. Exod. 33:19–22 NKJV.

4. William Shakespeare, *The Merchant of Venice,* act 4, sc. 1, in *The Complete Works of Wm. Shakespeare* (New York: Doubleday, 1936), 469.

5. Ps. 22:2.

6. Denise Levertov, *Evening Train* (New York: New Directions, 1990), 5.

7. Job 13:15 NKJV.

8. Jack W. Hayford, ed., *Spirit Filled Life Bible* (Nashville: Thomas Nelson, 1991), 1702.

9. Hos. 6:6 NKJV.

10. Luke 6:35–36 NKJV.

11. Matt. 25:41–43 NKJV.

12. Matt. 5:45–46 NKJV.

13. 1 Cor. 3:19 NKJV.

14. See John 8.

15. Thomas Merton, trans., *The Wisdom of the Desert: Sayings from the Desert Fathers of the Fourth Century* (New York: New Directions, 1970), 43.

16. Jorge Lara-Braud, "Book of the Week," *The Presbyterian Outlook* 182:12 (3 April 2000), 12.

17. Victor Potapov, "The Fifth Commandment of Blessedness," *Parish Life,* March 1993, quoting Father John of Kronstadt, *Complete Works.* Posted on the website of the Russian Orthodox Cathedral of St. John the Baptist, Washington, D.C.: www.stjohndc.org/beatitud/9303.htm.

Chapter 6: A Mirror in which You See Yourself Whole

1. 3:2–3 NKJV.

2. David Hill, *The New Century Bible Commentary on Matthew* (Grand Rapids, Mich.: Eerdmans, 1990), 113.

3. Victor Potapov, "The Sixth Commandment of Blessedness," *Parish Life,* April 1993, quoting from the third ode of the Canon of Preparation for Holy Communion. Posted on the website of the Russian Orthodox Cathedral of St. John the Baptist, Washington, D.C.: www.stjohndc.org/beatitud/9304.htm.

4. Jack W. Hayford, ed., *Spirit Filled Life Bible* (Nashville: Thomas Nelson, 1991), 784.

5. Luke 10:27.

6. Henri Nouwen, *The Way of the Heart* (San Francisco: Harper San Francisco, 1991), 45–46.

7. Dallas Willard, *The Divine Conspiracy* (San Francisco: Harper San Francisco, 1998), 9.

8. Lawrence Kushner, *The Book of Words* (Woodstock, Vt.: Jewish Lights, 1993), 11.

9. Exod. 22:30–23:1.

10. Kushner, *Book of Words,* 51–53.

11. Stuart Hample, comp., *Children's Letters to God* (New York: Workman, 1991), np.

12. Luke 12:4–5 NKJV.

13. W. B. Yeats, "The Second Coming," in *The Norton Anthology of Poetry,* Alexander W. Allison, et al., eds. (New York: Norton, 1983), 520.

14. Pablo Neruda, quoted in Luis Poirot, *Pablo Neruda: Absence and Presence,* trans. Alastair Reid (New York: Norton, 1990), 80.

Chapter 7: He Who Loses His Life

1. Ps. 122:6 NKJV.

2. Benedicta Ward, SLG, trans., *The Sayings of the Desert Fathers* (Kalamazoo, Mich.: Cistercian, 1975), 210.

3. John 14:27 NKVJ.

4. Ward, *Sayings of the Desert Fathers,* xvii.

5. Thomas Merton, trans., *The Wisdom of the Desert: Sayings from the Desert Fathers of the Fourth Century* (New York: New Directions, 1970), 5.

6. Richard J. Foster, "Heart-to-Heart: A Pastoral Letter," *Renovaré,* November 2000: 1.

7. Bryan Van Dragt, *Journal of Clinical Psychology* 4, no. 2: 15–18.

8. Vv. 6–7 NKJV.

9. Dan Allender and Tremper Longman III, *Bold Love* (Colorado Springs: NavPress, 1992).

10. 1:15 NKJV.

11. Matt. 10:34–39 NKJV.

12. Matt. 23:29, 33 NKJV.

13. Matt. 10:39 NKJV.

14. Alfred Kazin, "A Prayer for Owen Meany," *New York Times,* 12 March 1989, sec. 7, p. 1.

15. Os Guinness, *Time for Truth* (Grand Rapids, Mich.: Baker, 2000), 44.

16. Timothy Jones, "The Uncensored Merton," *Books and Culture* 6, no. 6 (Nov./Dec. 2000): 25.

Chapter 8: Life on the Edge

1. Matt. 5:10–12 NKJV.

2. Walter A. Elwell, ed. *Baker's Evangelical Dictionary of Biblical Theology* (Grand Rapids, Mich.: Baker, 1996).

3.V. ess," *Parish Life,* May 1993. Posted on the website of the Russian Orthodox Cathedral of St. John the Baptist, Washington, D.C.: www.stjohndc.org/beatitud/9306.htm.

4. C. S. Lewis, *Mere Christianity* (New York: Collier, 1984), 139.

5. John Alexander, "American Values and the Christian Faith," *Radix* 28, no. 1: 14.

6. Vv. 15–18 NKJV.

7. Vv. 19–20 NKJV.

8. Rev. 2:9–10 NKJV.

9. 3 John 4.

10. Lewis, *Mere Christianity,* 97.

11. John 21:18 NKJV.

Transformation

1. Scott Cairns, "My Farewell," in *The Translation of Babel* (Athens, Ga.: University of Georgia Press: 1990), 61. Used with permission.

2. John 5:2–6 NKJV.

3. C. S. Lewis, *Mere Christianity* (New York: Collier, 1984), 154.

4. Augustine, *On Christian Doctrine,* quoted in *Invitation to the Classics,* Louise Cowan and Os Guinness, eds. (Grand Rapids, Mich.: Baker, 1998), 32.

5. Jer. 2:23–24 NIV.

6. Lewis, *Mere Christianity,* 153.

7. Carlo Carretto, *Letters from the Desert* (New York: Orbis Books, 1972), 92–93.

8. Jer. 1:16.

9. John 8:31–32; 14:6; 18:37 NKJV.